You Live and Learn.
Then You Die and Forget It All
Ray Lum's Tales of
Horses, Mules, and Men

by
WILLIAM
FERRIS

With a Foreword by Eudora Welty

Anchor Books
DOUBLEDAY
NEW YORK   LONDON   TORONTO   SYDNEY   AUCKLAND

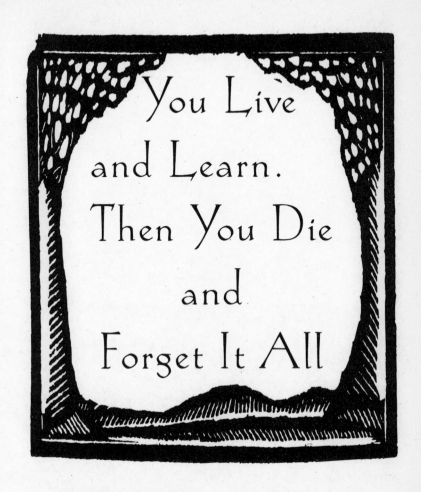

You Live and Learn. Then You Die and Forget It All

RAY LUM'S TALES OF HORSES, MULES, AND MEN

An Anchor Book
PUBLISHED BY DOUBLEDAY
a division of Bantam Doubleday Dell Publishing Group, Inc.
666 Fifth Avenue, New York, New York 10103

Anchor Books, Doubleday, and the portrayal of an anchor
are trademarks of Doubleday, a division of Bantam Doubleday
Dell Publishing Group, Inc.

Library of Congress Cataloging-in-Publication Data

Ferris, William R.
  "You live and learn. Then you die and forget it all" : Ray Lum's
tales of horses, mules, and men / by William Ferris. — 1st ed.
      p.   cm.
  Includes bibliographical references.
  1. Southern States—Social life and customs—1865– 2. Lum, Ray,
1891–1976. 3. Auctioneers—Southern States—Biography. I. Lum,
Ray, 1891–1976. II. Title.
F216.F47   1992
975—dc20   91-28554
                                                             CIP

Book Design by Claire Naylon Vaccaro

ISBN 0-385-41926-0

For three traders:
William Ferris, Sr., Ray Lum, and Dominique Rossi

Contents

Foreword by Eudora Welty
xi

Acknowledgments
xv

Introduction
1

School Days
11

Dog Days
27

Up and Down That Dog
69

Rattlesnakes, Coyotes, and Wild Horses
103

Eighty Thousand Horses
149

CONTENTS

When Mules Played Out
171

Letters
217

Bibliographic Essay
225

Endnotes
239

Foreword

by

Eudora Welty

Ray Lum was a Mississippi mule trader and a remarkable man. William Ferris has brought this book into being in the only possible way—by ear. That's the way Ray Lum had been telling it to him. Mr. Lum was above all a talker, listening to the way his tale went, keeping the ring true as he proceeded. His life as a mule trader and auctioneer, his stock in trade, his private well-being, his reputation—all were gathered in, all would find expression in his tales. They speak to the source of his pleasure in the world, and in this, all tale tellers everywhere are the same.

Ray Lum could afford to be, and he was, a spendthrift: with so many tales to tell, surely he'd be delighted—tempted—to tell them all, and why not? All the tales were his to tell; and all of them were true: not one would falsify the teller. They were all always available to him, carried around like currency loose in a rich traveler's pocket.

Thus we meet Ray Lum in the well-attuned company of his friend Bill Ferris: Ray Lum, a man born and bred to the practice of the country monologue.

Not all that long ago in any country pasture in America, standing contentedly motionless under a shade tree, a mule is exactly what you expected to see. At least you *didn't* expect *not* to see a mule. Today, your coming upon a mule in our landscape would be as rare as catching a glimpse of a distant cousin of his in the *equus* family, the zebra, trotting down the Interstate.

The mule is a sterile hybrid of a female horse and a male ass. (The hybrid offspring of a male horse and a female ass is a hinny.) The mule has a long head. The long face is somehow familiar; it might remind you of Disraeli. But the expression flickering along that lengthy graying countenance might be that of a cardsharp. William Faulkner has said that a mule would never allow himself to be driven through an opening unless he knew what was on the other side.

As Ray Lum knew, the strength and endurance of mules were put to use in the earliest days of settling the Delta in the state of Mississippi. Penetrating the wilderness of forest and canebrake (bear-ridden and panther-ridden) to hack out the first raw farmland, clearing and draining it, eventually planting it and harvesting it, could not have been accomplished without the mule. Mules worked in time to lay the railroads across America; they opened up the West. Eventually listed for shipment over the country were sugar mules, rice and cotton mules, levee mules, mine mules, railroad mules, mountaineer pack mules, all marketed by class according to need. Great numbers were destined for small barns, particularly in the South, where men such as Ray Lum made their livelihoods visiting from barn to barn, holding auction, buying and selling mules.

Mules should not be forgotten. They go back a long enough way —they have a history. The mule was named in earliest times by the Greeks, medieval bestiaries say. *Mulus* was their word for millstone, which the animal was put under the yoke to draw in a circle for grinding. (This, in fact, is what we may catch him doing today if we find him on some farm in a remote part of the American South, where the mule still grinds cane to make syrup for the farmer's table.)

Yellowed panoramic photographs still hang in city halls and county courthouses here and there, showing mules lined up, crowded collar to collar, every pair of long ears crossed with the pair on either side, posed at the head of Main Street: a team at the start of some ambitious project, about to hear the holler to begin. The date would have been seventy-five to a hundred years ago.

All over the country mules were put to work at the building of dams, railroad tunnels, bridges. They also moved like an army upon the scenes of disaster—tornado destruction, forest fires, earthquake. During the Great Mississippi River Flood of 1927, Ray Lum's barns and lots provided mules that labored to move thousands of endangered herds; and Ray Lum's mules took part afterward in the building of the first Mississippi River levees.

The equal to, and the answer to, emergency, the mule was ready for the frontier, for war, for disaster, and for better times. So he labored his life away. (And the mule's lifetime is twice as long as that of the horse, so we are told.)

Almost up until the peak of Ray Lum's career, the mule was an integral part of American life. He was a taken-for-granted source of national strength, unbeatable for working in the cause, and in the name, and in the achievement, of progress.

But progress, attained, came in on its own terms. It rode in with the tractor. The mule's career was over.

Mules have known battlefields for centuries back. A smartly barbered mule is portrayed in embroidery on the Bayeux Tapestry, the mount of a member of William's Court. This mule must have taken part in the coming Battle of Hastings—of course on the winning side. Back even farther, mules are figures in story and fable.

By tradition, the ass is both the beast of burden and the bearer of the innocent and holy. The ass carried the Holy Family on the Flight into Egypt. On Palm Sunday, Jesus rode in triumph into Jerusalem "even upon the colt the foal of an ass," and thereby communicated to the ass's back the marking of the cross which is borne there still.

The mule was a favorite beast for satirists to call on in holding our human foibles up to view. In La Fontaine's "The Mule Who Boasted of His Pedigree" (in Grandville's illustration for which the mule is wearing plumes and the Garter and displaying his coat of arms), we read:

A bishop's mule, full of snobbish vainglory,
Talked incessantly of his mother, the mare . . .

The mule lacks for the horse's beauty and romance. It is rather from his father's side that his greater gifts derive. He stands before us as deprived of the heroic as he is of the power to propagate: he has made himself into a comedian. And there is comedy's latent touch of sadness in his patient acceptance of mankind's burdens, of mankind's blows. Yet how often has it not been through portrayal of the character of the ass that great literature has brought human beings into touch with the poetry and humor and worship in our natures? The ass will live on forever in poetry and song. Elevated once and for all by Shakespeare, he is Bottom's Dream.

Indeed, the mule trader has undoubtedly helped to form our great oral tradition in the South. William Ferris, valuable folklorist, practiced discoverer and custodian of our living records, has seen in this life story an illuminating account of our not-so-long-ago past. It is all the more enhanced by being, as well, a reflective record of a friend.

This sensitive biography owes something in particular to William Ferris's affection for his subject. This shows, for one example, in the inclusion of a tale Lum told about his boyhood, one that is not about a horse or a mule or a wild horse, but about a coon. Out coon hunting by moonlight, the boy saw a coon sitting in a tree high out of reach, forever out of reach, against the moon—"a coon in the moon." Lum is endeared to us through this backward look, because he couldn't reach that coon, because he couldn't coax it down out of its tree, because he still remembers it, in its beauty and trickery. The coon might have been marked for his heart's desire. Ferris relays a country-poetic element in Ray Lum's telling, from its beginning—"It was a moon-shining night"—to the pronouncement that almost irresistibly furnished Ray Lum the signature to his tales: "That's right."

Acknowledgments

Ray Lum's life is best understood as part of the story of the American South and its worlds of mules, horses, and storytelling. This work is inspired by a belief that Lum's stories offer a rare view of the South and her people.

My study has evolved over the past twenty years, and I am indebted to friends who assisted me along the way. In 1970 my father, William Ferris, suggested that Lum was an excellent subject for an oral history. I followed his suggestion and in 1971 began work with Judy Peiser on a film and long-playing record with the same title, *Ray Lum: Mule Trader*. The Center for Southern Folklore in Memphis, Tennessee, produced both the film and the record, and Marie Connors, Jack Friedman, Diane Hamilton, Robert Jones, Carolyn Lipson, Barbara Moore, Jane Mosely, Joan Ruman Perkal, Bobby Taylor, George Edward Walker, and Carol Lynn Yellin assisted the Center with these projects.

Inspired by work on the film and record, I continued to interview Lum until his death in 1977. From 1972–79 I taught in the American and Afro-American Studies Programs at Yale University, where Susan Steinberg and Sue Hart located publications in Sterling Memorial Library and in the Beinecke Rare Book Library on topics ranging from cockney traders to southern mules, and Anne

Granger typed several drafts of the manuscript. A Yale University Morse Fellowship in 1974 and a Rockefeller Humanities Fellowship in 1978 provided generous support for my research.

At Yale, Walker Evans offered suggestions on my study of Lum, whose Natchez livestock barn he and Ben Shahn had photographed years earlier. Eugene Butler, Shelby Ferris, Sue Hart, Daniel Hoffman, Alan Lomax, Toni Morrison, Larry Powell, Diane North, and Robert Penn Warren each read drafts of my manuscript and offered helpful suggestions on it.

In Mississippi, Patti Black and Gordon Cotton provided important counsel on the project, and Black later used the manuscript as a resource in developing an exhibition and catalogue entitled *Mules in Mississippi.* Lum's half sister, Genevieve, and his brothers, Clarence, John, and Willie D., shared photo albums and stories of their brother. And Lum's old friends Eric Biedenharn, Victor Bobb, Lilias Chachere, Squire Harris, Elwood Jenkins, and Bill Lindley reminisced about their experiences with him. Charles Faulk and other staff at the *Vicksburg Evening Post* located early articles and photographs of Lum in their files, and blues composer and performer Willie Dixon reminisced about how as a child he learned to ride horses at Lum's stable in Vicksburg.

Ben Green and Elmer Kelton both wrote me of their experiences with Lum during his travels in Texas. And Howard Lamar and Clyde Milner helped me research worlds Lum encountered in the West. And Tom Verich and Sharron Sarthou located photographs and documents on Lum in my papers in the University of Mississippi Archives and Special Collections.

The University of Mississippi and Stanford University jointly provided support for my 1989–90 sabbatical leave at the Stanford Humanities Center where I revised and shaped the manuscript. I am indebted to Ken and Barbara Oshman, Gregor and Dion Peterson, Peter and Suzanne Voll, and Mary Wohlford who made my year at Stanford possible and to Bliss Carnochan, Mort Sosna, and the fine staff at the Stanford Humanities Center for their support.

Final work was assisted by John Kostmayer, James Magnuson, and Diane North who read the manuscript and helped me revise and focus its narrative. George Collier, Grey Ferris, and Duilio Peruzzi designed graphs, floor plans, and maps respectively for the book. Sidney Mintz and Richard and Sally Price shared resources on traders in the field of anthropology. And Roger Abrahams, Simon Bronner, and Bill McNeil suggested important folklore studies on traders and their folktales. Patricia LaPointe located photos and articles on Memphis mule traders Lum had known in the Memphis Shelby County Public Library and Information Center. Laurie Lawson printed my photographs of Mr. Lum, and Dannal Perry checked bibliographic entries. Mildred Kirkland gave to the University of Mississippi a collection of Lum's business files that was an important resource for my work.

During the last few years of his life Lum was recognized nationally as a storyteller and trader. Ralph Rinzler coordinated his weeklong appearance at the Smithsonian Folklife Festival in 1974. Patti Black featured him in a 1975 arts festival in Jackson during which Lum met Eudora Welty at the Old Capitol Museum and entertained her with his tales. Charles Davis, John Blassingame, Kai Erikson, Maynard Mack, Joseph Warner, and Joella Warner assisted with Lum's visit at Yale University where he shared tales with students on the Cross Campus and spoke to scholars at the National Humanities Institute in 1974. And Richard Bauman arranged for Lum to speak at the annual meeting of the American Folklore Society in 1975.

Martha Levin and Sallye Leventhal offered support and helpful suggestions on revisions of the manuscript. Their counsel and encouragement during the final year of my work were invaluable.

Over the past twenty years my literary agent Wendy Weil has offered encouragement and support for the project. Her friendship and counsel will never be forgotten.

My wife Susannah and our daughter Virginia understood and accepted my long hours of work on the manuscript by day and night. Lum is now part of our family, and his stories surface in conversations with a familiarity that he would appreciate.

To these and other friends who believed in my work and assisted in so many ways I offer heartfelt thanks and my hope that this book is an appropriate tribute to a man we all admired.

William Ferris
University of Mississippi

Introduction

Ray Lum was a famed southern storyteller and livestock trader who was born several miles from my home on the Big Black River sixteen miles southeast of Vicksburg, Mississippi. As a child, I imagined Lum must have arrived in the world full blown and talking. When I visited his livestock auction barn in Vicksburg the pungent smell of animals and the sound of his booming voice made deep impressions. He traded mules and horses with three generations of my family, from the 1920s to 1977, and his humorous tales were told and retold in our home.

Long after horses and mules had been replaced by automobiles and tractors, Lum steadfastly refused to give up the trader's life. In his eighties, he traveled each week to sales in an old Lincoln filled with "everything pertaining to a horse." He piled bridles, bits, and curry combs on the dashboard, covered the back seat with boxes of hats and boots, and filled the trunk with saddles and cans of ribbon cane syrup. When I asked about his health, he would reply, "I'm all right. I just need to have my speedometer set back. That's all."

Lum's life as a livestock trader was an important part of southern worlds where farmers used horses and mules to farm their land and to move their families in wagons. In this pre-industrial world he brought in livestock and set up financial agreements that allowed his customers to buy a horse or mule. When an animal was too old to ride or work, Lum exchanged him for another and charged his customer for the difference.

Over the course of his life Lum watched the rise and fall of horses and mules in the United States. Their number peaked at twenty-six million in 1920 and declined to less than four million by 1958. As their numbers decreased, most of the animals that remained were concentrated in the South.[1] The West was where tractors first displaced horses and mules, and Lum bought the animals and resold them to southern farmers. By the 1950s, however, southerners also replaced their mules and horses with tractors and cars, and Lum closed the doors of his livery stables and began to trade cattle.

A shrewd judge of both mules and men, Lum became a legend in the livestock world. Stockmen and fellow traders were struck by his humor and his rapid style as a bidder and trader. A West Texas newspaperman wrote that Lum:

> is known all over the cow country for his honest fair dealings and gentlemanly attitude . . . A letter addressed to him anywhere in Texas probably would be delivered. One man told us a few months ago when we were searching out the man's home address just to "back it to Mississippi or any adjoining state."[2]

From Stephensville, Texas, a friend wrote: "Ray, if we had you here we would elect you to Congress."[3] The notes and newspaper clippings that I found in Lum's scrapbook reflect the affection and respect others felt for him. Ben Green, a Texas trader and veterinarian, recalled in *Some More Horse Tradin'*:

> There was a fast mule and horse trader from Vicksburg Mississippi, by the name of Ray Lum . . . he might be a hard bidder and a mean buyer, but in years to come I would know that Ray Lum . . . was a good man to have at an auction barn because

he would put a starting bid on any kind of horse or mule that came in the ring.[4]

Lum traded with Green and remembered him fondly. "I used to run into Doc Green all over Texas. He wrote a book, and those stories in it are true as the Bible."

Western writer Elmer Kelton met Lum at cattle sales in Texas and remembers him as "a man who made friends easily wherever he went. With that broad smile, and a quick joke in that deep bass voice with the broad Mississippi accent, there was no way you could keep from liking him on first meeting . . . I have thought of him many times over the years. You don't meet a great many characters like him in one lifetime."[5]

Lum's presence was commanding. He was heavy-set and stood six feet tall. His clean-shaven face had a full quality—his blue eyes were deep-set, and grew smaller when he emphasized a point. He squinted and strained and then, to dramatize a story, his eyes suddenly opened and became quite large. If he wanted to stress that a person he spoke of was puzzled or angry, he moved his mouth, eyes, and eyebrows.

I often recorded Lum telling stories at the weekly livestock auction in Vicksburg. When he spoke, Lum would lean over so his shining bald head was visible, then raise up his eyes and stare at me boldly. He would stand close enough to reach out and touch me; his conversations were always very physical. His body rhythm was controlled as he would clap his hands, point, and slap his arms to make a point. When he spoke, he moved his hands back and forth as if adjusting a picture on a wall.

Like an operatic bass, Lum's voice could be heard at a great distance. When we entered a room, people stopped their conversations and listened to him. But with all of the imposing voice, girth, and gesture, he displayed the courtly, gracious manners of a southern gentleman. He was conscious of that role and was aware that customers appreciated his courtly behavior. New customers were surprised to discover this gracious, articulate manner.

When Lum spoke, he created his own theater, and tales of his trades were the heart of his drama. He linked these tales together as episodes in an epic. Horses, mules, and men paraded out as central characters in his tales, and he followed these animals and people from his first to his last encounter with them.

Lum wore well-washed and ironed western shirts and pants. He did not smoke, drink, or chew tobacco, and he never smelled like his animals. He wore a western hat and carried a stockman's whip across his shoulder. After breakfast the morning ritual demanded he put on each of his western boots. He reached down, grabbed a boot and grunted loudly as he pulled it on his foot.

Lum was deeply attached to the places in which he lived. During his travels across the South and Southwest he compared water levels in streams, movement of insects, patterns of plant life, and ways of antelope and buffalo. Born in Mississippi, he closely observed his native world and others he visited in Texas, California, and the Dakotas. He discovered that meat hung in dry salty air out West was preserved indefinitely, and western horses bucked harder than those he had known as a child. Back home in Mississippi these worlds inspired a vast library of tales that he shared with his customers.

His ability to quickly judge a situation and talk with speed at times helped him escape danger. In contrast to American frontiersmen whose boasts precipitated fights, he used his tongue to avoid violence. "I've been in a lot of tight situations, but I always managed to talk my way out. I always laughed and figured a joke was the best way out of a fight. I'm very fortunate to be here, I'll tell you that."

True to his dictum that "history repeats itself," he would connect tales of his past experiences with daily events and believed firmly that these tales helped him understand the present. "These are old stories [I tell], but they're just as true as the Bible. Things haven't changed. It's just a different crowd doing it. That's all."

Like every good storyteller, Lum knew how to leave his audience with the impression that the better part of the tale is left to come, often ending up with the phrase "To cut a long story short." After declaring "to cut a long story short," Lum would quickly describe the profit he had made in a trade and end the story.

The phrase is also apt in that it sums up Lum's personal essence; throughout his career he moved with speed. As a trader he could "lamp" or glance at an animal, and judge its value in seconds; as an auctioneer he prided himself on running the fastest sales in the world; and as a storyteller he related his tales "in a hurry! Like the goat, 'Ram, bam, thank you, ma'am.' " His tale might end, but his storytelling continued, and his favorite transition to a new tale was "back in business. Yeah, I was back in business then." Lum bought and sold his horses, counted his money, and, off on another trade, was sooner than not "back in business again."

Speed is essential for a successful trader, and Lum used short phrases or "telegraphs" to describe an animal's defects in his trades. If a buyer failed to understand these telegraphs and asked for a longer explanation or "letter," Lum dismissed him as an inexperienced "fellow whose bread ain't done."

As an auctioneer, Lum telegraphed a description of each animal that seasoned buyers understood. "One lamp burning" meant one blind eye, and "hitting on three" signaled that one leg was lame. "Angels," or those who did not understand these terms, would bid too high on the animal.

When I began to record Lum's stories in 1970, he conducted most of his business in the "Ketch Pen," a small room adjoining the Lum Brothers Auction Barn in Vicksburg. The room smelled of fresh leather, and customers came as often to hear his stories as to buy gear for a horse or mule. Every conversation reminded him of a story, and throughout the day he entertained customers with stories of his trades. He would interrupt a tale to wait on a customer, relate a story suggested by the customer's interest in a saddle or a bridle, and then return to the original tale with the question, "Where was I? Oh yes, so here come Uncle Dan MacBroom."

Listeners who gathered at the sale barn every Monday knew Lum's stories well enough to follow when he jumped from the middle of one tale to a second and then returned to complete the first. Lum's voice tone and facial expression changed constantly to dramatize his narrative. If a customer's attention drifted, he would turn to the person and ask, "Now what do you think happened then? Don't take all week. They don't take that long to hang you." Before the listener could respond, Lum was off again, having recaptured his attention.

An equally effective device was to place words in the mouth of a listener by quoting him. "Jimmy here says, 'History repeats itself.' Well, I'm inclined to agree. Definitely." Jimmy would be surprised and flattered at having been quoted, even if he had never said such a thing, and paid closer attention to the story that followed.

Customers moved in and out of Lum's Ketch Pen shopping for saddles and gear. When a customer entered the shop, Lum introduced him to a group of older men who stood like a Greek chorus in the background enjoying his tales. His audience was country people dressed in khaki shirts and pants who listened in rapt but relaxed silence as Lum spoke.

Lum learned early that a trader needed wit to survive, and he would often recall how mistakes in his early trades "woke him up." These lessons taught him to avoid being caught with an animal that he could not sell at an advantage to his next buyer. His philosophy was to trade with everyone he met and to do so fairly. He prided himself in always telling the truth, although he sometimes "handled it carefully." He might, for example, describe a blind horse as "not looking very good." Lum recognized a trader's code of honor that he followed with pride, if with a wink of the eye. He reflected "with horses and mules I never did see when it was necessary to tell a lie. I could do all the trading I wanted telling the truth. I never saw the time when the truth couldn't fit in better than a lie." This ethical code was important because a trader with a dishonest reputation quickly lost his customers.

Often a stranger in communities where he traded, Lum would begin sales saying, "Gentlemen, I'm a stranger here, but I've got good horses to sell." For over sixty years he was respected as a man who never missed a trade and turned each trade to his advantage. While he traded hard with other professionals, with children he dropped his guard and dealt fairly to find them a riding pony. "If a child come in, I would get the horse that suited him and didn't cost too much money. But if another trader comes, you gotta be on your watch."

During each trade Lum reassured his customers with colorful stories about horses and mules. These tales focused and controlled the customer's attention and were as important to his profession as the mules and horses he traded.

Lum believed that a trader is born with an instinct for his profession. He began to trade as a child and never forgot the lessons of his early trades. As a teenager he worked as a road trader traveling the Mississippi countryside seated in a wagon or astride an animal leading a string of horses and mules that he traded with local farmers. These early travels launched Lum on a life of trading that carried him by car and train to livestock sales throughout the United States.

My experience with Lum mirrors my own relationship to the South and its culture. I first encountered him as a small child at my father's side when he and Lum traded livestock. My father was a farmer and he admired Lum as a trader whom he could never best. I both loved and feared my father and through his eyes saw Lum, a generation older, as one whom he respected and understood. When he began to farm in the 1930s my father bought his mules from Ray Lum. I grew up on our family's farm in the 1940s and remember four elderly mules that were still used to plow a garden and haul wood in a wagon. After their death only tractors worked the land. A blacksmith's shop filled with tools and a shed with planters and cultivators once pulled by mules bore testimony to their passing.

My father looked forward to his weekly trips to the livestock auction in Vicksburg where he often left me listening to Lum's tales while he looked at cattle and spoke with friends. I sat in awe as Lum entertained his audience with stories of his trades that chronicled a world distinct from my own. After one of these visits, Daddy remarked to me with a smile, "The only way you won't be beat by Ray Lum is if you don't trade with him."

Later as a college student during the '60s I supported the Civil Rights Movement and found myself painfully at odds with Lum's world, a world I deeply loved. I associated him with both the beauty and the darkness of traditions with which I was wrestling. As an undergraduate student at Davidson College in North Carolina, I often heard his voice in my ear. I wondered how he would feel about my newly discovered ideas. When I came home from college during vacations, I always spent an afternoon with Lum to reconnect with his world.

In the late '60s while a graduate student in folklore at the

University of Pennsylvania, I rediscovered and understood better my culture as I filmed and recorded black blues musicians, storytellers, and folk artists from the Mississippi Delta. By 1970 I was teaching English at Jackson State College, and my father suggested I record Lum, whom he felt was unique as a storyteller.

I thought long about Daddy's suggestion and tried to imagine Lum and me together in a room. I remembered my first visits to his auction barn as a child and how the man had both attracted and frightened me. He was intensely familiar to my world as a white Southerner, and I knew that in facing him I would face myself. I took my father's advice and in 1970 began a quest for Lum and through him for my own identity. The search has lasted over twenty years.

While teaching American and Afro-American Studies at Yale in 1974, I brought Lum to meet my students so that they might also discover his world of southern storytelling. By that time I had recorded many hours of his tales and knew their power, but I was uncertain about how he would be received by an Ivy League audience.

On a clear fall day Lum sat on Yale's Cross Campus in a swivel chair I had brought from my office. Sterling Memorial Library towered over his shoulder as he spoke uninterruptedly for eight hours to hundreds of faculty and students. I tethered an aged horse beside Lum, and he dramatically auctioned the animal each hour for the audience. A student produced the Yale bulldog mascot during the afternoon, and Lum sold him in mock auction. Bart Giamatti, who then taught in the English Department, sat beside me for an hour and remarked that Lum brought to life worlds he had first discovered on the pages of Faulkner's novels.

My study of southern culture helped me understand how Lum's life bridged the disparate worlds of black and white, of old and new, of South and West, all of which he chronicled through his tales. Within his stories, Lum brings us face to face with people rarely seen on the pages of history.

When I began to interview Ray Lum in Vicksburg in 1970, he was seventy-nine and I was twenty-eight. Beyond our common bond with my father we knew little of each other. Lum was flattered that a younger man was interested in his life, and I saw him as a father figure. Although elderly, he was exceptionally vital. At times I drove him in his old Lincoln to livestock auctions, taping his conversation along the way, and he would talk about the countryside and speak freely about his travels as a trader. Different locations evoked different stories and different ways of speaking: at the auction barn he recalled livestock sales; driving in the car he reminisced about his travels; and when I brought old photographs to his home to trigger his imagination, he could easily talk for an hour about a single photo.

As a southern storyteller, Lum was unique. He required no effort to interview. From the first time I spoke with him, his tales flowed like a river, and there were many times I felt overwhelmed by the vast wealth of his stories. I know full well that there was much material still unrecorded at his death.

In 1984 I deposited over fifty hours of recordings, several thousand photos and color slides, several hours of 16mm film, and numerous letters written by Lum in the University of Mississippi Archives and Special Collections. As I combined and edited the tales that follow from transcriptions of my recordings, I tried to recapture the rich sound of Lum's voice. Where he repeated stories, I examined each version and pieced together a single tale.

The book is divided into two major sections of Lum's narrative. First we follow Lum's experiences from childhood to old age. We watch him learn from his early trades and mature into one of the nation's best-known livestock dealers. Then in the second section Lum reflects on a lifetime spent as a trader and explains how he judges horses, mules, and men. Throughout the narrative his colloquial expressions are explained in footnotes.

Among the oral histories I see as a model for this work are the translation from Celtic to English of Tomas O'Crohan's *The Islandman* and Theodore Rosengarten's *All God's Dangers,* a portrait of Nate Shaw, a black Alabama farmer.[6] But Eudora Welty's classics "A Worn Path" and "Why I Live at the P. O." set the highest standard for capturing the spoken word in print. Welty's eye for detail in her fiction evokes on paper a magic that I tried to preserve in Lum's tales.

9

Ray Lum died at 8:45 P.M. on December 17, 1976, at his home in Vicksburg. He was a great southern trader, and his rich, story-laden voice preserved a world that might easily have been lost. Within his stories I discovered a rich, memorable portrait of southern people, places, and animals that Lum deeply loved. This book is dedicated to Lum and to the familiar sound of his voice.

School
Days

Ray Lum was born on June 25, 1891, in Rocky Springs, Mississippi. One of nine children, Lum's sisters and brothers were Fanny Marie Lum, Edwina Lucy Lum, Willie B. Lum, Robert Samuel Lum, John Hamilton Lum, Allen Erving Lum, and twins, Mozell and Zoranell Lum. Half brothers and a half sister by his father's second marriage were Clarence Earl Lum, Genevieve Lum, and Herbert Wilson Lum. As in many large southern families, grandparents served as foster parents, and Lum was raised by his grandmother. As a child he herded cattle, trained horses, and attended a local school for several years.

Rocky Springs at that time was a rural community of about seventy-five white and black people near the Natchez Trace. Originally an Indian trail through forests and canebrakes from Natchez, Mississippi, to Nashville, Tennessee, the Trace was later traveled by settlers in wagons and on horseback. In the early 1800s Rocky Springs was known for its tavern and for the famed outlaw gang led by Mason and Harpe who lived in the area and robbed travelers on the Natchez Trace.[7] In 1863 General Ulysses S. Grant and his

Union troops passed through the community during their march north toward Vicksburg.[8]

A country store, school, and church were centers for social activities in Rocky Springs during Lum's childhood. Tales of early settlers, slavery, and the Civil War abounded in the community.

Lum's father was a cattle drover, and to supplement his family's income, Lum picked cotton for "two bits a hundred" (twenty-five cents per hundred pounds) and peddled meat from his mule-drawn wagon on weekends. With money hard to come by, families often traded for goods rather than spend cash. So Lum's trading experiences started early.

With forests and the Big Black River swamp nearby, Lum learned early to hunt and fish. His love for the outdoors and his knowledge of both wild and domestic animals served him well later in his career as a trader.

Today the Rocky Springs community has largely disappeared, and the Natchez Trace is a scenic roadway maintained by the National Park Service. On one memorable spring day I took Lum back to his birthplace. We walked deserted roads, visited the old cemetery where his mother and many of his family are buried, and Lum remembered his childhood there. He called the cemetery a "marble orchard" and pointed with his stockman's cane to each stone that marked a family grave. When we came to his mother's grave, marked "Sue Ray Lum," he paused in a rare show of emotion and explained that as a special gift indicating her love for him his mother gave him her maiden name. Then he reflected, "I had forgotten how many of my family are planted here. I guess I'm lucky to still be in the land of the living."

I was born in an old log cabin June the twenty-fifth in eighteen ninety-one, down at the old post office where my grandmother lived. The old building still sits there. All the old pecan trees are still there. I believe they are. We lived in the Scutchelo Hills out from Rocky Springs where I stayed with my grandmother, and milked eight cows every morning. I remember at six I was a pretty good hand at milking. Grandma had sixteen little stragglers like me, and we was just like orphans.

My grandmother would put the butter down into this cistern. I can see that old well bucket now. The butter would go down in the cistern and would stay cool. My grandmother didn't buy many things. Most of the things that we ate, she grew right on the place.

We would take our cream cheese and put it down in a bucket. It isn't like the cream cheese you get now. You'd have to cut it with a knife, just like cutting hard butter. I can remember how I would pour cream and sugar over it, and I thought that was the best cream cheese in the world. My grandmother made that.

On a Saturday I would hitch the horse to the buggy and take the butter to Port Gibson. That butter would bring twelve and a half cents a pound. I got twelve and a half cents and would take that in trade. Never would see money. I was seven or eight years old then.

My grandmother was considered wealthy. She was one of those kind that held on to money. Just the necessities is all Grandmother would spend money for. I guess you would say she was from the old school. She had studied the old blue-back speller.

My grandmother had more peacocks than anybody in Claiborne County. I loved them. When they squall, you can hear them for three miles on a still night. And you know where they sleep at night? In the trees. Wasn't no damned fox going to get them. They slept up high. They don't have much head, but they must be smart.

I'd be lost in the woods and hear them holler, and I'd know which way to go home. In them days I'd get lost a lot when I was hunting. I started hunting when I was six years old, and I was a damned good hunter. I'd buy two shells for a nickel. Sometimes if there was two squirrels in that tree, I'd wait an hour or two, and when they'd get together, "bam," I'd kill them both. I'd kill two with that one shell. Then I'd carry them squirrels to Grandmother, and she would give me a nickel a piece for them.

Grandmother had sixteen children, and about half of them was girls. We would all go to school, but we also done our chores. We had our work cut out for us. Grandmother was a wonderful person. I was pretty small when she passed away, but I remember her. She was very cool and quiet and calm with everything that she done. Looked like us children all minded her and respected her.

We drove cattle, and my daddy would sit down on a horse good

15

and drive and drive. When you drove your cattle along the road, they didn't have no fences on either side. I was a little fellow and didn't have a horse. So I'd ride up behind Papa, and if a calf turned out of the road, I would go right down behind him just like a dog and drive him right back in. And my papa would whistle. He had a little old tune he'd just whistle all the time. If the cattle would turn out of the road, he'd still whistle. Back in the road, he'd whistle. He never did get excited. I've often wondered about that. He was awful cool.

Old Judge Barlow lived near us, and he was as big as Papa. Papa'd start to town on his horse, and he'd catch up with Judge Barlow in his buggy. "All right, Judge, slip over."

"Oh hell, Ed, there ain't room enough in here for you."

And there wasn't either. That Judge Barlow was as big as Daddy was, don't you see. Both of them was big, and they liked one another. Papa thought a lot of Judge, and Judge thought a lot of Papa. It just looked like people thought more of each other in those days than they do now.

My grandfather owned three hundred slaves, and when the slaves was freed, there were only two of them that left. The others stayed right there. So that gives you a pretty good idea of my grandfather. I don't think there's another record like that in the United States.

When the slaves was freed, them that stayed lived not a half a mile from Grandmother's home. They were Hards. Now Toad Hard is still living. Toad's daddy was Old Man Raymond Hard. We called him Uncle Raymond. He had been a slave.

When we walked six miles to school, we would go right through Uncle Raymond's yard. He was very friendly and had a long white mustache. Uncle Raymond was always glad to see us. He was over a hundred then, and he lived to be around a hundred and six.

Right over to the right of where Uncle Raymond Hard lived, that was where Aunt Mary Regan lived. Aunt Mary lived to be a hundred and four, and I went down there one day and said, "Aunt Mary, they say you like to play the piano."

"Oh yes. Come on in."

I went on in, and she could not only play the piano, but she could sing like a bird. If I live a hundred years, I'll never forget that sweet voice.

I was named Miles Ray Lum when I came along. They named me after my grandfather, Miles Ray. When I was six years old, I went to school, and the teacher says, "All of you children go there and write your initials on the board."

I was named Miles Ray Lum. So I put up "MR Lum."

The teacher said, "You been acting smart all the morning. Come over here!"

She taken a rattail switch and like to wore my britches off. I never got such a whipping in my life. She whipped the Miles out of me, and I haven't used Miles since. My sister was sitting back there dying laughing. I remember that just tickled her to death, me getting that good whipping. That teacher really worked me over. I was only doing what I was supposed to do when I put my initials up there. But sometimes you get in trouble doing right. That's the moral of that. You can get in trouble doing right.

When I got to be ten years old I remember on Saturday I would drive Miss Enid Richman, the schoolteacher, in her buggy. We had to cross Bayou Pierre, and if it rained and that creek was up, the buggy would float. So I would get to that bayou, and I'd say, "Miss Enid, it's pretty high there."

"Ray, I think we can make it."

"Then let's cross up here."

That buggy would float, and many a time Miss Enid would get wet. When we would come back to the bayou, I would get down from the buggy and look at the water to see if it had rose any since we had crossed it. Usually it would be about the same, and we'd come on across. I've often thought if we had drowned there, they would have never found us, you know. That'd been all there was to that.

I was always glad to get back from taking the teacher for her ride. I would carry the teacher backwards and forwards across the bayou. I imagine Miss Enid is gone on to her great reward by now because she was older than I was by a good bit. That was seventy-some-odd years ago, don't you see. So that was my school days.

Did you know you can run over a hog with a buggy? I used to

drive a horse and buggy, and the hogs would be sleeping in the road. You can run up on that hog with a buggy wheel, and the way he jumps up, he'll turn that buggy over. I had it happen. You know a damned kid will do anything. I saw the son-of-a-bitch down there and gave him the wheel.[9] That's the worst deal I ever did. The hog rolled over and tore up the buggy, don't you see. What kids won't do. I never say nothing because I was one of them myself, and I done the same damned fool things. Don't ever drive a buggy up on a hog.

I think a dog's a lot smarter than a hog. We used to catch wild hogs in Louisiana. We'd have a good dog lope out and grab one by the ear and jerk the son-of-a-bitch around. The dog would turn him around a few times, and right back to that bunch he'd come. They go by instinct, of course.

When I was a boy, we had two or three pigs, and they got to be so thin that we called them razorbacks. They'd go all over the neighborhood and eat the people's garbage. If the people didn't have anything for the hogs, they'd browse[10] around in the neighborhood, and the dogs would get after them. I've seen them outrun a good dog. When they get to running, they go so fast that they just float.

I was on Big Black River one day. I was about twelve years old. Here comes a duck flying over. Boom. Down he went in the water. I kept waiting for the current to bring him in, you know. It was cold, cold as it could be, and I finally gave up on my duck. I wanted the damn duck so bad, but I could see the current in that river, and nobody there but me. So I said, "The hell with the duck." I done like the fox that was jumping at the grapes and couldn't get them. He said, "Hell, they're sour anyhow."

So I said, "The hell with that duck. I'm going to leave him."

The son-of-a-bitch was just turning around in that water. I could see myself falling in the water out there and nobody to help. So I started on back. It was three miles back to Rocky Springs where I lived. I walked about two or three hundred yards from the river and was going on home. It wasn't over thirty or forty minutes before sundown.

I was twelve years old then. I was a good, big boy, and had a little single-shot shotgun I'd bought. I picked cotton for two bits a hundred and went and bought that little gun. I saw some hogs out there, wild hogs. I eased right up on them, and I said, "I'll just kill one of them pigs. Then I'll gut him and cut his head off, and I'll have some meat to take home."

Bam. "Whee. Whee. Whee." God Almighty, here come these hogs running at me. Oh, I never saw as many hogs, so I run up a sapling. This sapling wasn't any bigger than about four inches through. I climbed up that sapling, and it bent over might near within four or five inches of where these wild hogs were. They was just reaching for me. Mouths wide open. "Whee. Whee. Whee." If one of them had went around and hit the trunk of the little sapling, I would have been on the ground. I kept getting closer to them hogs all the time, and there wasn't no way to go back up the tree. It had already bent over. All I could do was say my prayers and hope that those hogs would leave. The little hog was lying out there dead as hell. I wanted to cut his head off and gut him so I could get started for home.

Well, they finally did leave. They finally did after they stomped all over my little single-barrel shotgun. I got down, cut the pig's head off, gutted him, throwed him over my shoulder, and lit out. I did get home with a little meat. Course it was dark when I got to Rocky Springs. It was three miles from there.

Since then I've been with wild hogs and lots of other things in the woods. But that was one experience that I didn't forget. I was about twelve years old, and I come damn near getting in that pile of hogs. Good God Almighty.

I remember Mr. Drexler run a store in Rocky Springs, and every time I'd get a nickel, I'd want to go in there and get me some candy. "Mr. Drexler," I'd say, "I want a nickel's worth of candy."

"Just a minute."

That was Mr. Drexler. He'd go back around behind the counter, take that jug, that whole jug. "Just a minute," drinking a goddamn big swallow. "What was it you wanted?"

"I wanted a nickel's worth of candy, Mr. Drexler," and I'd already give him the nickel.

He had a long white beard that was as white as the driven snow, but right down the center of it was a streak just about like a tie. That streak was where the whiskey would run down his beard, you know. It wasn't no question about how it got there. That whiskey leaked down, and that old man, he lived to be, I think Mr. Drexler lived to be in his nineties. I'd go down to Aunt Emma Lum's to stay all night, and I'd say, "Aunt Emma, I went by Mr. Drexler's today." I was about nine years old then. "And Mr. Drexler takes that old jug and turns it up, 'glug, glug, glug.' "

She says, "Oh, tut, tut, tut. Whiskey is going to kill Mr. Drexler."

And it did. But he was ninety-two before it finally got him.

Back then my father was buying cattle. He got a fat yearling there one day, and I suggested, "Papa, let's butcher that yearling." It cost two dollars, don't you see, the yearling did. We cut that son-of-a-gun up, and that yearling dressed[11] out at about a hundred and fifty pounds. We cut him up in steaks, and I taken the old family buggy and horse, and when I came back home, I had me eleven dollars and all the meat we could eat for a week.

Every Saturday after that we butchered a yearling, and the people looked for me to bring them meat. There wasn't no place you could buy meat in that part of the world. In Rocky Springs there was a few stores, but there wasn't any fresh meat. So they was all looking for me when I would come. I remember my biggest handicap with that meat was the flies. I kept the meat in a box at the back of the buggy, and it was hot. I would stop and get me a fresh branch off a tree, the one that had the most leaves on it. That was so I could keep those flies off of the meat. I remember that quite well. Flies was awful in the summertime. My biggest trouble was keeping the flies off of my meat.

I would sell all my meat and make a nice profit on it. In those days a dollar was worth about what twenty is now. I sold that meat to them for a nickel a pound. You could get five pounds for a quarter. As time went on, we started selling three pounds for a quarter. Went up just a little bit. The quarters would always give out before the meat. My daddy was buying them great big yearlings for two dollars a head. That was pretty cheap meat, you know. It cost us about a half cent a pound dressed. After you dressed it, that was about all it cost. I'd peddle it all day and sell all I could.

Once I carried a dressed lamb up to Old Man Bulrun. I said, "Mr. Bulrun, here's your lamb for two dollars."

"Where is the head? Where is the liver? Where is the lights?[12] Where is the feet? Where is the tripe?"

I was listening. I said, "Mr. Bulrun, I'll bring them to you in the morning."

"Well, in the morning I'll give you your two dollars."

I went back home, and I said, "Papa, those people are living on what we are throwing away."

We never was hungry no more after that. We'd throw the lights out maybe but keep all the rest. A lot of people would say those were tough times, but I guess you could say them was the good old days. Nobody had any money much. But nearly all the people would have something to trade. If they had a horse, they would trade it for a cow. There wasn't too many people that had money.

I used to set traps for minks and coons when I was a kid. I'd trap them, and I'd sell the hides. I'd get more for the mink hide than I could for the coon hide. I remember that. I'd get a dollar for a mink hide and two bits for a coon hide. I've stretched many a coon hide for twenty-five cents. Stretch it up nice. About once or twice a year an old peddler would come by buying hides, and I'd have my hides stretched just right. Sometimes he'd say, "I won't buy that because it's not stretched right." He learned me to stretch them right. I was just a kid then.

I remember one night Cleve Brown and I went coon hunting, and there was just one dog. We had this dog, and he treed. I killed three of them coons. Then I come to find out I was out of shells, and there was three more still up that tree. So Cleve says, "Ray, you keep them up there." I was about nine years old. He said, "You keep them up that tree, and I'll go back up to the store and get some shells."

It was three miles back up to the store. Well, I kept walking around and whistling. The dog was there, and it looked like Cleve would never get back. Finally, one of them son-of-a-guns come down out of that tree. I was hitting the tree and yelling and everything else, but he come on down anyway and run off. The other two stayed up in the tree though. So Cleve came back, and we killed them two in the tree. And the dog went out and treed the other, so we didn't lose any on that deal. The one that got out of the tree, we got him too. We got all of them. Got six coons that night, and we was ready to go in. This old boy, Cleve Brown, he was two or three years older than I was. He was the one that went and got shells while I kept knocking on the tree to keep them up there.

It was a moon-shining night, and you could put the moon on them. You didn't need no headlight. If the moon was over here, you'd just walk around, and you'd put the moon behind the coon. And when you shoot, you shoot right at the moon. There's his head sticking up there in the moon. You can kill him just as good that way as you can in the daylight. I never did miss one in the moon. I was a good shot in them days, you know. I could see like an eagle. I'd enjoy putting the moon on them. I don't care what part of the tree he's in, you can get the moon on him. You keep walking around until you get the coon between you and the moon. Put the coon in the moon, then you shoot at the moon and kill the coon. That's right. Them days there was lots of coons.

I was picking cotton and getting two bits a hundred. I'd pick cotton during the day and hunt coons at night. You know, there's not many people around today that remembers drawing two bits a hundred for picking cotton. I picked cotton for my Uncle Joe Jett[13] in Rocky Springs. J-E-double T. I remember I'd get ninety-eight pounds, and I'd say, "Uncle Joe, give me two bits for that. It's so close to a hundred."

He never would do it. Well, I can appreciate Uncle Joe now. He wasn't giving anything away. He was learning me. It was educational, and I love him today for what he done then. I was picking that cotton when I was seven or eight years old.

That hadn't been too long ago. I guess it was seventy-five years ago. That was what they was paying for picking cotton. And cotton brought three cents a pound. You got fifteen dollars for a good bale of cotton, but you'd take that in trade. Them was really rough times. Cotton was fifteen dollars a bale, and I got two bits a hundred for picking it.

Well out of that twenty-five cents a hundred I got, I bought a pair of goats. Henry Freeman, a colored fellow down there at Hankerson had a big pair of tall goats. So I said, "Henry, what do you want for those goats?"

"Two dollars. Dollar a piece."

"I'll buy them from you. Put the yoke with them."

"I won't put the yoke in."

Well, he wouldn't put the yoke in, so I ordered me some harnesses and got me a little wagon. By picking this cotton at two bits a hundred, I had enough money to get a little harness. I don't remember what the harness and the little wagon cost. I got all that from Sears and Roebuck. In them days Sears and Roebuck was a lot cheaper than they are now. I think that wagon and harness were less than nine dollars.

Well, anyhow, here comes a drummer[14] along, and he says, "Ray, what do you want for that little pair of goats?"

They wasn't little goats. They was big. Henry Freeman, this fellow I got them from, had pulled a bale of cotton with them. Those goats were the only transportation he had. They were broke good. This man, this drummer, he says, "I'm with Mr. Cohn down there."

Cohns was big operators. They was big merchants at Lorman, Mississippi. Their old store is still there. It'll be an heirloom there always. Anyhow, this drummer come by and said, "What do you want for those goats?"

"Twenty-five dollars."

I was thinking about getting me a horse then. He said, "Take them down to Mr. Cohn. He'll give you the twenty-five dollars for them."

"I'll carry them in the morning."

"No. Don't take them till Saturday."

Well, I didn't sleep much between then and Saturday. I was thinking about that twenty-five dollars and the horse I was gonner get with the money. So I got up early Saturday morning, about two o'clock, and start out with my goats. It's thirty-five miles from Rocky Springs to Lorman, and I walked every step of the way. I was afraid that if I rode in that wagon, I'd make my goats tired, and I wanted to get them to Lorman in good shape. I stopped at Port Gibson to pick up an old gray mare that rented for a dollar. I brought the old mare with me to have something to ride back to Port Gibson.

So I finally got down to Mr. Cohn's store in Lorman. I said, "Here's your goats, Mr. Cohn. Twenty-five dollars."

I had that twenty-five dollars on my mind. Walked every step of the way. I didn't get in the wagon, not one time. I didn't want those goats to be tired. I wanted them to get there in good shape. That was the way I was doing business.

"Naw. Twenty dollars."

"The man told me, the man that sells goods for you, told me that you would give me twenty-five dollars for the goats."

"Naw. Twenty dollars."

He stormed at me so many times he shook my shoes. I said, "Well, just give me the twenty dollars."

So I got up on the old gray mare and come on back to Port Gibson. The next day I come on out to Rocky Springs with the mail rider. He charged fifty cents to bring me home. So when I got home I had all the twenty dollars but the fifty cents that I had to give the mail rider to ride with him and the dollar I rented the gray mare with. I gave the money to my daddy, and I told him, I said, "That man wouldn't give me but twenty dollars for my goats and harness."

"That's all right, son. We will get you a pony."

When Mr. Cohn bushed[15] me out of that five dollars, he gave me a wonderful lesson. That you don't absolutely have to have, you can do without. I got along just as good with the twenty he gave me as I would have done with the twenty-five.

My father took that money and bought me a little pony. Before that I'd been driving cattle without any horse. I would just hop up behind Papa on his horse when I would get too tired and ride with him.

By the time I got my pony broke good, Papa began to give me a dollar a day. I wasn't getting but fifty cents a day when I was walking. After I got the pony, he give me a dollar a day to drive with him. I was getting along just fine.

One night I turned my little horse out in the road to graze. Next morning Walter Hall came by and said, "Your little horse is down at the sorghum mill."[16]

I went down to the sorghum mill and looked at him. I looked at that horse and said, "You'll never play that trick again," crying all the time. "You'll never play that trick on anyone else."

He had eaten so many sorghum chews[17] that he died. That was the first horse ever I owned. I came back and told my daddy I had lost my little horse. He said, "Never mind, son. We will get another one."

So I got a colt, and then I started to trading. I remember going out to Dr. Austin's at Bovina and trading the colt I had. I swapped Dr. Austin my colt for a big old horse, but the old horse that Dr. Austin traded me didn't have any teeth. Dr. Austin was a good horse trader.

Tom Kline was there, and he said, "You oughta not put that horse without any teeth on that boy."

Dr. Austin said, "Well, somebody has to learn him."

I always loved Dr. Austin, and I lived to sell him lots and lots of horses. Finally sold them to him by the carload. So Dr. Austin gave me one of my first lessons. Instead of disliking him for it, I liked him, don't you know.

Next time I swapped for a horse, I looked at his mouth. And I didn't look to see what he had been eating. I looked to see if he had any teeth. Yeah, he swapped me an old horse without any teeth, but that one didn't die. I swapped him off, and I kept a-swapping.

Dog
Days

In 1903 Lum and his family left Rocky Springs and moved twenty miles west to Vicksburg. There he worked in local stores as a delivery boy for two years and continued his schooling at night. Too poor to continue his classes for long, he soon relied on his wits to survive as a trader.

Lum's trading career began in 1907 when, at the age of thirteen, he bought a horse for twelve dollars and sold it for twenty-five. He later reflected, " 'I made one percent[18] profit,' as the Dutchman says."

As a teenager in Vicksburg, Lum earned the respect of city fathers, who appointed him the town dog catcher. During this period he met gypsy horse traders in Vicksburg. Gypsies were said to have the power to "hoodoo" horses because they could make a defective "plug" look like a fine animal. In his story of Little Eatum, Lum describes a common trick practiced by gypsy traders. A customer often traded for a horse that appeared healthy, and later discovered that the animal was defective. The gypsy trader would then revisit the customer, buy the horse back at a reduced price, and move to another community.

Early trades in Vicksburg prepared Lum for a career that spanned sixty-nine years during which he bought and sold thousands of horses and mules throughout the United States. As automobiles and tractors began to replace horses and mules in the South, elderly livestock dealers in Vicksburg feared for their future and sold Lum their barns and stock at bargain prices. By 1912, at the age of twenty-one, Lum owned five stables that housed hundreds of mules and horses. These stables allowed him to trade on a much larger scale, buying and selling trainloads of mules and horses. He then traveled with his stock by boat and rail a hundred miles up into the Mississippi Delta, where he sold horses and mules to farmers. He had come a long way from the first horse he bought in Vicksburg for $12.50.

Lum's livestock barn was a favorite gathering place for children as well as adults. Blues composer and performer Willie Dixon was born in Vicksburg and described Lum's China Street barn:

> *There would be a lot of horse traders around there, and a lot of us kids used to hang around there . . . they had everything going there . . . and to see those guys ride those horses like that was really something at that time. Yeah, I remember Ray Lum when he was quite a young man. I was a kid then myself.*[19]

Lum's livestock barns were always neat and well painted. His brother John's barn in Natchez was decorated with colorful murals that both Walker Evans and Ben Shahn photographed. Evans remembered the barn as:

> *a sort of shop-front that advertised itself as such, very naively, and it had a picture of some horses' heads that was an extremely moving and touching thing.*[20]

Lum's stationery featured a drawing of a horse and mule facing each other with the phrase "Ray Lum Dealer in Horses and Mules." In a letter bearing this letterhead dated December 28, 1932, Lum responded to my grandfather's newspaper inquiry about a pony. In a formal, professional style Lum wrote my grandfather:

> *I noticed your advertisement in paper to buy or rent a gentle pony for children. Useless for me to describe same as I have all kinds, ages, sizes and prices. Would be glad to rent or sell*

*you pony, and in case you wanted to rent a while to see if
pony suited would be glad to let rent apply on purchase price
of animal.*[21]

*From his stables Lum supplied hundreds of mules to dealers who
marketed the animals to farmers in twelve counties around Vicksburg. He borrowed as much as $250,000 from the bank to support
these trades.*

*During this period Lum recalls Theodore Roosevelt's bear hunt
near Vicksburg, and the Mississippi River Flood of 1927. The flood
covered 26,000 acres of land and destroyed $236 million worth of
property. Many farmers in flooded areas drove their stock to Vicksburg and kept them in barns and feed lots operated by Lum.*[22]

*Lum won contracts with the Army Corps of Engineers to supply
them with mules to build levees along the Mississippi River. Since it
was first established in 1879, the Corps had erected and maintained
levees along the Mississippi. By 1912 their levees extended along the
Mississippi and its tributaries for fifteen hundred miles, the length of
the Great Wall of China.*[23] *Lum's encounters with the Corps offi-
cials were not without humor, and once he successfully matched wits
with a colonel who claimed that mules leased from Lum had jumped
into the river and "committed suicide."*

*Though his trades later carried him from coast to coast, Lum
always considered Vicksburg his true home. He knew the city's streets
intimately, and as we walked together, he confessed, "These hills are
in my blood. I've seen pretty country from the Pacific clean to the
Atlantic, but this will always be where I want to lay my head."*

When I was twelve years old, my daddy moved us to Vicksburg. There was nine children, and my father's health wasn't good. So we kids all went to work, and I got me a job selling papers at two dollars a week.

Papa decided that I should go to school. I went to the Catholic Brothers and made arrangements for the Brothers to teach me at night. They charged two dollars a month for teaching me, but I worked at Holerfield's Grocery for two dollars a week, so I was all right there.

Brother Roberts was my teacher. I'll never forget him. I thought the world and all of him. He taken quite an interest in me, and he tried hard to see that I did learn something. I guess that was the best schooling ever I got when I went to that night school, cause I was paying Brother Roberts with my own money. Two dollars then was the same as fifty now.

When I worked at Holerfield's Grocery for two dollars a week, I waited on the customers, and then I loaded up the wagon and delivered the groceries. You wasn't only a clerk for two dollars a week. You delivered the groceries too.

I remember one day a bunch of gypsy women come into the store. They had on those long sweeping dresses, you know. "Meester, what is that way up on the top shelf?"

Pointing up to the top of the shelf, way up high, you know. I climbed up there, and I thought I had better look back and see what was going on. I looked back and saw they was filling up their pockets with can goods, and they had a dozen pockets in each dress. So I came back down. Didn't get what I went up to see on top of the shelf. Mr. Holerfield came in about that time, and I told Mr. Holerfield, "Those outfits they have on got can goods in every pocket."

"Oh, they wouldn't take anything."

"They've already taken it. They've already cleaned us out."

Mr. Holerfield was a good old fellow. He just couldn't believe that them nice gypsy girls were stealing his stuff. We finally got them out, and they like to taken the store with them when they left.

Well, time went on, and Mr. Holerfield says, "Ray, if you can get a better job, you do it. Two dollars a week is all I can pay you."

So Miss Kate Feeney come up one day, and she says, "Ray, George Smith wants somebody to work for him. What do you get down there where you are?"

"Two dollars a week."

"Well, George Smith will give you three."

So I told Mr. Holerfield that I could get three dollars a week from George Smith. Mr. Holerfield was a good man. He said, "Now you go right on. I don't want to hold you back. I can't afford to pay you more. You go on and get that three dollars."

A few days later I went over and went to work with Mr. George Smith. I ate good up there. I would eat dinner with them every day. That was the only good meal that I would get, when I would eat dinner up there with Miss Kate. At home I never had much breakfast and not much supper. There were so many of us in my family that there wasn't enough to feed us. So, anyhow, I would eat lunch up there every day, and I got alone fine.

A few days went by, and here come a fellow up there with a little horse. He said, "I want to sell this horse."

"What do you want for him?"

"Twenty-five dollars."

"I'll give you twelve for him."

To cut a long story short, he finally decided to take the twelve. I went in and told Mr. Smith that I had ten dollars, and I wondered if he could loan me two dollars. Fine. That was all right with him.

I put a halter on the little horse, tied him out there to the post, and went on with delivering groceries. That was the first horse ever I bought in Vicksburg. Before I left that evening, a fellow came by and wanted the little horse. He was gentle and about a two-year-old. I hopped up on him and rode him. I was a good hand. So I bounced[24] the little horse around.

"How much do you want for him?"

"Twenty-five dollars."

So he bought him. "I made one percent," as the Dutchman says. A few days later another fellow came up with a horse. I bought that one for fifteen. He was a little thin colt, but he was young. I tied him out there and bought me a peck of feed from Mr. Smith, the fellow I was working for.

The next day Mr. Smith says, "Ray, don't you think that you can make more trading than you can working here for three dollars a week?"

I said, "I just don't know, Mr. Smith, but I will sure try it."

Miss Kate had been so good to me and served such good meals, I hated to leave, but I taken the little horse out and went to trading, and I hadn't been without a horse since.

I remember I caught a deer in the Mississippi River about then.

I saw him coming across the river, and I got me a little old boat, paddled over there and caught him by the horns. I was about thirteen years old, but I was little for my age. I pulled him as long as I could behind me and got him tired. Then I put the deer in the boat and tied him. Just by myself. Nobody but me. He was about half grown. Well, that deer undressed me. That son-of-a-gun tore my shirt off when I put him in the boat.

We lived out there on Washington Street. So Mr. Johnson came out there, and Papa says, "My boy caught a deer the other day, Joel."

"Where is he? I want to see him." He come around there and saw my deer. "What'll you take for him, Ray?"

"Twenty-five dollars."

Well, he like tore his pocket off paying me for that deer. There was thousands of deer over where Mr. Johnson lived. I was thinking I was going to have to sell him to somebody else. I always loved Mr. Johnson for that, and he was tickled to death to get him.

I went up to Mr. Kline's place there at Valley Park once and went squirrel hunting. Went right across the river. Bam. Every time I'd shoot, I'd kill a squirrel. I never did miss, and I generally tried to get two of them together with one shot. I'd killed about ten or twelve squirrels when I started back. I had my dog with me that I'd carried from Vicksburg. I guess I was fifteen years old, maybe sixteen.

I started back on the path there, and something screamed. My hat raised right up there on my head. He screamed again. If you've never heard a panther squall, don't nobody need to tell you what it is. When you hear the son-of-a-bitch holler, you'll know. I knew it was a panther. I walked on a little further, and he screamed again. I walked a little faster, and he screamed again. Well, I looked back, and I saw the brush shaking behind me on the path. Paths like that, you use them a while, and then they grow up and cover over. When I saw that shaking, hell, I knew he wasn't no more than forty feet behind me then. I had a little single-barrel shotgun that I'd killed them squirrels with.

The son-of-a-bitch squalled again just like a woman screaming. Just exactly like a woman. I knew what he was then. I was awake. It was getting night. I knew where the cat was, and I knew my boat was right down the path.

I run a shell in the little old single-barrel gun I had and looked back, but I couldn't see him. The panther was covered up in the brush. Finally he squalled again, and this time he was much closer to me. So I said, "Well, I'll just give him these squirrels."

I threw those squirrels in that path, and he never did squall again. I never heard another whimper. I went on down, got my little skiff, and went back across the Sunflower River. Mr. Kline said, "I heard you shooting a lot over there."

"Yeah, I killed twelve squirrels, but I had to give them to that panther. He was squalling around there."

"You done right."

That was Mr. Kline. So the next morning he takes my dog and goes back there, and he kills that panther within a hundred yards of where I threw them squirrels. When the panther went up the tree, Mr. Kline shot him. He shot him through the head right above the ear. He knew where to shoot one. When the panther hit the ground, he killed my dog. The dog grabbed the panther and kind of shook him. You know how a good dog will do. A good dog will grab him and shake him to be sure he's dead, and that's when the panther killed him. He bit the dog on the head right through the brain, and that one bite killed him. That was the last of my dog.

But let me tell you about the dog days in Vicksburg. The dogs was biting people, and the streets all over town was crowded with curs and old mangy dogs. You couldn't sleep at night. It was the damnedest thing you ever saw. So Chief Grooms says, "How about you taking that job as dog catcher, Ray? Fifty cents a day for impounding those dogs."

I must have been about sixteen then. I had that job for about two years. After them two years you couldn't hear a dog bark, much less see a stray dog around Vicksburg.

I got me a mule and a wagon and put a crate on it. It looked like a chicken coop, but it would hold dogs. I found an old whelp in heat and tied her behind that wagon. Well, sir, when I would come back to the pound, I would have twenty dogs following her right on in. Some of them I would have to return because they had tags on them. That bait got the tagged ones and the untagged ones. That got the mongrels and the registered dogs both.

So that bait works awful good for a lot of things. There's a moral to that. I got some lessons awful early in life, and they was just common-sense lessons, lessons you pick up when you look to see what's going on.

The greatest dog lover lived out next to All Saints School in the Park.[25] He had a pack of these white-and-red Walker hounds. Many a time I'd pick up his dogs and just put them in the wagon. The next day I'd take them back to him, and he'd say, "How much I owe you, Ray?"

"Not a thing, Mister."

He was a fine old fellow. He loved dogs, and them days there was fox in that park, quite a few fox. His dogs would run a fox all night, you know, and never get out of the park. I can't think of his name. He was a good fellow.

I got along with all the people that had dogs. Mr. Thompson was on Grove Street out here, and he had bird dogs. I used to pick his dogs up and take them on out to Mr. Thompson.

"How much I owe you, Ray?"

"Not a thing, Mr. Thompson. I'm glad to do it for you."

And I was. He was a good fellow, and that man give me more bridles and more doggoned stuff. He give me a gun, by God. Made me a present of a gun. I hunted quite a bit. It was the best gun ever I had. That gun cost twenty-five or thirty dollars in them days. They cost a hundred now, don't you see. That's right.

But he was one of the nicest fellows, and when I'd get those bird dogs, I'd bring them on out to his house and put them around in the pens where he wanted them. So he always appreciated those things.

When I was catching the dogs, I had to furnish my own transportation. I had an old wagon and a big old brown mule that I bought from Old Lady Boury. I had give fifty dollars for the mule, and she had a knot on her leg when I bought her. So I was coming up Cherry Street, along about Cherry and South by the *Union Post,* and one of the manholes was in a rut in the road. This mule stepped on that, and down in there she went. She fell over and broke the shafts out of my wagon. But I didn't lose my dogs. I had that wagon full of dogs. So I pulled the old mule up and got her on her way. The next morning I hitched the mule back in the wagon, went up to the Court House, and I said, "Judge Henry, my mule fell in the manhole there. Just look at her."

"Oh my goodness."

He looked at the big knot first. The mule'd had that knot twenty years. Mrs. Boury had the old mule, and I had given her fifty for her. So Judge Henry went in, and he said, "Gentlemen, I have a little complaint here. This client of mine, who's working for the city and doing a wonderful job, he said his hundred-and-fifty-dollar mule"—I'd given fifty for the old mule—"fell down in the manhole there, and you see what it done to her," pointing over to that big old knot. Been on her for twenty years, you know. "I'll make a suggestion that you gentlemen pay Ray for his mule a hundred and fifty dollars without any further recourse. He is a city employee, and his wagon was damaged fifty dollars' worth."

Oh Lord, I was smiling. I'm telling you that judge was talking right down my line. Oh my goodness, Mr. Helgeson and those men, they went back in a room, and they decided to give me fifty dollars' damage on the wagon and paid me a hundred and fifty for the mule. I was smiling like a jackass eating briers.

So a few days later that same Judge Henry says, "Ray, I've got two thoroughbred horses out of Mr. Lawhorn's stallion down there, and I'd like to get them broke. Whatever will you charge?"

"You'll like the price, Judge Henry, and you'll like the way I break them horses."

When I sat down on Judge Henry's horse, that horse jumped, and I never had a horse jump so high. I got to whipping him and finally got him to act right. But don't let nobody tell you that a thoroughbred won't pitch.[26] I kept those horses six months. They was Judge Pat Henry's horses. I'd ride them every night, don't you know. When I got them horses broke good, I says, "Judge, whenever you are ready for your horses, they are broke good. Come down today, and you can see me riding and working them." Judge Henry was glad to do that.

I had a boil here on my hip, and I had a little thirty-eight-caliber pistol. That pistol scabbard got to bothering my hip, and I, like a damned fool, taken the pistol out and tied it on the saddle. That was the worst mistake ever I made.

It was night, and I was riding one of Judge Henry's little horses. I just tied the pistol on the saddle. Thought I had it tied secure. Tied it to the trigger guard. So this little horse breaks in two. He broke in two and lost his coupling pin,[27] and before he got through bucking, that gun went off and shot my hand. Right here is where that bullet went in, and up here is where it come out. There's a scar up here where it come out, and this finger is still dead.

I went up to the doctor with it the next day, and the doctor looked at my hand. It was black, just as black as it could be, and the doctor had an awful frown on his face. I was looking at him. So I went back up the next morning. There was a yellow streak in my hand, and I saw him kind of smile. Each morning I went up and saw some more yellow in my hand. He saved my hand, but that finger never got right. The bullet went in there and come out up here.

There was an old whore lived near the stable, and she told some of them, she said, "I shot Ray last night."

You know how whores are. If you don't know, I'm telling you. A damn whore, they want to talk, and when she said she shot me, two or three other whores, they got it and spread it around town. There was whores all around that barn where I kept my stock. I was there all day long and half the night, sometimes all night. I done most of my business at night. Where the town pound was, down at the end of Washington Street to your right there, they called that Whore Town, and there was whores all around, don't you see. A lot of Vicksburg was Whore Town.

Mr. Allen who ran the dairy out there drove eighty of his cattle into the city one night. The mayor called and said, "There are about eighty of these cattle eating up the flowers and everything."

I just eased out there, whistled and drove them cattle out to the pound. I know I was a good hand from the time I started because my daddy was the best cow driver I ever knew. So right down through Washington Street I came with those eighty cows. It was about one o'clock in the morning when I put those cows in the pound.

Here comes Mr. Allen down. He was a nice man, just as nice as he could be. He says, "I don't blame you, Ray. You're just doing your duty, but I'd like to have you push those cows out about milking time."

All right. I got behind them. I walked them right through Washington Street again. On back out, and they was right on time to milk. They didn't lose a stroke. Mr. Allen was a man that had lots of influence.

Mr. Allen was a registered Irishman. He was full-blooded Irish, and his wife, Effie Green, was Irish too. They had a goddamn bull there, and Effie got to scratching the bull. But when she moved away from him, the son-of-a-bitch butted her a time or two. She told Mr. Allen, she says, "Don't go out there where the bull is. He'll hurt you."

So he went out there. "Get out of the way, you son-of-a-bitch."

The damned old bull moved out of the way. Effie said, "Well, if you had on a dress, he'd do you like he does me."

So Mr. Allen comes in the house and puts on Effie's dress and goes out there, and the son-of-a-bitch knocked him down, broke his leg, and rolled him under the house. Come goddamn near killing him, don't you know. Yes, that was Mr. Allen. I knew him like corn bread. That was Effie's husband.

I lived right back of the old ballpark, and a bunch of gypsies came in town below the park one day trading horses. Here come one of them riding up there on a big tall giraffe.[28] He says, "What have you got to trade?"

"Oh, I got a nice bay mare here."

"Come down to the camp and see if we have got something you want to trade for. We got lots of horses down there."

So I got my little bay mare and went down, and they had the prettiest little white horse that you ever saw. I finally traded for the little white horse. They had him washed and pretty. Had to give them my mare and ten dollars' boot.[29] So I bought the pretty little white horse and put him back of my barn.

It wadn't twenty minutes before I thought about that little horse and got out my brush to polish him a little. But when I come up to him, here he come flying at me with his mouth open, his teeth showing just like an alligator. So I reached down and got a two-by-four and combed his head. He fell, and I remember this fellow with me said, "I believe you killed him."

"Well, he wadn't a very good horse anyhow."

I saw him rolling his eyes around and knew he'd be up in a minute. So when the little old horse got up, I taken ahold of him, slapped him side the head, and led him around the lot. I wadn't but sixteen, but I was a good hand with a horse. I taken ahold of him and pulled him on up and slapped him aside of the head again a time or two. He was a pretty little white horse. I knew I had something.

It wadn't but about an hour until here comes a gypsy man and another gypsy and another one, three of them. "Meester, you know where Meester Smith is?"

"Yeah. Right here."

There was a lot of Smiths around there, but I knew I was the Smith he was looking for. I was awake. He looked down the hill there and saw this little horse.

"Oh, you got Little Eatum."

"Well," I says, "he was Little Eatum, but he's not anymore."

"Let's see you catch him."

I still had that two-by-four in my hand. "Come here you son-of-a-gun."

He walked right up, and I put my hand on him. He was thinking about that two-by-four. Little Eatum was converted, don't you know. I'd learned him some manners, and he behaved himself.

Oh good God, those gypsies dropped their feathers. They thought I would want to give him back after he tried to bite me. When they saw I had him tamed, they turned around and didn't stop running till they got back down to the gypsy camp. They was the sickest gypsies you ever saw.

Well, sir, it wadn't an hour before here come the old gypsy queen with nine or ten more gypsies. "Oh, you've got my little angel. Are you good to him?"

"Yeah. Awful good to him."

"Mister, how will you trade for that little horse?"

"I don't want to part with him. I've got attached to Little Eatum."

"If you come down to the camp, we will satisfy you."

"I'm pretty well satisfied now."

"Meester, Meester, what will you take in cash money for that little horse?"

"Five hundred dollars."

There wadn't any horse bringing five hundred dollars then. "Oooh, you must think we are crazy."

"Well, I don't know, but I don't think I want to get rid of Little Eatum."

"Will you come down there and pick out what you want to trade for?"

"I will do it in the morning at eight o'clock."

"We got to leave here at seven in the morning. We are leaving in the morning at seven."

"I will be down there by eight o'clock."

So at eight o'clock I went down, and, sure enough, they were all packed up and ready to go. Here they come. The gypsy queen came out, and she just loved that little horse and petted him so. The more she loved him, the more I thought how many horses I was gonna get from her.

They had a sorrel horse there that they had got from a good friend of mine. I said, "I will give him to you for that sorrel horse, that little mare, this gray mare, this bay mare, them six head."

"You must think we are crazy."

"No, I don't think you are crazy. I don't want you to have this little horse. I want to keep him for myself."

So I began to get on him to go. "Mister, we will bring them up."

They brought all six of them horses up. One of them I sold later for a hundred and fifty dollars. And the gypsies lit out.

That was their taw. That was their meal ticket. They wadn't going to go off and leave Little Eatum. They made their money with him, you know. I guess I kept Little Eatum longer than anybody else. Oh, those gypsies really helped me.[30]

The gypsies always kept a horse like Little Eatum that they could catch back. They'd trick you out of a good horse and give you a snide skin[31] for the good horse. I got to where the gypsies didn't have too much on me.

After the gypsies left I started to running the stables in Vicksburg. I was at the corner of South and Washington streets one day when I met Jim Moore, an old black man. "Mr. Ray, I want to sell you my barn and this equipment here. I want to sell you everything that I've got."

"I don't know whether I have got enough to pay for it."

"Oh yes you have. I have to leave here. I've got asthma, and the doctor told me that I have to leave."

"Well, figure it up, Jim, and I'll see whether I have enough to buy it. Let's start right here. What about this horse?"

"Fifty dollars wouldn't be too high for that horse, would it?"

"No, fifty dollars is all right for that one."

He went right on down the line with the horses and got down to the buggies. He had some good Babcock buggies. "I'm going to put them buggies and their harness down at twenty-five dollars a piece, the buggies and the harness."

"That's all right."

When he got through, I think all of it was fifteen, sixteen, maybe seventeen hundred dollars. Poor fellow; he had asthma. He was just as black as ink, and he had a handlebar mustache. He was very likable. I give him his money, and when he was getting ready to go, I shook hands with him and said, "Don't you stay away too long. You get well because I'll be ready to give this outfit back to you when you come back."

And I meant every word of it. I says, "You hurry up and get over that asthma," and I was hoping he would. If there ever was a good man, Old Jim was it. He shook hands with me, and then he cried. That was the last time I saw him. He told me where he was going. He was going some place in South Texas. Somebody told him it would cure him there, don't you see. He had asthma. But he never did come back. So I figured he died, you know. Bound to or he would have come back.

Before he left, he said, "Mr. Ray, I hope that you will keep these men working here. I have had them here for a long time."

"I will keep them. I'll keep every one of them and hire more." Which I did. I kept them all and hired more.

"Wait a minute. There is another request that I want to make of you. Old Dr. Birchett, that's his old gray horse. The horse is forty-one years old, and when he dies, I promised Dr. Birchett I would bury him."

"I'll tend to that, Jim. Where does he want him buried?"

"Out in the pecan grove." S. C. Regan had this pecan grove outside Vicksburg. "There is a pecan grove, and he wants him buried in that pecan grove, buried right under a pecan tree."

"I'll tend to it, Jim."

Sure enough, the old horse died at forty-two. Dr. Birchett's old gray horse, the horse Dr. Birchett finally replaced with a car, lived to be forty-two. Dr. Birchett had so much love for the horse that he just left him there and paid board on him. And when the horse passed away, we carried him out there and buried him. Sam Regan wanted him buried right beside a pecan tree. Well, a lot of people would ask, "Why would he want him beside a pecan tree?" People that want to know that, I just won't answer them. You see, Mr. Regan figured that tree would have more nuts on it, and I don't know but whether he was right too. Anyhow, we know it will be well fertilized with that two-thousand-pound gray horse under it, don't you see.

Old Man Regan would give us five dollars for bringing a dead horse out there and burying him. You didn't get your five dollars till you buried him. You'd haul him and bury him for five dollars. That was S. C. Regan that'd do that. And right where you buried that horse, he'd plant a pecan tree. Right there. Okay. Mr. Regan lived to be a ripe old age, and I used to carry mules and horses out there on a dray[32] and bury them. I'd plant him wherever Mr. Regan wanted to plant a pecan tree.

So I went to trading horses in Vicksburg and had a good business. People would come in from the country, leave their buggies and horses there in my barn, and I'd take care of them. They would pay me fifty cents for feeding their horses, unhitching them, and hitching them back up. I didn't care anything about that fifty cents. I was making money trading. I was glad to have them come 'cause I would wind up trading with some of them.

If you owned a horse and didn't want to keep him home, you'd leave him in the stable and pay about fifteen or twenty dollars a month. And when you'd go out, you'd go down there for your horse, and the hostler[33] would hand him to you. Then when you come back, you'd get out of your buggy and go home. That is the way it was done when I had my stables in Vicksburg. Even after cars come in, a lot of people still kept their horses. All of them didn't get cars at once, you know. But when cars started coming in the 'twenties, most of the Vicksburg traders decided to sell out.

It wadn't long until here come Mr. Roach walking up there. "Ray, I want to sell you my barn." It was up on Washington Street. The building still sits there and has the appearance of a livestock barn, just like it did seventy-five years ago.

"Oh," I said, "Mr. Roach, I would like to buy it the best in the world, but I don't guess that I have enough money to buy it."

"Yes, you got enough money. I'll fix it so you can buy it."

"Well, all right, Mr. Roach. Let me count my money and see whether I have enough to pay you."

He put them Babcock buggies that cost in them days a hundred and something, put them for twenty-five dollars a piece. Some of them were new. Had one or two brand-new ones. Put surreys for twenty-five dollars a piece. Put the harness at ten dollars. Lot of it was brand-new harness. A lot of those horses was Kentucky horses that he had give a hundred-fifty to two hundred for. He put all those horses at fifty a piece. Boy, you talk about being in business, I was in business then. I had something to trade on then.

While I was at the Roach Stable, here comes Old Man Levy from down on China Street. "Ray, I want to sell you my barn."

"Mr. Levy, I don't think I have enough money to buy it."

"I'll fix it so you can."

I knew he had been asking five thousand dollars for it. I said, "I will buy it if you put it down cheap enough."

"I'll take thirty-five hundred dollars."

To cut a long story short, I bought his barn for three thousand dollars. He said, "I want to stay there about two weeks."

"Perfectly all right. I'll stay here at the Roach Stable for the next two weeks."

Well, the fall of the year was coming, and I wanted to get the Levy stable fixed up. When I got that barn ready for mules, I was in business.

While I was in that China Street barn I remember the little blind Boudron boy and his sister used to come and sit on the bench at the barn. He was around about five years old, and his sister was about four. One evening I walked by. The Boudron boy was blind, and he says, "Mr. Lum." He knew everyone in the barn when he was five years old. Said, "Mr. Lum."

"Yeah?"

"I can tell you how many mules is in the pen there."

"All right. How many is in there?"

Lacy had just run the mules out. The mules had hit the floor and were running. He said, "There is fourteen."

We counted them, and there was fourteen. He said, "I can tell you how many is in the next pen. Go down there and let that bunch out."

The mules hit the floor, and he said, "There is fifteen."

Lacy said, "That is the Christ Child," talking about the Boudron boy.

Of course, I knew he was doing it from sound. Them mules would hit that floor, and the floor was wood, because they slipped too much on concrete. It was planks, and the mules would run on it and make an awful racket. That child was just five years old and could already tell how many mules was in the pen. So when Lacy would see him coming, he would say, "Here comes the Christ Child."

Well, I kept that stable a long time. I had that stable when, I don't remember what year it was, snow got about ten or twelve inches deep in Vicksburg. It was so much weight till that barn just folded up. Each side come together, and they said the crash sounded like cannon shooting. I had a hundred and fifty mules in that little barn. It was just stacked full of mules. Right out into the street they went. Stampeded, of course. But we got every mule back, and I think about the only damage was one mule that had an ear half cut off.

When I was down on China Street, a fellow came up and said, "Mr. Ray, I want to buy that horse and buggy from you. Let me feel out that horse. Let me try him a little."

"All right. Be careful with him there. That horse is green."

So he drove up China Street and started back down. Something happened. I don't know whether part of the harness got loose or what, but, anyhow, the horse run away from him. The fellow got his wheels astraddle the guide wire on the telephone pole, and he went up to the top of that pole with the buggy. He was a big fat fellow, and when he spilled out, he was lying on his back. I thought he was dead, and I said, "Jim, call the undertaker to take him away."

The man jumped right up from where he was laying and said, "I'm not hurt. You don't need to do that."

"Uh huh."

After he come under his own power he walked on to the barn, and I give him a drink of whiskey and straightened him out. He was all right. Didn't have no bad effects. I told Jim, "That's one time it's a good thing he was fat." It didn't seem to hurt him any.

A trader named Romega was right down the street from me. The boll weevils[34] had just come to Mississippi from Texas. Then there was MacAdams trading down on Grove Street. MacAdams had a load of Tennessee mules, and Romega was bringing his mules in from Texas. MacAdams was an Irishman, and he was like all Irish. They think of something. So a customer came around and looked at Mr. Mac's mules and told Mr. Mac, "I've got some mules cut out at Mr. Romega's, and I think I'll just go back and buy my mules from him."

"Well," MacAdams says, "if you want to buy those mules and get boll weevils all over your place, you just go right ahead."

The man dropped his walking stick and swallowed his tobacco. "Oh my goodness. You think they will carry boll weevils?"

MacAdams said, "They got hair on them, haven't they? How do you think them boll weevils got to Texas?"

The fellow went back around and told Romega he didn't want them mules. Then he went and bought Mr. MacAdams's mules. MacAdams's mules come out of Tennessee.

People would come into those barns from the hills outside of Vicksburg. "How much for them mules, Ray?"

"Five hundred dollars."

"I want to make a hundred-dollar deposit. Will a ten-gallon keg hold them?"

"That's all right. Bring it on."

They would bring a ten-gallon keg of whiskey and give it to me instead of money. A ten-gallon keg was worth a hundred dollars.

46

Ten dollars a gallon. Some of them called it white lightning, don't you know. They all got to seeing who could make it the best, and we had good whiskey. Vicksburg had good whiskey.

One day a man come into the stable and said, "Mr. Lum, I don't think you've been feeding that horse of mine."

"If you don't think I fed that horse just look at your bill."

That satisfied him. Telling that reminds me of an old fellow named Lawrence Bianchi who had a little iron-gray horse. You know, a horse is born black, but as he gets on, he gets iron-gray, then he gets white. He dies white. So Lawrence had this goddamn horse down on the street, and all night long it was cold, raining and sleet. An officer come by and taken the horse up to the city pound and told Judge Wagner how thin the horse was.

Judge Wagner was awful thin too. So, anyhow, Lawrence came up to court, and the judge says, "Mr. Bianchi, I'm going to fine you five dollars for cruelty to animals."

"Judge, I feed that horse twice a day all he can eat."

"Well, he sure doesn't look like it, Mr. Bianchi."

Mr. Bianchi says, "Judge, do you eat regular?"

"Yeah, all I want to."

"Well, you're as thin as that horse."

That judge was so skinny until he couldn't tell if he had the bellyache or the backache, don't you know. Good fellow, too. He was judge here for a good, long time. That's been sixty-some-odd years ago. I don't know if he fined Mr. Bianchi or not.

About two o'clock one morning the city barn in Vicksburg caught afire. This old mule knocked some gates down so he could get out, and when he got out, he was on fire. The back end of him was burning. He run right to the old man's house that had been working him, and he burned up right at his door. That man never did work for the city anymore. He just retired. His mule was gone. He loved that mule. No, he never did work for the city anymore. That's a true story, just as true as the Bible.

I was down at the street corner once, and a fellow said, "Mr. Ray, I want to buy a horse."

That was the Frenchman that came out of New Orleans and married the Hope girl out here. He said, "I never rode a horse in my life."

47

"Well, fine. Take that one there. He's never been rode in his life."

So he laughed. Full-blooded Frenchman. He said, "What will you take for him?"

"A hundred and fifty dollars."

He pulled out his money and paid for the horse. He said, "Now I want to board him here."

"Okay. That will be twenty dollars a month."

He would come over and pet that horse every day. I got the horse from Dan Cole, and he was as wild as Old Man Dan was. He was a red roan and a pretty horse.

So Frenchie would pet him, and finally I came back there one day, and he was on him. To cut a long story short, it wasn't but a day or two before Frenchie was riding him around in the barn, and it wasn't but another day or two until he rode him out here to the park. Frenchie was his name, and he was a full-blooded Frenchman. Well, when he got over to the bridge, this horse had never been to a bridge, and he put his brakes on. So Frenchie came back in and said, "Mr. Ray, I got out by the bridge with that horse, and he wouldn't go. So I scolded and scolded him."

"Well, it's getting late. I'll ride out there with you, and maybe I can help you." When we got out about fifty yards from the bridge, I said, "Here, you take my horse, and I'll take yours."

When his horse stopped at the bridge, I got off and combed his head with a two-by-four, right between the ears, and down he went. He rolled his eyes all around. Frenchie said, "Mr. Ray, I believe you killed him."

"Well, he wasn't a very good horse."

When the damn horse got back up, I just touched him with my heels and rode right across where he'd been stopping. I rode him back and forth across the bridge five or six times, come on back and give him to Frenchie and said, "I don't think you'll have no more trouble." He kept that horse for as long as he stayed here, and he never did have any more trouble with him.

We had a mule that was white-legged, a good mare mule. Perce Hubbard, a fellow that worked for me, rode her all the time. We got to calling her "Fox Trot." Well, Fox Trot rode more like a horse

than she did like a mule. She'd fox-trot, don't you know. I'd rather
ride her on the road than any horse I had.

So one day a fellow come along and said, "Ray, I'll give you four
hundred dollars for that mule."

"Well, just a minute."

Perce said, "If you sell that mule, I'm going to quit."

I told the man, I said, "I'm not selling the mule," and I went
right on. I don't remember who I did let have her later on. Oh yeah,
I sold that mule later on for five hundred dollars. I give Perce a
hundred dollars and bought him a suit of clothes. Made him happy,
anyhow.

I never did have one like her again. She had feet like a horse
with a white mane and tail, and she'd just fox-trot. She was a
beautiful mule with four white legs. Unusual mule. She was more
horse than she was mule. I understand she was out of a jack,[35] but
she was outstanding. You find them like that once in a while.

She was like that mule Mr. Thorn had. Mr. Thorn worked for
the government for years and years, and he had a mule that had a
long mane and a long tail too. He never did roach[36] that mule's tail
or his mane, and he drove him till he died. Most people roach a
mule's mane and tail to keep it from looking like a horse and to
keep it from being so bulky. His mule's mane was long, and his tail,
oh my God, he had an awful pretty tail. He kept him nice and fat.
He wouldn't cut a hair off that mule. You know, there's some people thataway. They'll be thataway, and you don't change them. He
was a good old fellow. I liked him. I liked nearly everybody in
Vicksburg. They had to be an awful stinker for me not to like them,
and I traded with damn near all of them.

I remember one fellow lived right out from Vicksburg. He
wanted a gray horse just like the one that Stonewall Jackson[37] rode.
So I went to St. Louis, and I bought a big, tall gray horse. In them
days a tall horse wouldn't be worth any more than a vinegar recipe.
If you got a vinegar recipe, with one nickel you can make four
gallons of vinegar.

Well, anyhow, I found a big old tall horse up there, and I
bought him for thirty-five dollars. Good God, you'd have to get a
ladder to get on him, don't you know. He was awful tall. So I

brought him here. Here comes the man down for the horse, and I says, "Here's your horse. He's just like the one that Stonewall Jackson rode."

This fellow looked at him and says, "Yeah, and I'm not right sure he ain't the same damned old horse." He bought him anyway, and everything was all right.

I've had every kind of a horse there is, I guess. And there's not many kinds of horses I haven't traded. I sold a man a little mare once, a pretty little mare. She wadn't over thirteen hands[38] tall. Just as pretty as a doll. He loved her. So she brings a colt, and the colt kept growing and went right up to seventeen hands high.

I don't remember what they bred her to, to get that giraffe. It was just a freak of nature, that big old thing coming out of the little bitty mare, you know. But those things happen.

For a long time those big horses didn't have any value. But I was in Chicago once, and this officer rode up on a big, tall horse. Something started happening way down the street, and he says, "I've got to leave you."

He could see what was going on a mile down from there. I could see then why they needed tall horses. And down in New Orleans they use them for leading racehorses. They're exercise horses. They ride those big giraffes that used to not be worth any more than a vinegar recipe. But time changes all things, don't you know.

I remember I had a saddle once with a radio in it. The radio was up under the pommel.[39] You would just turn the son-of-a-bitch on, and you would think you was in the house. I rode it lots of times and had fun with it. I'd ride up and be talking to a man and turn it on. He'd say, "Where is that music playing?"

"I don't hear any music."

"You don't hear no music?"

"Hell, no."

"Goddamn, I'm leaving here."

He thought sure as hell there was spooks around. It was playing real low, you know, real low. It was a good son-of-a-gun. I don't remember who I let have that saddle. It was about a three- or four-hundred-dollar saddle 'cause it had that radio in it. That's the only one ever I saw like that.

Speaking of saddles, I was up at Buck Starter's Rodeo. I got a lot of saddles up there. I stopped up at Starter's, and he had a pretty bay horse. I'd bought a load of horses from him, and I said, "Throw that damn bay horse in. I'm going to give you a hundred for him."

"That's my baby's horse."

"The hell it is. Well, what do you want for him, Mr. Starter?"

"Give me a hundred and a half for him."

"I don't want to do that."

"That's my baby's horse. I shouldn't let you have the horse at all."

"Well, I'm going to give you a hundred and a quarter to throw that son-of-a-bitch in."

So he did. He was a fifteen-and-a-half-hand bay horse. Weighed about eleven hundred pounds. Pretty as a doll. I brought him on here to the barn and started the sale. When he bounced in the auction, I said, "Here's a horse that I got from Buck Starter, and he said it was his baby's horse. I saw his baby, and his baby is six-foot-four. I don't know anything about this horse, and I'm not going to recommend him, but he's a pretty horse. A hundred and fifty. One seventy-five. Two hundred. Sold for two and a quarter."

Well, the man that bought him, about a week later at the next sale, I looked down there, and there was that same man. I kept looking at him. He was just sitting there like he was froze. So when the sale was over, I walked over, and I was kind of nervous, you know. Imagine how you'd be with a man sitting there froze. I knew there was something on his mind. At first I didn't recognize he was the same man that bought the horse. So I went down and said, "There's something wrong with you, and I don't know what it is."

"I came here to kill you."

"Well, I hope you'll change your mind."

He never changed his expression. He said, "I came here to kill you. That horse you sold me killed the only boy that I had. Knocked his brains out against the tree."

So, naturally, you know, I expressed my sympathies and said I was sorry and all. Said I was so sorry, and I was. I got him to go in the cafe and take a drink of coffee and finally had him eat a good dinner. But he come there to kill me. He wasn't wolfing. He was telling it just like it was. That horse was from Starter's Rodeo. Buck

Starter made a good saddle. It was a hard son-of-a-gun, but it was a good saddle.

I guess some of the best trades I made was right here in Vicksburg. I remember one time Joe Luster says, "Ray, what do you want for that bay mare?"

"I don't know, Mr. Joe."

"Saddle her up there."

So I saddled her up. "Sit down on her."

I kept sitting in the saddle, but after a while the saddle was down on the ground. Joe Luster laughed. I looked back at him, and I said, "Well, Mr. Joe, maybe you oughta get another one."

I had eight or ten horses and didn't care which one I sold. He said, "No, she's all right. I want her. I don't want her to ride nohow."

He was going to hitch her to a buggy, you see. She was a good work mare. I thought he wasn't going to take her after she done all that episode, you know.

Mrs. Platt had an old mare. Mrs. Platt's named Bob, and her husband was named Elmer. So she says, "Ray, Elmer and I are going away on a trip."

Elmer's gone, you know. Bee stung him in the eye, I believe it was. Something like that. Well, anyhow, she had an old bobtailed mare, and she says, "Ray, Elmer and I are going away on a little trip, and we want to put our mare out there in your pasture. There's nothing in there to bother her, is there?"

"Well," I says, "I don't know. There's an old jack in there. He's got one eye and one ear and no teeth. I don't think he'd bother your mare, Mrs. Platt."

Off she and Elmer go on the trip. All right. They come back, and she says, "Ray, how much I owe you for taking care of my mare?"

"Not a thing. Not a thing."

Half the time I never charged people for taking care of their horse. So about six months went by, and she called me up and says, "Say, Ray, you owe me twenty-five dollars."

"Yeah? What is that for?"

"Doctor Best charged twenty-five dollars for performing an abortion on that mare to take the mule colt from her."

"Uh huh. Well, that makes us even. That's my jack fee. That's what I charge as stud fee on that jack."

I remember she said, "You son-of-a-bitch."

Course I didn't charge nothing on the jack, you know. He was old and one-eyed and one-eared. Didn't have no teeth, and the old mare was the same way. But there was the colt. That was the damnedest thing I ever heard of. Nobody would believe it if they saw the old mare. She had a carved[40] tail, tail no longer than an inch straight up, and they had it docked, you know. So I said, "That makes us even, by golly. I charge twenty-five dollars stud fee for that jack." I don't think she expected me to pay the twenty-five dollars. They was making money, and they had money too.

I knew Old Man Watt all along, and Jim Bell was the boy he had by a black woman. Mr. Watt sent Jim Bell off to school and give him a good education. I liked Mr. Watt. I'd stop and trade with him, and he was a nice old southern gentleman. After Mr. Watt passed away, Jim Bell, the boy that he raised and educated, was killed right at the gate going into the home. I knew him, and I liked him mighty well. He was an awful good fellow.

So they brought a black detective in here from Tennessee. He come and stayed about three days, the detective did, and found out what he wanted to find out and left here. The supposition was that a good many of those people owed Mr. Watt money, and they thought that after Mr. Watt died, Jim Bell would try to collect it. But they didn't know Jim Bell. He wouldn't have thought about it. Jim Bell didn't want to be killed. I knew him like corn bread. He was just as nice as he could be, and why they had to go and kill him, I'll never know.

These are all things that happened a good many years ago. I was under twenty-five when all that was going on, so that's been a long time ago. Let's see, I'm eighty-five now. That was about sixty years ago when Jim Bell was killed right at that gate on the road. I never pass that gate and look at it that I don't think about where he was murdered.

That's been going on ever since Hector was a pup. Been killing people ever since. That's what it was, cold-blooded murder. That's how Jim Bell left here, and his wife stayed here for several years after that.

My brother John told me there was a time at Natchez that every white man had a black woman, and I said, "Well, I'm not sure that Vicksburg wadn't near 'bout the same way." That went on for blows.

One old man in Natchez, his wife had four children, and John says, "Ray, there isn't a damn one looks like him."

I said, "Do they look like the chauffeur?"

John said, "Quite a bit."

"Well, he'll have to raise that chauffeur's salary because he is doing all his work."

There was a fellow here named Sharpin, and after a while people got to calling him "Mr. Hairpin." I knew him awful well and we did a lot of business together. I remember they passed a law that you couldn't kill any sheep. You couldn't kill any sheep or cattle or hogs, and people were about to starve to death for meat. They was saving the meat to send to the boys in the army, and all you could kill was goats.

They had dropped the bomb on Hiroshima.[41] It was around that time, don't you see, and you wasn't supposed to kill a damned thing but goats.

Mr. Sharpin called me and said, "Ray, I got four hundred head of sheep up here."

"Goddamn it, I wish they was goats."

"Well," he says, "they're cheap."

When I first got there, I met the fellow helping him, and I said, "Which way is Mr. Sharpin?"

"You mean Mr. Hairpin?"

"You bet. That's who I mean."

Here come Mr. Sharpin. All right. We walked down there about a hundred yards and come to two men working on a piece of machinery. One of them come running over and says, "Mr. Hairpin, I can't work with this fellow here."

"You both quit then."

That was all he said. He never changed steps. Never quit walking. We went on down and looked at the sheep, and when we got back, both the men was still working. As we started down to the sheep, I saw a dead sheep laying out there to the left. I looked over to the right, and I saw another dead sheep. I never opened my mouth. I never said a word. I went on, and before we found his herd of sheep, I'd seen five dead.

"Well, we've seen enough of them. They're all alike here. What do you want to do, Mr. Sharpin?"

"What do you want to give for them, Ray?"

"Three dollars."

"You'll never get them."

"Then let the dogs kill them all."

I hadn't mentioned the dogs, don't you know, but I knew what killed those five I'd seen. I said, "I'm going to give you three and a half for them, and I'll haul them right now before the dogs kill the rest of them."

He never said a word. I called and got the trucks to haul his sheep. I had about four hundred sheep when I got to Vicksburg. We started killing them and put two hundred in the icehouse that evening. I told the icehouse man, "I want to put these goats in here."

The icehouse man never said a word. He didn't know the difference. If he did, he never said anything. The next day the icehouse man called me and said, "Mr. Lum, I want you to come out here. The government inspector's here, and he says two of them goats is sheep."

I went out there and said, "Goddamn, that son-of-a-bitch has killed my two pet sheep. God Almighty! I'll run him off when I get back."

I got to cussing so and raising so much cain that the inspector left. He went on out of there. We got him out of the way, don't you know, and went on down to the barn and finished killing the sheep and brought them on to the icehouse. The first man I called was at Greenville. I told him what I had, and he said, "How much are they, Mr. Lum?"

"Thirty-five cents a pound."

Before the next day was over, I was selling them for fifty cents a pound and didn't have enough to go around then. Some of them dressed a hundred pounds. They were big sheep, and I sold them for goats. I didn't have a goat. There wasn't a goat in the country. I had already killed every goat I could find.

I had good credit, and the First National Bank here at Vicksburg never turned me down. They let me have whatever money I wanted, and it took a good deal to handle mules. I remember one time there I owed the bank a hundred and seventy-five thousand dollars. George Williamson was president of the bank, and he said, "Ray, we can't let you have any more money. You owe a hundred and seventy-five thousand dollars now."

"But the government owes me that money for the mules they leased from me, and if the government is no good, by God, your dadgum bank is no good."

I just went on back to the barn. Mr. Burnside come in from down at Newellton. Mr. Burnside was what I considered a good businessman, and I told him about it. He said, "Did George Williamson tell you that?"

"He sure did."

So he went up to the bank, and when Mr. Burnside came back, he said, "Ray, you can go back to the bank now and get all the money you want."

"I'll see him in a few days."

I went ahead and bought four or five more trainloads of mules. I owed that bank a quarter of a million dollars for mules before the government began to pay. But when they paid, I settled with the bank and everyone else.

I furnished mules to dealers in about a dozen counties around here, and I had a big business right in Vicksburg too. I kept two or three barns full of mules all the time. And my brother John had a barn in Natchez that had been operated by a Mr. Cock. Flavoris A. Cock. "What's your name, Mr. Cock?"

"Flavoris. Flavoris Cock."

That was his name. That was the man whose barn John bought. Cock had written on a sign outside the barn, "Mares and Mules and Horses." I never saw a sign like that before. I'd of just said "Horses and Mules." That'd cover all of it. You know, you've got mares when you've got horses. I guess more people asked for mares than for horses. That sign stayed there for years.

Mr. Cock wore a hat. The old devil said the Indians told him never to wear a hat, and don't do nothing but fish and hunt. He said he'd strayed a little from that path. He caught himself wearing a hat. I guess he still done that when he died.

Mr. Cock had every kind of picture you could think of on that barn. And inside he had a life-sized horse painted on the wall. Some fellow came there and was broke, and Mr. Cock fed him. He told Mr. Cock he wanted to do something for him, and he painted this life-sized horse. When he got through painting it, somebody offered Cock two thousand dollars for it. Cock says, "I wouldn't sell it to anyone," and when Mr. Cock went on to his great reward, that horse was still there.

I got kicked once in Natchez. A mule kicked me right in the middle of my shoulder. The fellow with me yelled, "Look out, Mr. Ray."

I saw the doggoned mule when I went in the pen. I saw his ears laid back,[42] and I saw his eyes, and I knew he was a kicker. I knew what he'd do, but I forgot about him. The fellow hollered, "Look out, Mr. Ray," and that mule kicked me right in the back.

That night I caught the train and went on to St. Louis. The next day I bought two hundred and fifty head of bulls, and when I was bidding on them bulls I was lying on a stretcher. I laid right on the stretcher, bought the bulls, and shipped them over to Montgomery, Alabama. When I got to Montgomery, I was better, of course, but I lacked a lot of being out of the woods.[43] I was almost paralyzed from that kick in Natchez.

I'd buy young, green mules and send them out on the levee, and them mules would come back fat. The mules hauled willows to make mats for the riverbank. All that was done by the Army Corps of Engineers.

I'll never forget one incident that happened on the levee. A colonel came in one day and said, "I got bad news for you, Mr. Lum."

"Yes, Colonel, what is it?"

"Six of your mules jumped into the river and drowned, and we want you to know that the government is not responsible for those mules drowning."

"Oh, the mules committed suicide, did they?"

"Yes."

"Where are you from, Colonel?"

"Connecticut."

I saw his bread wasn't done,[44] and I got away from him. Down to Judge Pat Henry I went. "Judge, I want to go about this right. I had six mules on the levee that the bank caved off with. The mules went into the river and drowned with harnesses on them. That colonel from Connecticut told me the government wouldn't pay for them."

"Ray, a mule won't jump in a river, will he?"

"If you run one up to the bank, you might go over his head, but he's not going in."

"Don't you worry about that colonel. You just put your bill in for those mules. You will get every dime of it."

"I told the colonel that mules didn't commit suicide. There never was a mule known to commit suicide."

"Ray, you know more about mules than he does."

"Yeah," I thought to myself, "and about a lot of other things too."

It wadn't two weeks until I got twelve hundred dollars. That was two hundred dollars a piece for my mules and harness. I had my money for my mules, and I was back in business.

I kept the government supplied with mules. They acclimated the mules on the levee and gave me better mules back. People would come from the back part of Georgia to buy them mules when they come in. I kept two hundred there on the levee every year.

Those levees was all built with mules, and you could smell those mule camps before you would get within two miles of them. When you got there and pulled up the collar on one of them mules, you could see what you was smelling. God Almighty, both shoulders would be rotting with sweat, don't you know. When a mule died, they would throw him right in that levee, and when a man got killed around there, they covered him up just like the mule. That went on. I've seen it all.

I bought the Dan Cole cattle for the first rodeo that Vicksburg ever had. Old Man Cole had some five- and six-year-old steers that hadn't been penned but a few times. So I went up to Old Man Dan and said, "I'd like to buy those steers from you."

"I don't want to sell them."

"Uh huh. Well," I said, "we got a rodeo coming, and they will break every one of them to pull a cart and ride them."

"Well, by God," he says, "you can have them."

I bought his steers and he agreed to help me drive them down to the old fairgrounds. I went to the Cole farm the next morning, and Old Man Dan had those steers penned. There was forty of them. He was a good hand with cattle. A monkey man would have turned them out, and they would have scattered like a covey of birds. They would have went in every direction. But Old Man Dan just walked in the pen. "Ooooheee!" He would throw salt in the air, "Ooooheee!"

He threw the salt up in the air, and I saw them steers throwing their tongues out licking. "Ooooheee!" Cattle love the taste of salt, and they went for that salt the way a horse goes for sugar. Finally Old Man Dan said, "Ray, let them out. I'll go ahead of them, and you follow."

We drove the cattle right on to the pens where the rodeo people were. They give Mr. Cole thirty or forty tickets 'cause he had a large family, and they rode every one of those steers and worked them to carts. That was the first good rodeo we ever had in Vicksburg. Nearly everybody come, and they had it out at the old ballpark.

Nobody but Old Man Dan and me could have brought those steers in. "Ooooheee!" He'd throw that salt in the air, and you could see steers way in the back sticking their tongues out. And when Old Man Dan would come to my barn, I'd always notice him sticking his tongue out, licking around.

I remember one day Old Man Dan came to town with his horse and buggy and was driving down Washington Street when he run through the red light. The officer grabbed him and said, "What are you doing running that red light?"

"When I see red, I think it means danger, and I try to get out of the way."

That was Old Man Dan. They said he made good whiskey. He made good whiskey, and he consumed a good bit too.

I used to put a carload of mules on the big boats and go up the Sunflower River. There was no trouble to put seventy-five head on. The roustabouts would load them.

Two of those rousters would carry a mule kicking and bucking right up the gangplank. They could have led the mules, but they didn't. The mule might weigh a thousand or fifteen hundred pounds, and they'd carry him kicking and all. God Almighty. Every once in a while he'd kick a rouster and over in the river he'd go. The mates was just rough as hell on those rousters. I can hear them hollering at them now. "Pick up that mule, you sons-of-bitches." It could have been done a little easier without all the hollering.

That was when they had John Louser, the old roustabout who could pack a five-hundred-pound bale of cotton. I've seen him load many a bale of cotton. He'd carry a bale of cotton by himself. Old John Louser was one of the best rousters on the river, but he was just one John. They had to have more.

One time I bought a blind bull from a woman at Eagle Lake. "Mr. Ray, I'm going to sell that bull."

"I'll give you six dollars for him."

"Yes, sir."

I was driving the bull back when I met Dr. Keiger's hostler. He had the prettiest little black horse you ever saw. "Mr. Ray, how will you trade me that little mare you riding on?"

I had an old black mare. She wasn't no account. I'd swapped her about twenty or thirty miles up the road that day, and I was sick of her. He said, "How will you swap me that mare for this pony?"

I looked at him, and he had the prettiest black pony you ever saw. He was worth two of that old mare I had.

"Give me ten, and I'll trade with you."

He like to tore his pocket off, getting that ten and handing it to me. I slipped my saddle over on his little pony. I had just bought that blind bull from the woman there. I give her six dollars for him. That bull would be worth three hundred dollars today.

I didn't go a hundred yards until I come to a draw. It was a low place where the water come across the road, and the water was awful deep. When this blind bull got there, instead of going on across, the son-of-a-bitch turned and went right on out into the lake with me kicking and yelling behind him. To cut a long story short, before I knew it we was over a hundred yards out in the lake, and when I kicked my little horse, he went down. I almost cried. God, I loved that little horse. And the hell of it, I had a hundred-and-fifty-dollar saddle on him that I'd bought and paid for. I cried about losing my horse and saddle too. So I had to hold to the damn bull.

My tears didn't start to get dry before that little horse jumped up and, I'm not exaggerating, his feet cleared the water. How he done that I'll never know. He was strangling to death, you know, and the son-of-a-bitch come up and jumped. When he come down, I taken him by the bridle, turned his head toward the bank, and the blind bull followed him. The three of us went on back to the bank, and everything was lovely. I remember that like it was yesterday. I was so proud of my little horse when I got him and my hundred-and-fifty-dollar saddle back. I was back in business again.

When the boat come in to get me, I had this bull that was blind and weighed fifteen hundred. The bull cost me six dollars, way less than a half a cent a pound. When the boat come in and they lowered the gangplank, I says, "Captain, load that bull there first. He's been pulling back a little."

He says to the rousters, "Pick up that bull."

They picked him up, a fifteen-hundred-pound bull. They picked him plumb up off the ground, held him in the air, and carried him on the boat. That was the way they loaded him.

Old John Louser was in on that deal. John Louser-Rouster they called him. He was there that day. He was a rouster that was noted to everybody that knew about boats. When he'd go up the gangplank, he'd rock. He could throw a bale of cotton on his shoulder and trot right up the gangplank with it. John Louser lived to be a ripe old age, and I knew him all down through the years.

During the flood of nineteen twenty-seven, I had alfalfa hay in Vicksburg stacked a hundred yards high and two hundred yards long. The people sent their cattle in here to get them out of the flood, and I fed three thousand cattle out there at one time. If they wanted to sell them, I'd buy them. If they didn't want to sell them, I'd give them back their cattle when the flood released, and they carried them back home. One man came to Vicksburg from Tallulah, Louisiana, and somebody says, "Are you living over here now?"

"No, I just come over to milk my cows."

He lived twenty miles away in Tallulah, but he was a dairyman, and his cows were over here. In 'twenty-seven that water leaked from here almost to Monroe, Louisiana. That was one of the big floods.

Teddy Roosevelt come here after the flood. I remember it like it was yesterday.[45] He spoke down at the Court House, and when he finished his talk, he had everybody following him. Vicksburg people liked Teddy, and the whole town went Republican that year.

I think any place Teddy was, he was at home. He just called an ace an ace and a spade a spade. He didn't ring no bells about it, and whatever he called, it was generally about that way.

Franklin was all right, but I always liked Teddy the best. I thought Franklin done wonders for a man who was paralyzed and then could go ahead and be President of the United States as long as he was. It's like that saying, "There's so much bad in the best of us, and there's so much good in the worst of us, it hardly behooves us to believe in the rest of us." That's just as true as the Bible. There's some good in everybody.

Getting back to Teddy Roosevelt, when he got to Vicksburg, the first thing he done was go on a bear hunt. He went up to Panther Burn, got an old colored fellow that was a bear hunter named Jim and come back to Vicksburg with him. Other hunters wanted to go, but Teddy wouldn't take nobody but Jim.

"I've always hunted alone," he says, "and I'd prefer to go just with Jim and his dogs."

On they went to Louisiana. They went right over to Tallulah, and when they got up north there about fifteen miles, Jim said, "This looks like where we might find one."

They put the dogs out. It wasn't thirty minutes before the dogs bayed in the briers. The bear was standing up on his haunches, and Teddy says, "Jim, I think I'll shoot him right in the eye."

The bear was seventy-five yards from him. Bam! The bear turned over and started to roll, and the dogs ran right up and grabbed him, you know. When the son-of-a-bitch quit rolling, Old Jim turned him over, and, by God, that eye was asleep. That's how good a shot he was. He had shot him square in the eye, just exactly like he said he'd do it.

Teddy says, "Jim, we might get another one while we're here."

That was the first one, and they put the dogs right back out. The bear was thick as rabbits then. Maybe they weren't that thick, but there was plenty of bear. Jim said it wasn't half an hour before they had another one bayed. When Teddy shot him, he didn't move anymore. He was a dead shot. He shot that first bear in the eye, and the other he shot in a different place, but neither one moved after he shot.

I knew old Jim. I said, "He didn't shoot but once?"

"No, sir. That man, one shot was all he needed."

After he left, Teddy sent several bears to be turned loose over there. After a few years, here come the bears swimming the river and coming on into Mississippi. They come into Vicksburg, and there was a few people here that their bread wasn't done. They run and got a big shotgun and killed them, you know. Charlotte Wilson lived out there, and one come to her house. She said, "Mr. Ray, I fed that thing there for about two weeks. I hated when he left."

He was there every morning, and she liked him, you know. I said, "Well, I hope that he ain't one of them they killed."

So many people would run and get two guns. Boom! Boom! Boom! Shooting the bear, you know. They advertised in the paper that the bear was coming back and not to shoot them. Those was the bear Teddy had turned loose. Teddy was a genius on animals, and he thought them bear would do awful good there. They would have if they hadn't crossed the river.

Down on the river was where Old Captain Tom had his whiskey boat. He sold his whiskey, and he made four million dollars while they was trying to find out whether the boat was in Mississippi or Louisiana. Every time they'd say "Louisiana," he'd say "Mississippi." If they'd say "Mississippi," he'd say "Louisiana." And while they was farting around with it, he just kept making money, don't you know. He was working with Governor Bilbo.[46] If you go out to shoot a fool, don't shoot Bilbo. Save your ammunition. His bread was done. They was trying Bilbo in Jackson, and somebody said, "Bilbo, we going to send you either to the penitentiary or the governor's chair."

He said, "I'll make a damn good man at either place."

And he did. He got to the governor's chair.

Bilbo bought a farm down in South Mississippi, and Captain Tom built him a castle on it. He done all that for Bilbo. Of course, Bilbo kept Captain Tom's whiskey boat going for four years.

The world had gone bone dry. It was in Prohibition. You couldn't buy liquor nowhere in the United States, and Captain

Tom was running whiskey everywhere. People was going over there and coming back, not with a bottle, but with a grip.[47] You could buy grips and go in and fill them up with whiskey. That went on for four years while they was trying to decide whether his boat was in Mississippi or Louisiana. You know how much they were trying to decide. Captain Tom would say he was in Mississippi, then say it was Louisiana, just switch it back and forth, don't you see. All the time he was making money and had no business in either place. Captain Tom was in his bloom in those days.

When Captain Tom passed away, it was the largest funeral ever in Mississippi. I don't know whether it was the largest in the United States or not, but it was the largest one in Mississippi. I attribute that to those customers of his. No matter how sorry, how dirty, or raggedy a trembling old drunk was, Captain Tom would say, "Give that son-of-a-bitch a double jigger."

Them's the people that caused that funeral to be so large. A lot of them drunks didn't stay thataway. A lot of them people straightened up and made men. A lot of fellows that he gave a drink to got to be lawyers, doctors, and everybody else. Everybody don't stay a drunk. So I attribute that to Captain Tom having that big funeral.

Mrs. Lum's daddy was a MacIntyre, and he come here from Hopkinsville, Kentucky. I remember trading horses and mules up in Hopkinsville, and there was a fellow named Bill Orphus. Old Bill would give you the shirt off his back. He run a saloon, and sometimes a fellow would come in there about half drunk and say, "Bill, you take one on me."

Bill'd just register it up and not drink it. Some of them'd say, "Bill, you gonna take that man's money?"

"Well, he'll come in here someday and want a drink, and he won't have the money."

It made good sense what he done. He made a fortune selling booze and never did touch any himself. He said, "Whiskey was made to sell. It wadn't made to drink."

Mrs. Lum's family come on from Hopkinsville to Vicksburg. After we got married, she was in the undertaking business, and I was in the livestock business. An old boy come from Texas to see me, and when he got back home, somebody asked him, "Did you see the Lums?"

"Yes, I did."

"How're they doing?"

He says, "Ray is in the livest business, and his wife's in the deadest business, and they make a good pair."

I look back sometime, and I wonder what become of all that money. My wife was a builder, and she built a whole end of Vicksburg. She built and sold houses, and it didn't make no difference whether you had the money or not. Just put a payment down and move in, don't you see. A lot of times she would sell our house while I was away trading and move into another one. I'd go to Texas and be gone two or three weeks at a time. When I got back to Vicksburg, I'd stop at the tollgate out at the Mississippi River bridge to use their phone, and they'd say, "What you stopping here for?"

"Hell, I got to find out where I live."

I remember Mrs. Lum and I was up at Long Lake gar[48] fishing, and we tied our line to a jug and put a bell on it. The bell started ringing, and I got into the boat to get the fish. He was caught in the mouth and leaped like a horse. When I got to the bank, I pulled him, and he just slid right on up.

The next morning they had a gar rodeo, and I carried the son-of-a-bitch down there. They were giving a prize for the biggest gar, so I carried mine down and weighed him. He was a big son-of-a-gun, a hundred and seventy-five pounds.

"Oh, boy," I said, "I know I've got it now."

The man said, "What you got, Ray?"

"Oh, I got a good one, a hundred and seventy-five pounds."

"Mr. So-and-So just weighed one in at a hundred and eighty-five."

That settled it. Prize went to him. But don't think that a hundred-and-seventy-five-pound fish don't give you a lot of fun. When you catch ahold of him to pull him out of the water, he's a lot of trouble. They have that gar rodeo every year.

I had a fellow named Squire that worked for me a long time. The best one on Squire was when he run into Old Bull's head. Squire said he was picking cotton. I guess he was. He was twelve or fourteen years old. Squire was like a lot of folks. He was grown when he was a boy. He started early. Squire was down picking cotton, and a man was going to bring them cotton pickers back to town in his pickup truck. When he started driving back, he picked up a big black man that had a sack in his hand. So he gets on the truck, and there was twenty or thirty men already on it. This big black man weighed about two hundred pounds. Squire looked down and saw blood on the end of the sack and says, "You been hunting?"

The man said, "No, I hadn't been hunting. That's Old Bull's head. You want to see it?"

"Yeah."

He just emptied the sack out, and there rolled this black man's head. Had it cut off right even with the neck. Just rolled like a ball. The truck was running forty or fifty miles an hour. Squire said them other passengers on that truck was just like birds. They began to fly in every direction. Everybody left but Squire and the old man, and into town they went. The driver didn't even know the others were out of the truck. This fellow driving had to go to the jail, and this old man that had the head says, "I'm going to take this in to the sheriff. You want to go with me?"

Squire says, "Yeah."

In goes Squire with the man to the sheriff. The man says, "Sheriff, I got Old Bull's head."

"Let's see it."

He rolled it right out on the rug. Sheriff said, "You can put that back in the sack."

The sheriff locked him up, and that was the last of the man that killed Old Bull. He lost his marbles, don't you see. Didn't nobody like Old Bull 'cause he was a bully. This crazy fellow just killed him and cut his head off.

Pete and Armane Robinson were the ones that I let have green mules.[49] Mrs. Powers come in and told me, she said, "You better go down and get your mules from Armane and Pete Robinson. It's against me to tell you this because they're doing my work, but they're going to kill your mules."

"I'll get them, Miss Charlotte, and thank you."

They wouldn't feed them and would tie them up to the fence post and beat them all the time. They beat the mules. But they wasn't the first ones. My grandma'd sell Lisha Hard a mule on credit, and he'd beat him to death. It took him six months to do it, but he'd finally kill him. He was mean to a mule. Grandma'd send him to cut stove wood. She'd say, "Bring in some stove wood, Lisha."

If there was a tree in the deepest hollow, Lisha would cut that one, and then he'd beat his mule to death trying to get the log out. A fellow like him, if he had the money, he'd have been a good customer. He'd wear a mule out in seven or eight weeks.

Mr. Lawhorn was one that didn't never abuse a horse. He would polish his horse's hoofs. He'd do everything to make him pretty, and he'd always ride him in a walk. I remember we'd be riding horses and walking, and he'd say, "Let's rest them a minute," and we'd let the horses canter. That was the way you'd rest them from a walk. It always amused me.

Mr. Lawhorn had one horse he called Tim Finnegan, and, oh, he was fond of that horse. He would get a horse and love him, and he wouldn't part with him. He kept Tim Finnegan with him till the horse died of old age. I sold two hundred horses while he was riding one horse. He was a good rider, but he didn't trade after he'd get hold to his horse.

There are people that get attached to a horse and just keep him. I never remember keeping one. The better a horse he was and the more I loved him, the more money I'd get for him. I never did think about keeping him. I figured I knew better than to fall in love with a horse. I'd love him, but I loved the trade more.

Up and
Down That
Dog

Ray Lum's first trades outside Vicksburg were in the Mississippi Delta. Bordered on the west by the Mississippi River and on the east by hills of wind-deposited loess[50] soil, the Delta extends three hundred miles north from Vicksburg to Memphis. For centuries Mississippi River floodwaters each year deposited the rich Delta topsoil that was cleared and planted in cotton during the nineteenth and the twentieth centuries. A distinctive Delta world developed on white-owned plantations where blacks worked with their mules to plant, cultivate, and harvest crops.

Delta culture is celebrated in the literature of twentieth-century writers such as Eudora Welty, Richard Wright, and William Faulkner and in music by bluesmen such as B. B. King, Howlin' Wolf, and Muddy Waters. Lum discovered in the Delta a frontier culture where fortunes were quickly made and lost, and gambling and violence were common.

In 1907 Lum first entered the Delta, at the age of sixteen, moving his stock on a sternwheel steamer up the Sunflower River. He later traveled the Delta as a road trader and, astride a mule or horse,

71

he led a string of livestock that he traded with local farmers. At times Lum traveled in a mule-drawn wagon with a black hostler who rode well and skillfully demonstrated stock to customers.

As Lum's reputation grew, he shipped large numbers of horses and mules into the Delta on the Southern and the Yazoo-Delta railroads. The Yazoo-Delta Railroad engines with the initials "Y-D" written in bold letters on their sides inspired the railroad's nickname, "Yellow Dog." Lum recalled that he "traded all up and down the Dog."

The Yazoo-Delta and Southern railroads intersected in the small Delta town of Moorehead, known as the community "where the Southern crosses the Dog." W. C. Handy remembered hearing blues played by a lone guitarist in the Delta town of Tutwiler who sang, "Goin' where the Southern cross the Dog." Handy was inspired by the music to compose his "Yellow Dog Blues."[51] And Memphis artist Carroll Cloar's celebrated painting, "Where the Southern Cross the Yellow Dog" (1965), depicts a lonely scene of a black man and woman crossing railroad tracks in Moorehead.

Lum was familiar with these isolated Delta worlds and often traveled their roads alone with his livestock. He visited Mound Bayou, an all-black town in the Mississippi Delta that was established by Isaiah Montgomery in 1888. Montgomery was inspired by Booker T. Washington's conservative philosophy of moral and economic race development.[52] Lum respected and worked with many blacks and recalled with pride the sales he made in the Delta with a black trader named Joe Wicks.

In 1915 the price of cotton began to rise, and Delta farmers paid top dollar for their horses and mules. Lum bought stock in St. Louis and Fort Worth and shipped it to Delta towns such as Clarksdale and Indianola where he auctioned the animals before enthusiastic buyers.

The Delta has always been known as a frontier area where gambling and fights were common. During his trades Lum saw one of his close friends murdered and held the bets during a wagered fight between a bulldog and a monkey. His skills as a trader and auctioneer matured and helped him survive dangerous encounters in the Delta.

In 1917 he moved from Vicksburg, the southern tip of the Delta, to its northernmost point in Memphis. The two cities are intimately associated with Delta culture, and David Cohn once wrote that the

Mississippi Delta "begins in the lobby of the Peabody Hotel in Memphis and ends on Catfish Row in Vicksburg."[53]

At that time Memphis boasted the nation's largest mule market, and each day thousands of animals were sold in large auction houses. Through his sales in the Delta and his purchase of livestock barns in Vicksburg, Lum had become a prominent figure in Mississippi livestock worlds. Memphis was famed for its livestock dealers, and rather than risk trading on his own in this new world, Lum accepted an offer to work as an auctioneer for Darnell and Berry, one of the leading auction houses in the city.

Before each sale Lum looked over his mules and memorized identification tag numbers on animals that had defects. When these mules entered the ring, he used trader's slang to note their problems. "One lamp burning" signaled a one-eyed mule and "hitting on three" a lame animal.

By the age of twenty-six, he was considered one of the city's finest auctioneers and was close friends with veteran auctioneers such as Colonel M. R. Meals. Meals was a legendary mule auctioneer who worked for Owens Brothers Commission Company in Memphis. He weighed 350 pounds and lived in the Chisca Hotel, which was frequented by stock buyers. By the time he was forty-eight, Meals had sold over 1,200,000 mules valued at $168,000,000. During his career he auctioned in twenty-seven states and often conducted large auctions in other parts of the nation. His record sale of mules was in January 1939, when he sold 1,274 animals in one day.[54] Traders such as Colonel Meals provided colorful models for Lum, who quickly established himself as one of the finest young auctioneers in Memphis.

T he Delta was a booming place for mules in the 'thirties. If you didn't have mules, you wasn't in the farming business. Those farmers bought them by the hundreds. Some good farmers had a barn that would hold fifteen hundred mules, and they'd ring a big farm bell every morning to call the men to work.

Every town in the Delta had a mule barn and a livery stable. They looked to me and Red Nelson, another trader, to supply them with mules. Red brought most of his mules out of Missouri, and mine come from Texas. The Nelsons and the Rileys were families of

Irish traders that intermarried, and they dealt strictly in mules. They had barns in Cleveland, Tutwiler, and Clarksdale, and they would charge out two or three hundred mules at one time to a plantation.

Red was like me. He didn't have no education, but he could figure in his head faster than you could do it on the calculating machine. He was real smart, and he always had an answer for you. He could make you think a horse was well broke when he was wild. That was Red Nelson.

Around 1909 I went to buying horses, and I would move those horses up to the Delta by boat. I would put a load of horses on the boat and go up the Sunflower River. Old Man Klaus, that has got boys here in Vicksburg, lived up the river. He said, "Ray, why don't you put your horses with mine?"

At that time the boll weevil had hit the country, and it was eating up the cotton. The people in the hills was all broke, and they was selling mules cheap. So Mr. Klaus goes to Natchez, buys a load of mules, and brings them up to Vicksburg. In the meantime, I bought a team of fire horses from the city. They had begun to bring in the fire engines and wadn't going to need the horses anymore. I gave the city a hundred dollars for two great big bay horses. They were just as pretty as dolls, slick as buttons and blood-based[55] with a black mane and tail. I put those fire horses with my other horses and Mr. Klaus's mules, and we went up the Sunflower River. When we got off the boat, we stayed with an old fellow. I wish I could think of that old man's name because there might be some nephews of his living yet. This old man had long whiskers, and before night would come, him and Mr. Klaus would be at the table playing poker. I'd go to bed at ten o'clock, and when I would wake up in the morning, they were still sitting there playing.

I had put my two big fire horses out in a little shed. I was so proud of them and didn't want them to get hurt. One morning, I guess it was five-thirty, just at the break of day, they rang a bell for the workers to go to work. They rang it just about daylight.

So that bell goes "ting-a-ling-a-ling," and as it did, these horses kicked the side of the shed out. The shed fell down on them, and they run for three quarters of a mile. I walked down there and got ahold of them. I talked to them and petted them for a half hour and finally got on one and led the other one back. They were still scared because of that shed falling on them. The poor things finally settled down. One had a pretty deep cut, and I put coal oil on it. Before I got my horses straight, here comes a man riding in a buggy with good horses. Says, "What will you take for that pair of horses?"

"I don't know what them horses is worth. These were city fire horses in Vicksburg. When they rang that bell this morning, the horses wanted to go to the fire. So they kicked the shed down and run off with it."

All my life I've heard, "A horse trader'll lie to you." I'd listen to them and laugh. I never did see where the truth wouldn't fit better than a lie. It always fitted better. I told him exactly what had happened to the horses.

"These horses were fire horses in Vicksburg, and I don't know whether they would suit your purpose or not."

I had some horses that I would rather have sold than my pretty pair of fire horses. I knew that I would sell them and sell them pretty quick, and I knew that I wouldn't get any more like them.

This old man says, "What will you take for those horses?"

"I will take three hundred dollars for them."

That was two percent[56] on the hundred I paid for them. He liked to tore his pocket off getting his billfold out. Just stripped out three one-hundred-dollar bills and handed me the three hundred dollars for the horses. I put two good halters on them and fixed them up for him. We was on the Sunflower River, and I said, "Not many people are going to find me down here on this river. If you tell people about these horses, I'd appreciate it."

"I'll send you some customers, and I'll be back."

Only two or three people passed by a day on that river, and it was kind of lonesome. I asked him to tell people about my horses, and he did. A lot of customers come. Of course, a lot of them come and wanted a pair of fire horses like Mr. Uh Huh. Well, I didn't have any more of them.

I sold all my horses in about three days. I sold my horses and was ready to git back on the boat and come home. I was about eighteen then.

All that time Mr. Klaus kept playing poker with the old man. I don't know whether he was winning or losing. When we got back to

Vicksburg, Mr. Klaus paid me off. I had sold all the mules he had carried up and sold my pair of horses too. I was in pretty good shape. I said, "Mr. Klaus, you are a wonderful person, but I don't believe I will go up the Sunflower River with you anymore. I've got enough money to buy horses now."

He thought for a minute, Mr. Klaus did. He was a good man. He said, "That's all right. I don't blame you. If you need any money, just go down to the bank and tell them I sent you."

I don't remember who was president of the bank then, but it seems like it was the old tall, slim man that lived out on Washington Street. He had a nice family. What was his name? Had a pretty daughter. I remember the daughter well. Oh, I wished I could call the old boy's name. He had a son. He had a daughter. I liked them all. They were the nicest people, and when I would borrow money from him, he would always say, "Is that enough, Ray? If you need any more, you can come get it."

"All right. Thank you."

I think I borrowed five hundred dollars from him. I didn't need to borrow any more. I wound up going to Fort Worth, Texas, and buying fresh horses, and then I went on up in the Delta again to sell them. Two or three years had gone by, and I had got in pretty good shape.

John Dandigger, a German there at Fort Worth, said he had a hundred government reject horses. They was horses that he'd showed the government, and they didn't take them. They was just as fat as town dogs. Pretty as dolls. They had eaten their heads off. The government had vaccinated them against every known contagious disease. Them horses wouldn't pick up a nail.[57] You couldn't make them sick. You could ship one across the world, and he wouldn't sneeze.

"What will you give me for those horses, Ray?"

"I'll give you fifty a piece for them."

"Well, I'm going to sell them to you."

I give John fifty a round for his hundred horses, loaded them up on the train, and started for Clarksdale. That was in nineteen-eighteen or nineteen-nineteen. That was the year that cotton went to a dollar-five cents a pound.[58]

I got on the train. The horses was up front, and I was back in the caboose riding in the loft. I had been listening to an auctioneer in Fort Worth selling, and I lay back there and practiced. "Hey! Fifty dollars. Fifty-five. Sixty dollars. Sixty-five. Seventy dollars. Seventy-five. Eighty dollars. Eighty-five. Ninety dollars. Sold to Oscar Gould for a hundred-dollar bill!"

The little old redheaded Irish conductor on the train come up and said, "Hey, what are you doing up there?"

"I'm selling them horses up in front, the horses you got up behind the engine."

"Well, sell another."

That was just what I wanted him to say. I wanted to get some practice so I could do it when I got to Clarksdale. It just tickled him to death to hear me selling them horses.

He looks out the window, and there were some people digging ditches. This little Irishman said, "Looka there. Them people down there digging that ditch are breaking their backs. They oughta have a piece of machinery doing that. A piece of machinery is not worth as much as a man's back."

"Well, if they got a piece of machinery, what would those people do for a livelihood?"

"By God, let the government take care of them."

That was sixty-five years ago, and it's all come to pass just like he said. After he got through, I laid back and kept selling my horses. I was nineteen years old. I got to Clarksdale and unloaded my horses. There hadn't never been an auction in Clarksdale before. That was along about nineteen-eighteen or -nineteen, during the war, you know. The war was in full blast at the time. The government bought fifty thousand horses, and these were their rejects. They were just as fat and pretty as dolls.

I got to Clarksdale on a Wednesday and unloaded those six or seven carloads of horses, and the first thing I did was get out handbills and bill out the auction for Saturday. Then I went up to the bank to get a teller to clerk the sale. I introduced myself, told the banker who I was, and I said, "I've got a hundred good horses I want to sell here Saturday. What'll you charge me to send a man down there to keep books?"

"Twenty-five dollars. And we'll give you a cashier's check for the money." That's how things worked in those days. Just think about that now. "We're gonna take the checks you get for the horses, give you a cashier's check, and charge you twenty-five dollars."

I shook hands with him, and I said, "You're what I call a gentleman."

Sure enough, the day of the sale came, and he had the best clerk in the bank down there. Just as smart as he could be. That was the first auction they had in Clarksdale. We had the auction over on a lot. I had rented a barn, but so many people came that you couldn't get them all in the barn. So I moved my wagon outside, got up in the wagon and got me a box and a stick, and I started to selling horses. When the smoke cleared away and the last horses were sold, they brought about three hundred and fifty dollars a head. I cleaned up. When the sale was over, I didn't own a horse. I had them all in my pocket. I was in business. I rented two or three barns while I was there and went right on back to Fort Worth and got more horses.

Nineteen-ten was the year cotton sold for a dollar and five cents a pound. You could grab any little fellow there and shake four or five hundred dollars off of him. They all had money up in the Delta. Money was cheap, awful cheap.

I remember going over to Merigold to eat dinner with Joe Fink. He asked me to come over and eat dinner with him. He had a goose hanging up there, and grease from the goose was dropping down in this pan. I said, "Look at that, Mr. Joe. There's a wiggly[59] in there."

"Oh, damn the wiggly. It's the goose that we're after."

Did you ever see goose grease? It's just as pretty as clear water. I went on in and ate the goose and forgot about the wiggly out there in the grease.

That year Joe was buying cotton and giving a dollar-five a pound for quite a bit of it. The next year, to show you how fast things happen, the very next year cotton dropped to a nickel a pound. The day it went to a nickel a pound, Joe Fink stuck a thirty-eight up to his temple, and that was the last of my friend. That was the last of Joe Fink. He couldn't take it.

I didn't have a better friend. I sold him every mule he bought, and he bought mules for all the country around there. Bought them for other people. Everybody loved Old Joe Fink. He'd made all that money, but he oughta realized that he couldn't take it with him. I don't know why he took his life. That was the last of Joe Fink. That was one of the bad things that happened. I don't like to tell them bad things. I'd rather tell the good things that happened to me in life.

When cotton went to a nickel a pound, Mr. Dakin lived up in Clarksdale. He was a good man and bored with a pretty big auger.[60] So he goes into the bank in Clarksdale. He pulled off his four- or five-carat diamond ring, throwed the ring out on the table and says, "You're looking at a broke man. That's all I've got."

The banker said, "Mr. Dakin, put that ring back on. You go right on and go to trading. You're not broke."

In other words, he was going to loan him some more money. And Mr. Dakin did go right on. Ten years from the day he tried to give the banker his ring, he was back in business and making money. He went to trading with me, and we put on a cattle sale in Clarksdale. Them was the first cattle sales in the Delta. There wasn't no cattle up there till we started bringing them in.

When we got ready to have the first sale, I was partners with Mr. Dakin, fifty-fifty. He says, "You people that came to buy cattle," says, "I want you to buy just what you want. Buy all the cattle you need, go down to the bank and sign a note for them." They all bought cattle, and they all paid for them. I was selling yearling[61] cattle, and they made money.

I first met Bud Doghitt in the Delta at Clarksdale. I loved Doghitt. I thought the world of him. Every pair of mules I'd bring in, he'd buy them. He'd give me whatever I'd ask for them and tell me to get a better pair if I could. You could never get them too good for Doghitt. I remember one time Doghitt says, "Ray, can you get me a pair of sorrel[62] mules with white mane and tails?"

"Yeah, and they'll cost like the devil, Mr. Bud."

His name was Doghitt. So I got them mules, and they was eleven hundred dollars. That just suited him fine. One day he come in with those pretty mules to get them shod. He stood there himself with the mules 'cause he knew how he wanted them shod. Up comes a showman with two little bay suffolks. Most of them suffolks were sorrels, but these were bays.[63] Weighed about fifteen hundred a piece. They was made good as you'd want to see a horse made. This showman says, "If you're not in a hurry to get those mules shod," he says, "I'd like to get my horses shod." And he says, "I'd appreciate that."

Doghitt was a man that was accommodating to everybody. He said, "Go ahead and shoe his horses."

The showman looked over and saw that pair of mules Bud had paid me eleven hundred dollars for. He said, "You've got a nice pair of mules there."

Bud says, "Yup." That was about all he said, "Yup."

"I'll bet you these horses can outpull your mules."

Doghitt throwed me a hundred-dollar bill, and this man that had the horses, he pulled out a roll, and looked like to me after he pulled off a hundred-dollar bill you couldn't tell he had nothing taken off. He had several more there. Bud says, "How do you want to do it?"

"Just hitch the single trees⁶⁴ together."

While they was getting the teams together, I saw them little horses looking around at the mules, and I said, "Bud, your money's turned to water."

"Oh, the hell with that. The hell with that."

There was no use saying anything to Bud. He'd throwed away several bets like that, you know. When I said, "Your money's turned to water," he didn't smile. Didn't laugh. Didn't talk very much.

We got them hooked together, and this showman that had the horses, he said, "Whenever you're ready, Mr. Bud."

He was as cool as a cucumber, you know. Bud moved his mules up first. He took a little advantage, and when he did, the mules pulled the horses back about ten steps. But when those horses got straight, they dragged those mules over about fifty feet. Doghitt said, "Give him the money, Ray."

The man says, "Maybe your mules didn't have a fair chance, Mr. Bud."

"The hell with that. Give him his money, Ray."

That settled that deal. That's the kind of man Doghitt was. No argument with Doghitt. They had called Doghitt just a few days before down to Drew, Mississippi. There was a man that had killed nine people and was hiding back in a dredge ditch. There was nine people laying out there, and somebody says, "Can't you get to him with dynamite?"

No, they couldn't do it. Well, Doghitt just blazed right around in front of them. This fellow shot him, and when he did, Doghitt turned around and shot him right between the eyes. Back to Clarksdale Doghitt went, and he got all right. He got well. That finished that deal.

But this one day he left the barn and started over to get the mail. My cousin Clint McKay come by and said, "Ray, you tell Doghitt don't cross Ellie Chapman's path. He'll kill him."

"I hope he don't do that, Cousin Clint."

"Well, the reason I'm telling you is I thought maybe you could talk to him."

"Cousin Clint, Mr. Doghitt's a man you don't tell nothing to. Nobody can talk to Mr. Bud."

Clint McKay, the man that was talking to me, had about a dozen notches on his gun. It wasn't five days after he told me that, Mr. Doghitt stepped up on the porch to come and get his mail. Bud had started over to get his mail, and Ellie Chapman had told him, he said, "If ever you cross my path. If ever you cross my path."

I was standing at the barn door and saw Chapman step up there. They both had one foot up from the ground, and Bud Doghitt throwed his gun over and shot off Ellie Chapman's tie. He had one of these little bow ties. Chapman wore a bow tie. Doghitt just throwed that gun. Bam! Off went the tie. The next shot was Mr. Chapman's. I didn't see it. I'm glad I didn't. When he shot, he shot Bud right through the heart. It was just too quick. That was the last of my friend, Doghitt. I cried like a baby. My best friend was gone. I haven't had a better one. That's the way they go, you know. His wife said, "Ray, you sold my husband these mules. Can you help me sell them?"

"You bet I will."

I sold them for more than he give me for them. She was a sweet little woman. Just as sweet as she could be. Didn't have any children. That was the last of Doghitt. I sold his wagons and everything. That's what you'll do for a friend, you know. That was at Clarksdale. Back in them days, a man's life wasn't worth too much in that doggone Delta.

I carried horses and traded up and down that Delta. I shipped my horses in there by the hundreds, and I made plenty of money at Clarksdale. You could go down anyplace in the Delta and sell a load of horses in a day. That was before the car days. There wasn't too many automobiles around then in nineteen hundred and nineteen. People were using horses and mules.

I went to Valley Park when there wadn't a tree cut from Valley Park on out to the Sunflower River. It was all in swamp. I remember one time, it's been a good long time ago, Wes Young killed a depot agent there at Valley Park, and Dr. Bettow was there. Dr. Bettow was a cousin of mine, and he called Clint McKay at Port Gibson. Clint came up, and the depot agent was still laying out there, laying out there where he had been killed. When Cousin Clint got in, he said, "Bettow, have you got something I can ride?"

"Yes," he said, "I've got a mule. Mule rides good."

Clint was a good hand. He could ride anything. He got the mule, and Dr. Bettow says, "I'll just go with you, Clint."

They rode about five miles out. There was just one path, and the underbrush had grown up so that it was covered. You couldn't see the path. Dr. Bettow said, "It's about five miles down there to the killer's house."

Clint got on the mule, and rode down this path. He got down there about five miles and saw a light over in the house. He walked up and kicked on the door. The man inside said, "Who is it?"

"Come out, Wes," he said. "This is Clint McKay, and I came after you."

"I'm not going with you, Mr. McKay."

"Yes, you're going."

He kicks that door open and shoves that gun in his belly. Cousin Clint put him out in front of his mule and trotted him all the way, five miles back to Valley Park. That was Wes Young. He had killed the depot agent, and the depot agent was still laying out there. When he got back, they tried him right there at Valley Park. In them days they didn't have a lot of mess about a big trial. After they tried him, they hung him, and then they buried him the next day. They did bury them in those days, don't you see.

When I rode up in the Delta, I traded with everybody I met along the road. I remember I went into Indianola with Crip Reynolds, and there was thirty white men in that jail. They all got their hands up and waved, "Hey, Ray! Hey, Crip! Hey! Hey!"

Every damned one of them was in there for murder. And we'd shot craps with every one of them up and down that Dog, you know. That was the railroad they called the Yellow Dog. Crip and I tied up our horses and went on down to the restaurant. On the way, here come Purdom, and I said, "Hello, Mr. Purdom."

He never said a word. And Crip Reynolds says, "How is your little old horse we sold you, Mr. Purdom?"

I said, "We'll stop by again the next time we come by, Mr. Purdom. Might have something you like better."

"It's immaterial to me whether you stop or not."

I saw Purdom was crazy and had come to town to kill somebody. I saw he was off his rocker. I was a good-enough judge of human nature to know what that crazy man had on his mind. Oh, good God, he could have killed us right there. Crip started to say something, and I grabbed him and said, "Come on. Let's get out of here."

"What are you jerking me for?"

"That son-of-a-bitch is fixing to kill us."

And just as we walked in the hotel where we were going to get our meals, "Boom! Boom! Boom!" Six or seven shots. I said, "Let's go, Crip. I bet that's Purdom."

We went around there, and he had killed Claude Hicks and Little Jim Hutchinson and some other man. I knew all three of them like corn bread. All three of the ones he'd killed was from over at Rocky Springs.

The next morning I rode through town and went by the jail. "Hey, Ray! Hey, Crip!"

I talked to the officer there, and he said there was thirty-one in jail. They was all in jail for murder. And every one of them had traded with me or played craps with me down the road, don't you know. Yeah, Purdom says, "It's immaterial to me whether you come or not."

Crip and I kept on trading up through the country to Belzoni and then went to Moorehead where the Southern crosses the Dog. Those were the two railroads, you see.

Once there was a white boy and a colored boy fighting in the war. They was in the army, and they was down in a foxhole. Shells was bursting all around. So one of them says, "Lord God, I wisht that I was back at home."

"Boom! Boom! Boom!"

Raining bullets, and shells bursting all around. And this other boy says, "Where is your home?"

"Where the Southern cross the Dog."

"You from Moorehead too!"

Oh man, they throwed their arms around one another. There wasn't any need to be sad anymore. They rejoiced over finding somebody they could talk to. It just happened that both of them was from Moorehead, Mississippi. They loved each other then. Them shells was popping, and they was praying in them fox-holes.

Sometimes I wonder how I lived through it all. A lot of people got hurt in fights. I laughed a lot and figured that was the best way out of a fight. I remember little Caney Bayou Smith was at Delta City, and every day he came to town, he'd get drunk. He had to have a fight or two before he went home. I had my mules in a lot over there, and I knew everybody in town. Caney Bayou came up there and said, "I want to fight you, and I want to whip you."

I knew damn well that he wasn't going to leave town until he had a fight. I said, "Yeah, I've been thinking about you too. You come back here at six o'clock this evening, and I'll whip you good."

I threatened him good and then forgot all about it. I wasn't worried 'cause I was in good shape, and Caney would always come up half drunk and say, "I'm gonna fight."

He'd had two or three fights that day, but he wanted to whip me. I said, "You come back here at six this evening."

It wasn't dark before my hostler said, "Here come that man."

I had forgot all about him and went ahead with trading. Never even thought about Caney Bayou Smith. Goddamn, when six o'clock come, here he come. He was a man that didn't leave there without a fight. Here he was rolling up his sleeves, and I said, "Well, I was looking for you. I'm so glad you come. Look, you stay right here 'cause I've got to go eat supper."

Well, you know about what I done. I went and ate my supper, and when I come back, the son-of-a-bitch had gone. That was Caney Bayou Smith. He wasn't going to leave without he had a fight.

Another time I stayed overnight with my horses right on the Sunflower River. I didn't know it was Caney's house. I remember he come in about two o'clock in the morning, and he went down and shoved his head down in that river. He stuck his hands down in there, and mud was all up to his elbows. It was the worst damned gyp[65] water on earth, that water in the Sunflower River. He called his wife, woke her up, said, "Get them children. Bring those children down here. I want them to take a drink of this. This is the best water on earth."

And it was the worst gyp water. I couldn't drink it with ice in it, and there wasn't that much ice in those days. "Come down here, I want them children and you to take a drink of this water."

She brought them down at three or four in the morning. What a drunk won't do. Good little fellow when he was sober. Once in a while I would catch him sober. That was in Delta City.

One of the toughest people I met in the Delta was Wildcat Stevens. I rode into Leland with a string of horses, and when I went to put my horses up there, Cat come in. He didn't know I was there. He come in, and I was glad to see him. When he started to walk in, I hollered at him, "Hey, Cat."

Called him Cat. Cat was a man that didn't carry a gun. That little old marshal in Leland had a stable, and I was using it for my horses. But this part of his stable where you come in, this part was locked. So Cat come up one day, knocked the lock off, and put his horse in a stall.

Here comes these two officers, both of them with pistols. They come up, and they didn't know Wildcat Stevens. He had just moved to Leland a week or two before. He just went over, slammed them guns out of their hands, just that quick, and throwed them over in the ditch. He had done already brought his horse out, and he just ignored the officers. He says, "Ray, I'll see you tomorrow. I'll be back in about eight or nine o'clock."

There was the officers' pistols over there in the grass. Those were officers in the town, you know. He said, "I'll see you tomorrow."

"You bet. I'll be looking for you, Cat."

And the next day he was right back. He didn't pay no attention to those officers.

Cat came to our livestock barn in Vicksburg one day, and he had a little boy with him about three years old. Mrs. Lum was there that day. Mrs. Lum and I was staying at the barn. We had our living quarters at the barn until we built our home. Anyhow, Cat comes in, and his little boy, coming about three years old, followed him. Here comes a cat running right under the barn. And, goddamn, right under the barn his son went. You never saw a dog go under there no faster. And when he came out, he came out with the cat right in his hands. Mrs. Lum said, "That's a chip off the old block."

So that was that. Little fellow was three years old, and never saw that cat before in his life. When he come out, he had ahold of him, don't you see. That was Wildcat Stevens. He never used a gun, but oh good God, he was powerful when he'd take your hand. I guess he's dead and long gone. I don't know, he might be living yet. You can't tell about them kind of people. He might be living. I bet that little boy is living, the one that got the cat.

One of the best trades I ever made in the Delta, I was traveling with Squire Harris, and we pulled up to a house at Belzoni. I hollered at this lady and said, "Does your husband have something he wants to trade?"

"He wants to see you. Come here. He wants to see you."

"Where is he?"

"Down in the well."

I looked down at him, and I said, "Hey, there. How you getting along? You taking it the hard way, are you?"

He said, "Yes, I am."

And he commenced to climb out of the well. I figured he was taking my picture. He was sizing me up, and I had done sized him. I was awake. He wanted to see if I was a gypsy. If I was a gypsy, he was going to keep on digging. I had a bunch of horses with me, and he said, "I've got to make a crop, and that's all the horse in the world I've got."

The man was almost crying. I mouthed his horse while he was talking. I flipped his lip and saw he was a five-thirty, five and a half years old. I felt his eyes, and they wasn't soft. I knew his eyes was all right, and I said, "Git up, man."

When I spoke to the horse, he stuck his foot out and began to groan. And the man says, "He's lame in every foot he's got."

I kicked him and saw it was his front foot that was lame. His wife and four or five little children was standing around there. I said, "Squire, take hold of him there and git him up." I clucked to him. His front foot was still out. "Uh huh. How would you like to have that white mare there for him?"

I had a good white mare I'd swapped for down the road somewhere. I got her and four or five others. She was throwed in. She didn't cost nothing. He said, "Oh, would you give me that horse for him?"

He cried. I said, "You got to make a crop. I guess this gray mare here is worth about fifty dollars, and she'll work. I'd be happy to give her to you for that horse, and I hope you have good luck with her."

I guess that white mare was a ten-year-old. She had a little gray around her hoofs, from her knees and hocks down. I didn't have to mouth her to know how old she was. I said, "Well, I hope you have good luck with her."

I never saw a fellow that appreciated a horse any more. He put his arms around me, and his wife was happy too. He said, "Mister, you don't know how happy you have made me. I don't think you can get him to go anywhere."

"Yes, sir. Well, I'll do best I can with him."

That was one of the best trades ever I made. I had my wagon up there with Squire, and I said, "Let's get this horse on out of sight."

So Squire and I go back and get the crippled horse. We led him about two hundred yards away from the house, and I said, "Squire, get your pick there. Let's see what we can find."

Say, we didn't pick a minute before we found a nail sticking, not exaggerating, a half inch out of that horse's foot. I had turpentine in my wagon. So I went and got that turpentine. I said, "Pull it out easy, Squire."

While he pulled the nail out, I poured turpentine right down the nail. I had an old piece of tin—I don't know what it was doing in the wagon—and I said, "Let's cut that piece of tin and see if we can fit it on the hoof."

We cut off a piece to fit the hoof. We put a shoe on the horse and took cotton and stuffed it down inside the tin.

On we went with that horse, and when I looked back, he wasn't even limping. Walked just as straight as a soldier. Before he would hop on three feet, and the man thought he was crippled for life.

Let's see. How far did I get with him? Somewheres up the road about the Dog, I run into a man there. "What do you want for that horse?"

"I don't know what he's worth."

"I'll give you two hundred and fifty dollars for him."

Horses was high then. They was selling good. "Well, I don't guess I'd want to do that. I think he's a better horse than that." I hadn't felt the horse out too much. "Squire, set down on that horse and show him to this gentleman here." I said, "You can ride him without a halter. You can ride him just with a string. He's one of the best broke horses you ever saw."

The fellow said, "Well, I like him."

So Squire rode him up, turned him around, and rode him back. He was a five-thirty, coming a six-year-old. I said, "What are you going to give me for him? You see he's a good horse."

"I'll give you three hundred dollars for him."

I thought, well, there's no use to deprive him anymore. He looks like a good man. "All right, I'm gonner let you have him."

That was the last of him. I put a lot of horses away in good faith.

I was at Indianola, and I had just finished a sale. I sold a hundred horses and mules, and I was tired when the sale was over. They'd all paid for them, and here come a fellow running. "Hey, Mister. Mister, that mule you sold me, he grabbed at me."

"Yeah? Bit at you, did he?"

"No, he grabbed at me with his foot."

"Oh well. That'll never do. That'll never do."

And that same day I'd found a horse that wasn't paid for. The mule was worth about twice what the horse was, so I said, "He grabbed at you, did he?"

"Oh yeah. He grabbed at me with his foot and tore my pocket out."

"Uh huh. Well, that will never do. Give me ten, and I'll give you that good horse for him. He won't grab at you."

The damned mule was worth about two horses, but he wanted to get rid of that mule that grabbed at him, you know. So he give me the ten and lit out.

Another buyer come before he got away. I wanted to get him out of the way so I could price that mule to the buyer. That was a good mule. There was nothing wrong with the mule. He just knew that fellow was afraid of him. A mule's a pretty good judge of human nature. They got an instinct.

I was trading at Mayersville, and I was riding one mule and leading eight or ten mules and horses. I pulled into Mayersville 'cause I had to stop at the store there to get some sardines and crackers. This old man named Meat Myers was running the store, and up comes an organ-grinder. He had this organ grinding and making music, and his little old monkey was dancing around. Old Man Myers had a great big bulldog that was sitting down looking at the little monkey with his head between his paws. The organ-grinder kept a-grinding.

Old Man Meat didn't give the organ-grinder anything. He didn't give him any nickels or dimes. He didn't like that monkey. The little monkey kept a-dancing and all. When the monkey got over pretty close to the bulldog, Mr. Myers says, "You better not let your monkey get close to that dog. That dog will kill him."

"This monkey can whoop that dog."

"What?"

"Yes. This monkey can whoop that dog."

Oh, the fat was in the fire. "Would you bet on it?"

The organ-grinder run his hand in his pocket, pulled out a fifty-dollar bill and handed me the fifty dollars. Well, Mr. Myers like to tore his pocket off getting his fifty out. When he handed it over, I said, "Your money's turned to water, Mr. Myers." Talking to the man that had the bulldog, "Your money's turned to water."

I knew better. I'd had a monkey. They got ready, and the organ-grinder said, "Get your dog ready."

Mr. Myers said, "He's ready."

He had the big old bulldog back there, and the little old monkey was jumping around. "Cheechee. Cheechee."

The organ-grinder asked Mr. Myers, he says, "You wouldn't mind him having that little pencil, would you, something to kind of protect himself?"

"No, you can give him a cord of wood if you want to."

The organ-grinder give the monkey the little pencil. "All right, he's ready."

"Turn him loose."

Old bulldog surged at the monkey, and the monkey just hopped right up on his back and started jooging him in the ass with that pencil. Kept shoving that pencil in his back end. Well, the bulldog knocked two slats off the fence, run right in under the house, and the little monkey jumped up on the porch. Here the monkey come back. "Cheechee. Cheechee."

The old organ-grinder had done that before and was smart. He says, "Ah, maybe the bulldog didn't have a good chance. You want to give him another try?"

Old Man Meat says, "Give him the money, Ray."

He wasn't going to argue about it. He done seen enough. That settled that deal.

I had a little old monkey once. He would go up a tree, shit in his hand and throw it at you. I'd have a devil of a time trying to get him down. I swapped the son-of-a-gun for a bulldog and swapped the bulldog for a horse. You just have one monkey in life. You don't ever want the second one.

Another experience I had up in that Delta was with a bear. I stayed all night with a man at Blanton who had this good bear. After I put my horses in his lot, I was in eating supper—and I was hungry. Here comes something shoving around under the table, and I said, "What the hell is that?"

"That's my pet bear."

"Well, fine. How old is he?"

"A year old."

"What does he weigh now?"

"Two hundred pounds."

He pushed me around. I wadn't very hard to move over, you know. I give him room, and he come right in under the table. He was a huge son-of-a-gun. I looked over, and the man was feeding him.

Next morning I went out, and I got my rope. I was a pretty good hand with a rope and still am. The old bear come by, and I just dropped the rope around his neck. When I did, it scared him, and under the house he went, rope and all, you know. The man said, "Now you've lost your rope."

"That's what you think."

In about five minutes I picked up the rope and pulled it on out. That bear could take his paw and beat you taking it off. Don't ever try to take a rope off of a bear. It's a lot safer to let him take it off.

That's like when I tie a yearling's hind feet to work on them. Somebody would say, "Wait. I'll take that rope loose."

I would tell them, "You let that rope on his hind feet alone. You get away from there." The damned fool was going to get his jaw kicked off.

That man's bear at Blanton ran away one day. I was over there a few months later, and I said, "Where's the bear?"

"Ray, he left. By God, he's gone." He was about to cry.

Nearly a year went by, and he was out squirrel hunting. He looked, and there was his bear in a tree. He talked to him, and when the bear come down, he carried him home. But he found him too late. The bear didn't live but about a week after he carried him home. He'd depended on that man for his food too long. All that was at Blanton. I forget that old boy's name.

I had a good sorrel horse I got down there from Lot Fortner. A man here who was going to run for sheriff says, "What do you want for that horse?"

"Two-fifty."

"Will he pull this buggy?"

"I don't know whether he ever was worked to a buggy or not. He's a horse that I got from Lot Fortner, and they called him 'Dixie.' "

He hitched him up to his buggy, and when he said, "Git up, Dixie," the horse run up and run back and kicked out his traces.[66] The fellow said, "You owe me five dollars."

I didn't tell him to hitch that horse up, and I didn't tell him the horse was broke to a buggy. But I said, "Yes, sir."

I began to pull out my pocketbook, and four or five other buyers was round then. I was glad they were. Wish there was some more. I just handed him the five dollars. He was going to run for sheriff, and I thought to myself, "You son-of-a-bitch. You aren't going to get far running for sheriff."

I didn't tell him to hitch that horse up. He just asked me if the horse worked a buggy, and I told him I did not know.

Mr. Gibbons was a blind man that I showed a five-year-old mule. A five-year-old mule has got a shell on the side of his mouth. Mr. Gibbons put his finger in the mule's mouth. I saw him finger the mule's mouth, and I saw him feel his eyes. You can tell a weak-eyed son-of-a-bitch. If you put your finger on his eye, and it goes down, that'll tell you if he's blind or weak-eyed. Mr. Gibbons had his fingers on the mule's eyes and done felt his teeth. Done felt both of them. "How old is them mules, Ray?"

"They're five-thirties,[67] Mr. Gibbons."

"Uh huh. Tell So-and-So to go down there and bring up my pair of mules."

He sent word to his manager to bring up the mules. Nearly everybody had a manager in them days. So he brought up this pair of mules that was just as fat as they could be. Oh, they were fat. He said, "Ray, how would you trade them for these mules of mine?"

"Mr. Gibbons, I can give you a hundred dollars for those old mules, and I've got to get four hundred and fifty for my mules."

"That'll be three-fifty difference?"

"Yes."

"What have you got in a good saddle horse?"

"Oh, I've got the best."

I had the horse that the man who was going to run for sheriff had hitched up to his buggy, and when he said, "Git up," the horse just run up and right back and broke his traces. That was the horse I got from Lot Fortner. Lot had gotten him from Old Man Roach. Old Man Roach got them horses out of Kentucky. Old Man Roach was Lot's daddy-in-law, and Lot got them horses and swapped them to me.

Mr. Gibbons had done got the mules straight. He done traded for the pair of mules. Now he's at the horse and says, "Is that a good saddle horse, Ray?"

"I think he is. He come out of Kentucky. I got him from Lot Fortner at Vicksburg, and he got him from his father-in-law there. That's a Kentucky horse, and he's really a nice saddle horse."

I'd done got his pair of old fat mules. Give him a hundred for them. So he says, "I've got a mare here, and I want you to take her in trade."

"That'd be all right. I'll be glad to."

So he sent for her, and here she come. Just feeling along. Her feet was that long. I said, "Mr. Will." His name was Will Gibbons. I said, "I see she's been a great mare. She's been a good horse."

I was flipping her lip all the time and saw she was a twelve-year-old. Mr. Gibbons said, "How old do you think she is?"

"Oh, about twelve years old."

"That's exactly how old she is. I bought her."

I give him my horse in trade for fifty dollars in boot and his mare. I had profit.

It had been raining, and it was muddy. So Squire and I got up the road a little piece, and I said, "Squire, let's see what we can do for that mare."

All right. We went to work on her, and we give her a manicure. We padded her feet. We done everything we could to her hoofs. We put gasoline in them and trimmed them till she was sore. She had long hoofs that looked like they never been trimmed before.

When we got to Rolling Fork we pulled up in front of Mr. Meek's office. He had a pretty daughter. I remember his daughter. I was single then. So we pulled up there in front of his office, and he said, "Ray, what do you want for that mare?"

"Mr. Meek, I better not let you have that mare. I got that mare from Mr. Will Gibbons down there, and she's awful sore 'cause her feet was all growed out, and we had to trim them. I don't know whether she'll ever be well enough to do you any good. I'd rather not let you have her, Mr. Meek."

"My daughter likes her awful well."

"Well, anybody would like her. She's fat, and that's the prettiest color in the world." I said, "Mr. Meek, I'll be back by here in the next week or ten days, and I'll bring you what you want for this nice young lady. I'll bring her a good horse and show it to her."

I never did say anything about selling it. I never told a man I'd sell one in my life. I always said I'd be glad to show it to him. I said, "Let me bring her another horse."

I walked over to the sheriff's office, and here comes the sheriff out. "Ray, what do you want for that mare?"

"I don't want anything for her. I got her from Mr. Gibbons, and she's sore in her feet. I don't want to let you have her."

"Well, by God, my money's as good as anybody's."

"Yes, sir, it sure is. Your money's good as anybody's. But let me tell you a little bit more about this mare. When I got her, her feet was that long, and we trimmed them till they bled. I don't think you'd want this mare. Why don't you let me bring you one when I come back through here next week. I'm going to St. Louis to buy some saddle horses."

Most of the horses I had then come from right around Mississippi or come from Texas. He said, "Well, all right."

He didn't like it a damn bit, though. He didn't like it because I wouldn't let him have that sorrel mare. Squire was with me. I left Rolling Fork, and on up we went to Panther Burn. I still had my sorrel mare that I got from Mr. Gibbons, and she was as pretty as a doll. When I got up to Panther Burn, here come Hughey McKenzie. Hughey says, "Ray, you know Mr. Johnson don't allow traders to stop on his place. The last one that passed through tried to steal from him."

"Well, that's fine. I don't blame him, Mr. Hughey. I'm going on up to Mound Bayou."

Mound Bayou was the place where all the black folks lived.

Nobody there but black folks. I said, "I'm headed to Mound Bayou anyway."

"Well, you stop when you get off this place. There's several men here that want horses, and you've got what they want."

"Well, I'll tell you what I'm going to do. I'm going to give you five a head for every buyer that you bring up there."

"I'm not going to charge you nothing."

"Well, don't bring them then. I want to pay you 'cause I'm making money."

I was just a little kid the last time he had seen me. I'd growed up and got to be about nineteen by that time. "Well," he said, "I'll bring them up there."

"And I'm going to give you five a head for every one you bring."

I never did get to Mound Bayou. I sold all them horses right there at Panther Burn. They bought them all right there. I sold all my mules and give Mr. Hughey five a head for bringing up them buyers from Panther Burn. The sale started, and the first buyer said, "What do you want for that mare there?"

"Oh, that's Mr. Gibbons's good saddle mare. She cost a lot of money." I had her and fifty already, don't you see. "That mare's worth a lot of money. I'll have to charge you a good bit for her."

"What you got to charge for her?"

"Three hundred dollars."

He liked to tore his pocket off giving me the three hundred dollars for that sorrel mare. I went ahead, and before the day was gone, we was out of horses. All I had was the wagon, and I had to borrow a pair of mules to pull my wagon back down to Rolling Fork. I wanted to leave my wagon back in Rolling Fork.

I went to St. Louis and bought my next horses. The horses I had just sold had come out of Texas. I saw those Delta people had plenty of money, and the horses in St. Louis were prettier and were different breeds. So I come in with a load of horses from St. Louis. Well, you talk about ringing a bell with horses, I really rang a bell. I sold that load, and then I doubled back and went to Fort Worth. I bought two or three loads, and run into this big old black trader there named Joe Wicks. Joe said, "Mr. Ray, let me go back with you to Rolling Fork."

He had heard I was going to Rolling Fork, and I said, "All right, Joe."

"I got two head I want to put in with yours."

"That's all right. Stick them in there."

Joe's bread was done. He was a good trader. He weighed about two-fifty and had a good, heavy mustache. So we got down there to Rolling Fork, and I remember that first night the horses was in the railroad pen when the gate broke down, and all the horses got out. We penned them back up in a few minutes, and a black woman there said, "That pen will hold them if you put your rope across here."

When we got them penned Joe says, "Mr. Ray, you going uptown. Bring me back some dinner." Told me what he wanted. And he says to the woman, "What do you want?"

"Get me a can of snuff."

Joe says, "Don't you want something else?"

She said something else she wanted, and I brought it on back to them. They had the rope across where the horses couldn't get out. The next morning we got ready to have a sale. We billed the sale, and here come these black traders. One of them says, "Mr. Ray, I'll give you five hundred dollars for that horse there."

Joe says, "Mr. Ray, let me wait on that gentleman."

"You bet. That's all right, Joe. That's fine."

I figured I might get three hundred for the horse he wanted. Calvin Miller was this man's name. So we talked a while, and finally I said, "Calvin, I appreciate you coming and offering to buy the horse from me. I know you're going to find something you want to buy, and Joe wants to sell it to you. I haven't told Joe, but I'm obligated here. I've advertised to sell these horses at auction. Several done already looked at the horse, and if I had a-done what you want me to do now, the horse wouldn't be here. They'd done bought him. Now, I hope you understand."

"I understand, Mr. Ray. That's perfectly all right, but don't sell that horse till I get the last bid."

Calvin Miller was a great big black man, weighed two-fifty, fine-looking man, and he had a brother who looked a good deal like him. He was black too, and both of them had a heavy mustache.

The whites was there and a good many blacks too. Cotton was a dollar and something a pound. Son-of-a-bitch, they had money up in that Delta. When the time come to sell, Joe brought the horse Calvin Miller wanted out first. Joe was tending to all of the horses, getting them in and getting them out of the ring. He could do as much work as three men. Shit, he didn't ring no backup bells,[68] and I went to work on the son-of-a-gun. Calvin had seen me sell at auction, and he just put his hand on my hand when the horse he wanted come in the pen. I knocked off the son-of-a-bitch at three hundred and fifty dollars. I cut the auction short and sold him to Calvin for just three-fifty.

Old Joe liked to fell out. Oh hell, he knew I could have got six or seven hundred dollars for the horse. His friend, Calvin, had already offered me five hundred for him, and I told him I couldn't sell him before the sale started. Joe was glad to see that. We went ahead with the sale and made a barrel of money. After it was over, Joe said, "Mr. Ray, let's go back to Fort Worth."

I said, "I'll tell you what we'll do. You go to Fort Worth, and you buy every horse that looks good to you. I'm going to St. Louis."

"How should I charge those horses?"

"Tell them to charge the horses to Ray Lum."

"That's fine."

I went to St. Louis and got a load of horses. I come back with them from St. Louis and sold them in Rolling Fork. Joe wadn't with me. I didn't need nobody. All you needed was to get the horses. The money was there. Then I went on to Fort Worth, and Joe had bought some damn nice horses. He says, "I want to go back to Rolling Fork with you, Mr. Ray."

I knew most any place you'd go was good then. Cotton was a dollar and something a pound. But we come back to Rolling Fork and sold them just as high as before. But poor Joe taken sick and died. Joe died with the flu. They was all dying with the flu. I never thought more of any trader than I thought of Joe. Joe Wicks. That was his name.

When I left the Delta and went to Memphis in nineteen-seventeen, there was auctions going on all over the country. I was considered one of the best auctioneers, and I got calls from every doggoned place. I went to work at Darnell and Berry, and when I went there, that old man says, "What are you going to work for here a day?"

Me, like a fool, says, "A hundred and fifty dollars a day."

So he give me a hundred and fifty dollars for Monday and Tuesday. I got three hundred dollars. That was the worst deal I ever made when he give me that three hundred dollars. Before that I was buying a hundred and fifty horses a week, maybe two hundred, and shipping them around. I could have made more buying and selling horses than he was paying me, don't you see. If I hadn't been auctioning, I'd of been down there, buying horses. I'd go over, and I'd say, "Mr. Spinach, I bought two of your horses there. This horse's got a little blue in his eye here. Take off twenty-five dollars."

The horse might have a blue eye, and that would mean he was blind or weak-eyed. Well, you'd raise cain and all when I'd show you the blue in his eye. Then you'd knock a little off the price. There's something wrong on every one of them. There never was a sound one, and I was a good judge of horses. I was doing all that work auctioning, when I could have bought and sold for myself and made more money. But I always loved to auction, and I hadn't figured out yet what I was doing, don't you know.

This little fellow that was my ring man,[69] Harry Barnett, I can hear him now. "Come on, Ray! Come on! Come on! Come on!" Harry would start the bidding. When the mule hit the auction floor, Harry was looking him in the face all the time and kept a good fast auction going. When the gate slung open, "Hundred and a quarter."

Harry set the price, and he never backed off his price. I would auction, and Harry worked the ring. He brought the animal in and set the first bid. He was as good a ring man as I ever saw, and I seen lots of them.

But this little Harry, to give you an idea of how fast he was, if there was two thousand mules shipped to the livestock barn, Harry would own a thousand of them before they got to the auction. Say you would ship in with a load of mules. Well, Harry would catch you outside the barn and buy them mules from you before the sale started. By God, he was giving you all the money you wanted to make, and you'd sell them to him. That's how fast he was. Course I was auctioneer, and Harry and I was partners. I would sell them mules high as hell, and we would split the profit. People in Memphis said we had the fastest auction in the city, and at that time Memphis was the mule center of the world.

When it was time to eat lunch, I'd go look at my mules to see what was coming. If we had two thousand mules, we'd start with one and go to two thousand. At noon, when they stopped to eat lunch for thirty minutes, I would look over the mules that hadn't been sold. I knew which ones was coming through that afternoon, and I wanted to be as well acquainted with them as I could. I remembered each one by his number, you see. Had them all numbered.

I never did eat lunch. I would eat breakfast that morning and dinner that night. It wadn't nothing to have three thousand mules at our sale and finish them in two days. We never was over two days running and never went very deep into the night. I can hear this little Harry now, "Come on, Ray! Come on! Come on!"

He was awful to take a little nip, but oh good God, he'd work. He was the hardest worker ever I'd seen. He kept a little bottle of whiskey in his pocket that he called Little Mike, and cold sweat would be dropping off of him big as buckshot. I was rolling pretty doggone fast in them days, but Harry was one of them nervous kind that believed in being in a hurry. He'd say, "Come on, Ray! Come on! Come on!"

You didn't roll too fast for Harry. He could keep up with you. That stock gate never quit swinging, and I'd call every fault on the mule. I'd call it in a hurry, and if you wasn't listening, by golly, you was out of luck. I'd call it in a way that the buyers knew. An angel[70] that just walked in wouldn't know. "One lamp burning. Left lamp there dead" meant the mule had one eye blind. Say it all in a hurry. You didn't lose no time. "Little jack on this mule here" meant he was limping.

A thousand mules a day is about what we sold, and we never did turn a mule around. He come in one gate and went right out the other. In a fast sale you go quick as you can step. You don't ring no backup bell. You're going forward. When a mule come in, I called what was on him, and I called it right now. Most of the people I was selling to was dealers. People that didn't know the score, I didn't have time to wake them up. If they was asleep, I let them sleep on. But most of the people that bought the mules was dealers, so when I'd call a mule, "a six-year, one eye a little blue," I never did turn around. I just kept a-going. Called it just as it was.

One mule's tail went out. Another mule's head come in. Like, "Sold to you there!"

And I'd grab the next bid and go right off. I'd call everything on him, and what I called was put on the ticket. If you'd buy a mule and then go outside and find something wrong with him that wasn't called, you could bush him and turn him back. You'd give two hundred and fifty dollars for him and say, "The damned mule's got one eye."

"Well, discount fifty dollars off that son-of-a-bitch. Bush him fifty dollars or reject him, whatever you want to do."

It'd be up to you, you see. Some of them got by sometimes, but if something was wrong, I'd generally call it. I'd have inspected them, and if one come in, whatever was on him, I'd call it and throw it on the ticket. The buyer don't stop and look at the mule. He'd just buy him at what I called on him, you see.

I was a good auctioneer, but I never was as fast as Colonel Meals. He's dead now. Colonel Meals would sit back in the auction box, and he weighed three hundred pounds. Goddamn, he used to roll like a Cadillac. He was a wheel horse.[71] He was one of the best. I always knew he was a better auctioneer than I was, but some of them liked me the best. Old Colonel Meals and I was competitors, but that didn't make no difference. He sold for one company, and I sold for another. Sometimes he'd get through and come up where I was working. He'd say, "Well, you gonna sell that whole lot? Come on, rest a minute."

Then he'd go in and auction for me, you know. I'd do the same damn thing for him. If I went down to his place, I'd say, "Now push over, you son-of-a-bitch."

He'd just roll off there like a ball. We'd call each other a son-of-a-bitch, and after the auction we'd eat supper together.

Harry Corner was another auctioneer there at Memphis. Harry worked at Maxwell's, and he was damned near as good an auctioneer as Colonel Meals. I walked down there to see him, and I said, "Push over, you son-of-a-bitch. You'll break your neck. Goddamn."

I pushed him over, auctioned about thirty or forty minutes more, and finished up his sale. He said, "I'm glad you come along. I've had this crick in my neck all day."

I said, "Come on. I know where the best chiropractor in Memphis is."

We went on down and found the doctor's office. I said, "Doctor, take this fellow next. He's had a crick in his neck all day."

"Well, now, that's too bad. Sit down and rest yourself."

The doctor sat Harry down. He began to make his head roll, and then he popped it. "Oh, Doctor, you goddamn son-of-a-bitch. You tried to break my neck."

I taken ahold of Harry. "How much I owe you, Doc?"

"Two dollars."

"Here. Here's five dollars. It's worth that to get that crick out of his neck. Come on, Harry."

I just grabbed him by the collar. "Hell," he said, "that goddamn son-of-a-bitch tried to break my neck."

"The hell he did. Your crick's gone now. You're all right, you bastard. Let's go and eat a good steak."

We went on out, but he was still mad at the doctor. I said, "You Irish son-of-a-bitch. Are you going to be mad at the man for curing you? Goddamn."

Harry finally got to laughing. He finally got the good humor, you know, but he said, "That son-of-a-bitch tried to break my neck."

I said, "He done what he was supposed to do. He got the crick out of your damned neck."

Rattlesnakes, Coyotes, and Wild Horses

Ray Lum's move to Texas signaled a major expansion in his business as a trader and auctioneer. He had often traveled to Texas to buy livestock in Fort Worth, and his move to the state brought him closer to his markets there. While he continued to ship livestock to his livestock barns in Vicksburg, he significantly broadened his markets to include Texas ranchers.

Harry Barnett, Lum's partner and ring man from Memphis, and ten men from Vicksburg accompanied him to Texas. This staff joined thirty Texans who organized livestock sales for Lum in cities and towns throughout the state. Lum shipped each person stock and then auctioned the animals for them on a partnership basis.

Ellie Lum, his wife, moved to Texas with him, and they shared an apartment in Fort Worth. Mrs. Lum was born in Hopkinsville, Kentucky, where her father was a livestock dealer. When they first married, Mrs. Lum lived with her husband in an apartment in their livestock barn in Vicksburg. She later ran a real estate business and developed land they owned around the barn into Sky Farm Subdivision, Vicksburg's first suburb. She sometimes lived in one of her newly built homes and would sell it while Lum was away trading.

Lum remarked that before he returned to Vicksburg, he always called his wife to see where they were living.

A letter dated "7/17-50 Mon. night" that Lum wrote his wife from Texas has a formal, businesslike tone. On letterhead stationery illustrated with a bull, a goat, a sheep, and a bucking bronco from the Naylor Hotel in San Angelo, Texas, he describes his recent live-stock trades in detail:

> Dear Mother & Sonny,
>   Came in here this morning and attended the sale. Bought 9 bulls. Already had 4 here. Sent them to Stephenville to sell Wed. Will go to Abilene tomorrow. Looked at a Mr. Trimble's cattle this evening after sale. Didn't trade with him. Called Mr. Hughes. Nice chat. No business.

The pressures of travel and trades throughout Texas are felt as Lum concludes his three-page letter with:

> Well I am tired and will say good night and write again when
> I have a chance—Love to you and Sonny.
> Daddy

Lum enjoyed the Texas climate where air was thinner, rattle-snakes struck faster, and horses bucked harder than in his native Mississippi. He discovered West Texas people spoke less and often lived on isolated ranches. He traded with prominent ranchers such as Paul Waggoner who owned hundreds of thousands of acres.[72] Wag-goner developed Shorthorn and Hereford cattle and operated Wag-goner Arlington Downs Stables between Fort Worth and Dallas where he specialized in fine horses.

Between 1889 and 1903 the Waggoner Ranch grew to over a million acres in Foard, Knox, Baylor, Archer, Wilbarger, and Wich-ita counties. In 1900 William Thomas Waggoner gave each of his three children, Paul, Guy, and Electra, 90,000 acres of land and 10,000 head of cattle. Oil was discovered on the ranch in 1903. In 1909 Waggoner divided half of the ranch among his children.

Lum met Paul Waggoner at Waggoner's horse sale which also attracted famed humorist Will Rogers.[73] On the evening before the sale Rogers performed his celebrated riding and trick-roping act. Lum *appreciated Rogers's humor and was also impressed with his roping skill.*

Lum also bought horses on the King Ranch. He mentions Robert Justus Kleberg, a lawyer who represented Richard King, founder of the King Ranch. King established the ranch with a Spanish land grant of 75,000 acres in 1852. Kleberg married Richard King's youngest daughter, Alice, and managed the ranch most of his life. Kleberg crossbred Brahman cattle with Shorthorns to create the famous Santa Gertrudis breed. The Santa Gertrudis cattle were named for the creek on which the ranch headquarters sits. The King Ranch was also known for its horses, and in 1947 it had 2,900 quarter horses and 82 racehorses. Fifteen hundred miles of fence surround its four divisions, Santa Gertrudis, Laureles, Norias, and El Sauz. Water comes from 75 artesian wells and 225 windmills.[74]

From Texas, Lum shipped registered Hereford bulls into the Deep South, where they were welcomed by local farmers. At a memorable auction in Baton Rouge he was challenged by Earl Long, who questioned the value of his cattle. One of the most colorful politicians in Louisiana history, Long was a progressive who supported education and was one of the earliest advocates for black voting rights.[75]

Lum admired the famed Texas cattleman Charles Goodnight. With his partner John G. Adair, Goodnight developed a herd of 100,000 cattle on one million acres of land. His final years were spent at his ranch at Goodnight, Texas, a Panhandle town named for him.[76]

Texas German farmers impressed Lum because they kept their stock in good condition. He noted with interest that the German preference for beer distinguished them from Mississippians, who loved whiskey.[77]

Lum encountered several celebrated outlaws in Texas. He met Frank James outside a shoe store in Dallas. A bank and train robber, Frank and his brother, Jesse, were among the nation's most famous outlaws. Born in Clay County, Missouri, during the Civil War, Frank James joined William Clarke Quantrill's guerrillas. Frank and Jesse's career as outlaws began on February 13, 1866, when they robbed a bank and killed a bystander in Liberty, Missouri. Their celebrated robberies of banks and trains continued until April 3, 1882, when Jessie was murdered at his home in St. Joseph, Missouri, by Robert Ford as James stood on a chair adjusting a picture. Several months after Jesse James was murdered by Robert Ford, Frank James gave himself up and was tried for murder in Missouri and for robbery in Huntsville, Alabama. The James Brothers were said to have robbed from the rich and given to the poor, and juries in both trials found Frank James not guilty of all charges. He remained free until his death in 1915.[78]

Another famed outlaw whom Lum met several times in the West was Pretty Boy Floyd. Floyd grew up in the Cherokee Indian Territory of Oklahoma and became a Robin Hood figure for sharecroppers in eastern Oklahoma. He robbed banks from Kansas City to Ohio and remained at large until 1934 when F.B.I. agents trapped and killed him in a cornfield near East Liverpool.[79]

Lum admired Judge Roy Bean, the famed Texas judge who was known as the "Law West of the Pecos." As justice of the peace, Bean allowed divorces when marriages he had performed did not "take," saying he had a right to correct his errors. He died in his saloon on March 16, 1903, and is buried in Del Rio, Texas.[80]

One of Lum's best friends in Dallas, Frank Corolla, had his saloon destroyed by Carry Nation. Nation was a temperance champion who weighed 175 pounds and was almost six feet tall. She fiercely attacked saloon keepers and destroyed their businesses with her famed hatchet.[81]

During his travels in Texas, Lum was often accompanied by Squire Harris, his black hostler from Vicksburg. Harris was a fine rider who demonstrated horses to customers. Some of the towns they visited did not allow blacks to stay overnight. Harris quickly gained favor with Texans through both his wit and his riding skills.

Lum refers to both "black" and "Irish" gypsies. The "black gypsies" are Romany people who trace their roots to ninth-century India. Between 50,000 and 100,000 Romany gypsies lived in the South, with the largest communities in Texas, Arkansas, Georgia, Louisiana, Kentucky, and the Carolinas.[82]

Lum considered "Irish gypsies" the greatest traders he knew.[83] Irish traders traveled in two-family convoys consisting of three cars, each drawing a trailer with tents and furniture, and three trucks for stock. Often four generations traveled together and would camp in tents with two large carpeted rooms.[84]

Irish traders used a secret language or "cant" to conceal their conversations from outsiders.[85] Irish cant evolved from Gaelic, and traders spoke the language during business dealings. Many phrases dealt with horses and mules, and when Lum "partnered" in

*Texas with Irish trader Richard Riley he learned to use cant phrases
such as "cat eye" for a hundred dollars and "pound" for five
dollars.[86]*

*During their visit to the Lone Star State, New Yorkers Al Smith
and Jimmy Walker had vivid impressions of Texas. Smith served as
governor of New York, and in 1928 he ran as the Democratic candi-
date for president and was defeated by Herbert Hoover.[87]*

*Jimmy Walker was a popular mayor of New York City and held
the office until 1932.[88] Both Walker and Smith were popular figures
in Texas, and Lum's stories of their travels in the state were among
his favorites.*

*From 1922 to 1940 Lum traded throughout Texas. Unlike Mis-
sissippi, where mules were his primary interest, most of his Texas
trades were for horses. During his travels he encountered a dangerous
bulldog, ate barbecued rattlesnake, and went on a coyote hunt. He
grew to love Texas people as his own and regarded the state as a
second home.*

*Over the course of the years I talked with Lum, his great hope
was that I drive him to Texas to revisit the old friends and places he
knew so well. As a young man he frequently drove from Vicksburg to
Texas, and I regret we never made that trip together.*

W hen I left Memphis in 'twenty-two, I went to auctioneering
for Mr. Yount who owned a barn in Fort Worth. He was
getting a good many miles on his speedometer, and I did most of
his selling.

I shipped stock all over Texas. Harry Barnett and I come to
Texas together and was partners. Harry never did leave the city,
which was pretty smart. Wadn't no use to get out in the country,
'cause the city was where the stock came to be sold, don't you know.
I anchored[89] all over because I had men selling all over. There
wadn't a town in Texas that I wadn't familiar with, and Texas is a
big state.

Mrs. Lum's father was in the livestock business, and I carried
him to Texas too. Mrs. Lum and I stayed at Fort Worth in a big
apartment house there. I got my brothers, John and Robert. I
brought my brothers over, and I brought about ten more men from

Mississippi. I had thirty Texas boys working too, and I'd split with all of them. They all made money.

I remember one fellow, Will Worthy, said, "Ray, I think I'll just go to trading for myself."

"That's fine. Go right on."

I had plenty without him. In about two weeks he was back with me. The horses he bought lost money. I had them all working, and I split with them.

I already had those sale barns and the livery barns in Vicksburg.[90] I had four or five men working in Vicksburg, and I talked to them by phone every night. My brother Allen Lum was in Vicksburg in them days. Allen ran the Vicksburg barn, and I had Old Man Husband, Will MacBroom, and Lacy Childress from Yazoo City that were salesmen. I kept them full of mules, and they'd keep me posted on the phone each night. That went on for blows and blows. We had the best trade in the South with mules.

Texas is a big country, and there wadn't a town in Texas with as many as five thousand people that I didn't auction in. I got to all of them towns. I was the first auctioneer that went to having sales at night. We were getting so many sales that we couldn't get to all of them during the day. So I says, "Let's have them at night."

Our night sales was much better than our day sales. They was cooler. The temperature would get up to a hundred and twenty in the day, so them people really appreciated night sales.

When they'd have a sale, I'd go down and sell the stock for them. I made lots of money, and I think most of them fellows was honest. If they wadn't, wadn't no way I could keep up with them. I was splitting with them all. I had a big Irishman named Richard Riley working for me. Richard Riley was my foreman. He was about six-foot-four, an Irish trader. Had traded all his life. He knew a black gypsy better than they knew themselves. Them black gypsies, you know, was supposed to be good traders, but Richard was better.

The most interesting thing I run into was down in South Texas. Richard Riley was with me this day. He said, "Come on. Let's go over to this cave, this certain cave."

Richard was a registered Irishman, and you couldn't scare him

Lum children, Vicksburg, Mississippi, c. 1900, Lum Family Album.

Ray Lum, c. 1911.

Ray Lum, c. 1921.

Ray Lum auctioneering, Vicksburg, Mississippi, c. 1940, Lum Family Album.

Ray Lum auctioneering, Vicksburg, Mississippi, c. 1940, Lum Family Album

Lum sale barn, Vicksburg, Mississippi, c. 1940, Lum Family Album.

*Ray Lum standing beside western saddles, Vicksburg, Mississippi, c. 1950,
Lum Family Album.*

Ray Lum auctioneering, Vicksburg, Mississippi, c. 1940, Lum Family Album.

Ray Lum with boy, Vicksburg, Mississippi, c. 1950, Lum Family Album.

Storytelling in The Ketch Pen, Vicksburg, Mississippi, 1973.

Showing a pony, Vicksburg, Missis-
sippi, 1975.

Visiting with George Cowan, High-
way 61, 1974.

Visiting with old friends, Lorman,
Mississippi, 1974.

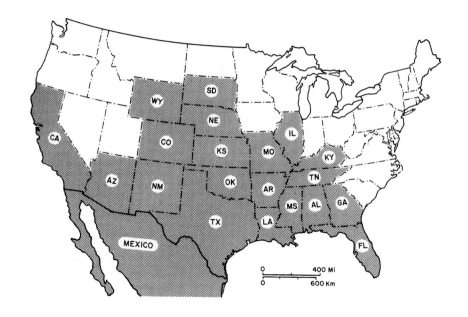

States in which Lum traded. (Map
by Duilio Peruzzi)

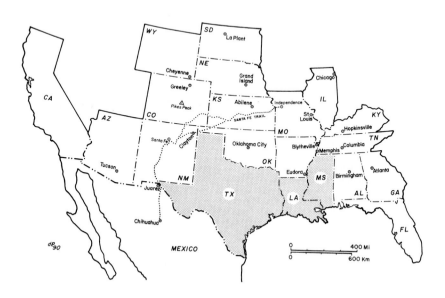

*Cities outside of Louisiana, Missis-
sippi, and Texas in which Lum
traded.* (Map by Duilio Peruzzi)

Locations of trades in Louisiana,
Mississippi, and Texas. (Map by
Duilio Peruzzi)

With the author, Vicksburg, Mississippi, 1975. (Photo by Teresa
Jordan)

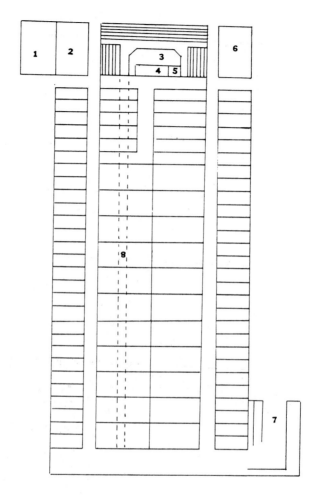

LUM BROTHERS AUCTION BARN
Vicksburg, Mississippi

1. Ketch Pen
2. Cafe
3. Ring
4. Auctioneer platform
5. Scales
6. Office
7. Loading and unloading area
8. Elevated walkway

Auction barn floor plan (Drawing by Grey Ferris)

with nothing. So we got over to the cave, and I said, "Richard, I'll be here when you come back, if you do get back."

"Hell, you're not going down?"

"No, I'm not thinking about going down in that cave. But I'll try to be here when you come back. Be damn sure you get back."

Richard went on down, and I talked to the man who was outside collecting money, charging you for going down. I was with him for a while, and I peeked down and saw, "drip, drip, drip," the water dripping. Richard finally came out, and he said, "You don't know what you missed."

"Well, you're out. That's fine. I'm glad you're back out."

"You ought to go down and see that."

"I'm not thinking about going down."

All the while, I seen the water, "drip, drip, drip," and knew that thing might give way. But Richard said it was safe. He brought back a lot of pictures from down there, and it just looked like icicles was hanging, don't you know, and water dropping over them.

Richard said, "They're not icicles."

"Well, that was water dripping off of them?"

"Yeah, definitely."

"Fine. I feel just as good or better than if I'd went in there with you."

I didn't have any idea of going in that mine. Richard Riley was an Irish trader, and he had a brother that was older than him that was ten times better. His older brother, oh good God, he'd rob every man he'd meet and do it with a pair of lazy, old deadhead horses. He'd say, "Here, Mister, let me give you this whip."

"I don't need no whip."

"Yes, you might need it."

Things like that. He was as smooth as he could be, and he lived to be a ripe old age. And Richard was good too. Of course, they had the same daddy.

I was with Richard when he swapped with a Dutchman at Temple, Texas. He swapped with this Dutchman and got his pair of pretty white mules, white as driven snow and fat as town dogs. Them German people keep their mules fat. They ain't going to have one unless he's fat. So Richard said, "I think I'll paint them damn mules."

See, a mule is born black and gets white with age. Richard just wanted to turn their speedometers back. I went on doing something else, and when I come back, I saw a pair of black mules in the place of them white ones we traded for. Well, that night those mules broke out of their pen, and after a while, here come the Dutchman, the same Dutchman that we got them from. He come up and said, "Boys, two goddamn mules are down there trying to push my gates down."

Richard said, "Well, son-of-a-bitch. Let's go down and get them out of your way."

Richard went right down and got them. The Dutchman didn't know his own mules. Oh, Richard had done a good job. That son-of-a-bitch, he could do anything. Make no bones about it, them mules didn't have a white hair on them. When he got through painting them, they were black as wolf's shit, and that's black.

You've heard of "Texas against the world." Well, that's near about right. Texans are a special breed of people, and it's just as much difference in West Texas and East Texas people as there is in daylight and dark. I like them both, and East Texans are just like we are here in Mississippi. But you get to West Texas, and they'll look plumb through you. They don't say a word. They treat you just as nice as can be, and they don't lock up a thing around their place at night. They leave out horses and mules, saddles and everything. No lock on the gate or nothing. If anything is gone, they'll know who got it. I've been to their houses when they've been gone three years, and if there's anything missing, they didn't send out no alarm or nothing. It would be back there in a few days. It would be put back there in its place. I never did know just how they done it, but they had a way of knowing how to get things back, and there wadn't much stealing going on in that country.

West Texas people are good judges of human nature. They don't talk much, but they'll treat you nice. But don't steal nothing. Don't take nothing that don't belong to you. They know everybody who comes through and know everything that goes on. If there's something missing, they'd figure pretty fast who would be the one took it, don't you know.

If you drive to San Angelo and go south, you can be riding

along in the heat and look up at the mountain, and there's snow up there. Right around Marfa. That's where it was. Marfa, Texas. You can be riding right down the trail here and look up on the mountain, and there's snow. It's hot as it could be down here where you are, and it's snow up there. That always looked funny to me.

Marfa was where I ate the rattlesnake. They was having this sale and served barbecue rattlesnake for lunch. They had other things there, and if you didn't want to eat rattlesnake, you didn't have to. I enjoyed it. This man said, "You know what that is?"

"I figure I do. Give me another piece of it."

It was barbecued snake, and it was delicious. It tasted better than fish and mighty near like frog legs.

In that country they have snake drives where they catch four or five hundred snakes and get their venom. They milk that poison out of them and sell it. I don't know whether they use the hide or not. Then they eat the meat. This man was having a cattle sale, and he served that snake with a wonderful dinner.

I came close to getting bit by rattlesnakes two or three times out there. I always wore boots when I was around snakes, and I've had fangs stuck in my boots several times. A snake don't hit too high up. So if you're wearing boots, you're pretty near safe with them.

A rattlesnake don't strike without warning you. Isn't that wonderful? I just hoped my hearing was always good when I was around with them 'cause they'll sing before they'll strike. I found out a lot about Texas rattlesnakes. A Texas rattlesnake'll hit twice in the time one here hits you once. It's the climate, the atmosphere, of course.

Just like them Texas horses. A Texas horse will break in two with you when you get in the saddle. When you sit down on a Texas horse, he'll pitch,[91] and then he'll go on and ride. They'll pitch with you. You'll get your good ride after he pitches.

You cheek[92] every Texas horse before you get on him. Pull his head around with the bridle or reins so he's looking at you when you get up on him. Don't go walking up to a horse and stick your foot in the stirrup with his head loose. If you do, bam, you'll find out you need another belly because that one's gone.

And them West Texas girls is raised so they can ride better than most men. I remember I pulled in once in West Texas to buy horses. I was buying horses for the government, and this man says, "I'll have to send my daughter over there with you." He had a little fifteen-, sixteen-year-old girl. I was twenty. And he says, "You two can gather those horses and pen them. Which horse do you want to ride?"

I looked out. I knew what was going to happen. I knew the son-of-a-gun was going to pitch with me, but them days I was a pretty fair hand. "I'll ride this little roan horse."

I cheeked him and set down on him, and he broke in two with me. He pitched off there around a hundred yards. I said to the little girl, "Do you ride this one quite a bit?"

"Oh, I ride them all."

That was all that was said. We went on ahead, gathered the horses and brought them in. I didn't see her when she mounted, but I'm sure hers pitched too. It's that air. They feel good. They're playing when they're pitching. He don't care whether he throws you or not. He's got to get that buck out. That's his exercise, you know. I always thought, "I wish he could get his exercise out without bouncing me around."

But you get to where you don't pay no attention to it. I was always thinking, "I'll step on a son-of-a-gun after a while, and it'll be a sunfisher."[93] That's one of them pitching horses that puts his back where his belly ought to be, and you ain't going to stay on him. Well, I never did step on one of them, so it was all right. But I kept thinking about it every time I'd get on a horse out in that country. They'd say, "There's nobody here but just this boy, and you're going to have to help pen the horses."

I never said "no" about it. I always rode their horses, but I always hoped that I wouldn't step on one of them sunfishers that throws their damn back under their belly. Ain't much way to stay on him. It's the climate, the air. Air's lighter there than it is here.

One evening I pulled up to a Mr. Bobb's place. He had a lot of horses. When I started into his ranch, here comes a man up and says, "Where's Mr. Bobb's place?"

"I think it's right on down this road. What's that you got in the car?"

"My dogs."

I looked over, and there was these three long, tall dogs. I said, "Them's greyhounds you got there."

"I'm a bounty hunter. I hunt coyotes."

"Well, that is interesting. You going to try to catch one before you get down to the house?"

"I thought I'd drive down this draw.[94] You want to make a little round with me so you can see them work?"

"You bet. I'd love it."

I got in his truck with him. We crossed a cattle gap and didn't go a hundred yards before he slapped, "bap, bap, bap," on the side of the truck. Them greyhounds was just like three birds, right over and right out. Wadn't three hundred yards before one of them had the coyote by the throat, one of them had him by the middle, and the other by the hind leg. They stretched him out, and they killed him. By the time we got there, the son-of-a-bitch was dead as hell. "Well, we'll try to get another one before we go in."

He just cut his tail off, throwed it behind the seat, put the dogs back in, and we went on. Drove two or three hundred yards more. The same thing again. He saw the coyote before the dogs saw him. So he slammed on the side of the car, and out they went, just like birds, over, right on down, the same deal. He cut the tail off the coyote, came back, and throwed it behind the seat. He got the dogs back in, and we went on back to Mr. Bobb's ranch. We got on down there, and they was just getting ready for supper. Mr. Bobb spoke to the bounty hunter, and he spoke to me. He knew I come to look at horses. He says to the bounty hunter, "I'm glad to see you. Been looking for you for several weeks now."

"Yes. I intended to get over here sooner."

"I bet you boys are hungry. I'll fix you a steak. Ray, do you like beef steak?"

"I love it."

He takes a windlass and lowers a quarter of beef down out of a tree. He didn't have no wife. He was just living by himself, and he kept that quarter of beef up in the tree. It was black as it could be. He cut a slice off, and I said, "How long has that been there?"

"Oh, I put that up there several months ago."

I didn't go into it any further. I was hungry that night, and I really enjoyed that steak that had been up in the tree. I don't know how long it had been up there. The air is pure there, and it puts a little crust over it like salt, and that preserves it. It'll stay up there for months and keep getting better all the time. He cut off our three steaks and throwed them right on the grill. Then he said, "I better cut off some of this so you can feed your dogs."

"No," the bounty hunter says. "I have their food."

He reached down in his little bag and took out three thin slices of bread. He had three dogs. He pitched them slices of bread over, and the dogs caught that bread. They had done already caught those two coyotes. I don't know how many more they'd caught that day. I said, "Aren't you going to feed them anything more?"

"That's all."

"Uh huh."

I didn't talk anymore to that man. I figured he knew what he was doing. That was the bounty hunter. He got twenty-five dollars for each of them tails. That was fifty dollars he made after we started out to get supper. I don't know how many more he stayed there and got, but that was interesting to me to see that.

Then I went out to buy a man's mules, and he wasn't there. I looked out and saw a damn snake as big as your leg. So I thought I'd chunk[95] a rock at him and make him move. When I went to chunk, the man come up and hollered, "Don't you hit my snake."

He come on up, and I said, "I never saw one that big before."

"That's my bull snake, and I wouldn't take five hundred dollars for him. We haven't got a rat on the place."

He was big as my right leg and twelve feet long. He blowed just like a bull. I apologized for chunking at his snake, and said, "I didn't hit him. I just wanted him to move a little."

Which was all the truth. I didn't have no idea of hitting him. But, oh good God, if I'd hit that damn snake, I wouldn't have got his mules or nothing else.

I got through with that deal and went on to the next ranch. I heard the man there had a pair of mules to sell. They didn't tell me about his having a bulldog. I went up there, and he wadn't at home. So I got out of my car and was standing near a fence with four strands of barbed wire. I walked over to within three feet of the fence when I saw this dog, this bulldog, and he wasn't saying a word. His tail stood up, and when he come through that fence, he liked to took that bottom wire off. He didn't even move his tail. I said, "My good man, what's the matter with you?"

I was getting my knife out all the time. I couldn't make it back to the car. I'd got too far from the car, but I had a sharp knife. I figured on cutting his damned head plumb off if he didn't kill me before I cut it off. I said, "Good man, what's the matter with you? Sit down there, boy."

He got as close as three feet from me, then he commenced to shoving them front teeth out and sat down. When he sat down, I began to back up a little bit, talking to him all the time. "What are you ruffed up about, big man?"

I never saw such a mouth on a bulldog. God Almighty, he was really something. Here come the man that lived there, and he was a damned sight more scared than me 'cause by that time I'd got back in my car. He said, "You didn't get out of your car, did you?"

"I'm sorry to tell you I didn't see the dog when I got out."

I knew then the damned dog must have killed somebody a day or two before because the man just turned white, and he was a red-faced man. "Don't you keep him tied up?"

"No, and we don't have nothing bother us around here."

I didn't say any more. I let it go like water, and I said, "How far are those mules from here?"

"Right there in the barn."

The man was just white as a sheet. I was judging him all the time. I figured that damned dog done killed somebody or tore him up. I said, "I guess you wouldn't think about selling him."

I was just making conversation. He said, "I wouldn't take that pair of mules for him."

He was crazy about the dog, don't you know. We went on down to the barn, and I bought his mules. I didn't have no trouble trading with him. He was still scared. He told me about another fellow that had a pair of mules, and I went over to see the next man's mules.

I done had more experience in that day's time than ever before with that snake and that bulldog. I don't know which one was the worst. I don't know what them snakes will do to you, but I don't think they'd hurt at all.

I was at Houston, and there was a man there named Frank Corolla that had a saloon downtown. I'd been talking to Frank around the time Al Smith was running for president and Jimmy Walker was mayor of New York. So Jimmy come down with Al right by where Frank and I was talking. Al said, "I'm tired."

Jimmy said, "I'm going to drive around and see some of the country."

"Well, go ahead."

So Jimmy went ahead to the car. Jimmy said to the man, "Drive me around here."

"Where do you want to go, Mr. Walker?"

"I just want to see the country."

That was Jimmy Walker. He rolled ninety miles an hour, you know. "Stop the car. What's that?"

"This is one of our rivers."

Not a damn drop of water in it. "This is your rivers. Uh huh. Go on. Pull over there. What are those?"

"That's some of our good cows. That is the Hereford breed of cow."

They was beef cattle and didn't have no bag.[96] "Uh huh. All right. Drive on."

On they went looking. He keep looking, and as far as he could see, wadn't a bit of grass. Just gravel. That's the way it is in that part of Texas.

So Jimmy had the fellow to drive him on and asked him all the questions he could think of. He tried to find out all about Texas. When he did get back to the hotel, Al Smith said, "Well, what do you think about Texas now?"

"Al, I'll tell you. Texas has got more rivers and less water, more cows and less milk, and you can see further and see less than you can in any country on God Almighty's green earth."

That was Jimmy's description of Texas, don't you know. You can go for miles and not see a drop of water in the rivers, and the cows had not a drop of milk. Well, when you stop to think of it, he saw a lot. When a man comes to your country, he sees a lot that we don't see. We just take it for granted. Jimmy Walker was awake.

Al Smith run for president the same year, and I won some

money on that deal. I bet against him, and I won. I forget who it was Al run against, but they didn't beat him too bad. Al Smith was a Catholic. That's what beat him. He talked like an orator, and everybody liked him. He was down in Texas where they drank a lot, and he said, "I'm for more whiskey and bigger bottles."

They wasn't electing Catholics president in them times, but he come nearer to getting it than anyone until Kennedy. Kennedy was the only Catholic put in office, and you know they killed him. So I don't think it's safe for one to run even now.

Getting back to Frank Corolla, Frank was raised right here at Vicksburg, and I run into him in Houston. Frank was running a saloon, and he said, "Ray, I'm so glad that you come down here."

"Nice to see you too, Frank."

"Come on and get a drink."

"I'll take a beer."

We both had a drink. I drank beer, and he drank whiskey. The next night, the night after I was with him, Carry Nation come in, and she took a hammer to every bottle of whiskey and every mirror in the place. I wasn't there, but a fellow that knew Frank told me. He said he come by, and Frank had his head bent over his arm crying. This fellow heard what happened, and he was Frank's friend. So he said, "Did they break up everything, Frank?"

"Yes, everything. All the liquor."

"Frank, why don't you go to preaching?"

Frank studied a while, and then he said, "I just may do that. You know that's been on my mind."

He'd already been thinking about it. Frank preached in Houston that next night, and he took in seventy-five dollars. The night after that it was a different story. He went to San Antonio, and when he preached, he took in just a little bit less than two thousand dollars. He was a natural, don't you see. He had a voice that was like a bull. God Almighty, he'd roll off the words.

Frank had a wonderful voice. He could sing like a mockingbird. Frank kept on preaching, and the hats got bigger. When Frank Corolla died, he was worth close to a million dollars. We buried Frank Corolla right here in Vicksburg.

My best trading was in South Texas. I would buy my mules in Kansas where tractors was coming in and sell them in South Texas.

There was all German people there. I think I made more money on mules with the German people than anywhere else. In Johnson City I run into a German, and he had a sign up on his livestock barn that read "Horses, Mules, Cattle and Sheep. Some to Sell and Some to Keep." That was his sign. I went in and met this young man and bought all the mules he'd sell me. He had good mules, but he wouldn't sell all of them. You couldn't buy them all.

That was a good country to buy mules in. If ever you'd find a German with a mule, the mule would be fat. He wouldn't have a poor mule. Both of them'd be fat. The German would be fat, and the mule would be fat.

What makes a Dutchman like beer better than anybody else? We drink whiskey, and they drink beer. And a six-year-old kid down there in that German country is as big as a twelve-year-old here. They're big healthy kids.

I was at Ballinger, Texas, trading with a German, a nice fellow. One day he come up and said, "Ray, I want you to meet my daughter."

"Hey," I said, "I'm going to guess how old you are."

And she said, "I bet you're going to miss it."

"You're fifteen."

"I'm eleven, Mr. Lum."

But you never talked to a lady that used any better English and was smart as hell about everything. Well, she married a week after that. So John Shenold come up the next day, and Walter Millen says, "What did you think about so-and-so's daughter? She got married, and she was just eleven years old."

John said, "Well, when they're big enough, they're old enough."

I was around there two or three years after that, and she had a baby. She was glad to see me and was just as sweet as she could be. You never talked to a finer woman. But she had her bread done at eleven. She was a grown woman at eleven. Some of them mature earlier. I think that's true of all nationalities. You'll find some people that mature early, and you couldn't find another girl in Texas eleven years old who had done as much as that girl had.

Old Man Suggs was a pretty fair trader out in that country, and I sold him a lot of horses. I ran into him one day, and I had a stud horse that'd drop his dipper[97] out, and it'd touch the ground.

Horses was selling high then, and this was a good-bred Suffolk horse. So I said, "Mr. Suggs, I want to tell you about this horse. He's a little heavy hung, and you might not want him."

"Oh, my folks have always been short on that anyhow, and I want him."

Well, of course, I let him have him. I don't think he ever got him to breed. He was out of proportion. He was too heavy hung to ever make connections. That was Mr. Suggs. S-u-g-g-s. A Texas rancher. He was a good man. I bought horses from him always. I swapped that one horse to Mr. Suggs for a bunch of his horses. That was a pretty good trade in them days.

I had an old boy worked for me in South Texas, and his name was Gene Dobson. Gene was one of my best men there. He would say, "You can call me an S.B.,[98] but don't call me lazy."

I rolled up to a little town where he was selling my stock. I had shipped Gene a load of mules to this town. I rolled up there, and he was fixing to lead the mules out to start the sale. This great big German that owned the local sale barn there was sheriff too. I walked up, and Gene was laughing and grinning, and there was the sheriff right beside him. Gene said, "This sheriff says he's going to shoot the first mule I lead out here to sell. Ha ha ha ha. Ha ha ha ha."

I was awake, and I knew that laugh. That was a death laugh. Knowing Gene like I did, I knew something had to be done and done in a hurry. I said, "Hey. There's no use in that. We'll just take the mules out to the edge of town. This gentleman's right. I don't blame him a bit. He's the sheriff. He's had this business here for years, and he's right. We'll just take these mules outside of town and sell them."

I never did quit talking. I went to leading mules, and we left. That settled the deal, saved Gene, made us money, and I didn't go back there anymore. You see, the crowd had gathered. Gene was laughing 'cause he didn't intend to git killed. This sheriff was a gunman and a good one. He was six-foot-six or seven, weighed two-fifty or sixty, and Gene was a little slim fellow. He said, "He's going to shoot the first mule I lead out here. Ha ha ha ha. Ha ha ha ha."

I knew what that meant. Gene didn't intend for him to shoot

the mule or him, either one. I got them mules out of town and had the best sale you ever saw. I apologized for everything that happened, sold them mules, went down to the bank and give the cashier twenty-five dollars to get me a cashier's check. He said, "Mr. Lum, I don't know some of these people."

"You're closer to them than I am."

He was in better shape to collect than I was, trading all over like I did. I give him twenty-five dollars and said, "If you have any trouble, here's my address."

We never had trouble with any of the checks. But if we had, the bank was in better shape to get the money than I was, living the way I did away from there.

That German was the sheriff there, and he told Gene, "I'm going to shoot the first mule you pull out there." Course he wasn't going to shoot the mule. Might have shot us, but he had no idea of shooting that mule.

I remember another time Gene furnished Mack Daugherty, an Irishman, some money to buy a load of horses. That was when I first met Gene Dobson. I was over in Mississippi at Clinton to sell a load of horses, and when I got in, here come Gene on crutches. He says, "Ray, this is all I've got left out of five thousand dollars."

He had give Daugherty a load of horses to sell, but after Daugherty sold them, he run off to Memphis, got drunk and spent all Gene's money. So Gene says, "Ray, after you sell your horses, I'll pay you anything you charge to sell mine."

"Well, you'll like my price. I'll tell you what I want you to do. You keep books for me."

I come to find out he was a hell of a good bookkeeper. I explained to him all I was going to do. Then I told the customers, "Mr. Dobson has got a load of horses here, and I'm going to sell his horses for him after I finish mine. When I get through, you can walk right up and pay him."

When I finished selling my horses and collected all the money for them, I said, "Now we're going to sell Mr. Dobson's horses."

I went to work on Gene's horses, and they sold awful good. I put him in the car with me and said, "How you going back to Fort Worth?"

"Ray, I'm going back on the train."

"I'm going to drive back tomorrow, so you can go with me."

So he come on to Vicksburg and stayed all night with me. And he was a partner with me as long as he lived. He was the one that went down with me to the place where the man was going to shoot the mule right between the eyes. Gene wadn't afraid of hell itself, you know. He walked forward all the time. Didn't back up a bit. And he was a gambler. He done every doggone thing. He didn't lose when he gambled, and he was a good judge of human nature. He was paralyzed when I picked him up that day at Clinton and sold his horses for him. He was on crutches, but he got over that. When people start making money, it'll cure them of a lot of things.

I was in Dallas once, and a fellow said, "Ray, you want to see Frank James?"

"You bet I do."

I went on up, and there was Frank James. I talked with him quite a bit. And that fellow that was with me, he said, "Ray, I'm not right sure that Jesse's not here too." He believed it. You know Jesse James was supposed to have been gone a good long time ahead of Frank.

Frank was at this shoe store there, and people come from everywhere to see him. I used to go by and see him when I was buying livestock in Dallas. Frank was fine-looking, six-foot-three, and, goddamn, much of a man. He was just as nice to talk to as you'd want, and I wondered whether Jesse was dead. I never did think Robert Ford killed him. I thought it was somebody else that they killed to save Jesse, don't you know. Robert Ford shot him. "Robert Ford, a dirty little coward, shot Mr. Howard and laid Jesse James in his grave."

Paul Waggoner was having a sale at Dallas and was selling eight hundred horses. Mr. Waggoner had the largest herd of quarter horses[99] in Texas, and it got so he had a surplus of horses. He owned horses, and he owned plenty of land. I don't know how many acres he owned, but they counted it by the mile. So he held his first horse sale at Dallas.

The night before the sale I saw Will Rogers do a show with his rope in Dallas when a cat run out on the stage. Will dropped the string. Horse people call a lariat a string. He dropped the string around that cat, picked him up, turned him loose, and that was all.

That's how good he was. A lot of people can't rope an elephant, much less a cat. But Will Rogers could rope a cat, and I saw that happen at that show.

I always think about Will Rogers. Will said, "I like every man I ever met." I thought it over for a while, and wondered, "Gosh-a-mighty, how could he like a lot of them old stinkers?" Then I got to thinking it out a little. He figured the man had a cocklebur under his saddle. He'd figure what made him an old stinker. He'd pick out what was causing that. So he said, "I like every man I ever met."

The next morning Mr. Waggoner had his horse sale, and Will loved horses. Over to the horse sale he went. Will said, "Mr. Waggoner, I'd like to feel of that little horse."

"Go right ahead, Will."

He sat down on the horse, a little sorrel horse. He rode him out, I'd say about fifty yards, and when he did, the horse stepped in a gopher hole and turned over. Will turned two or three somersaults. A young fellow with me said, "Reckon he is hurt, Mr. Lum?"

"No, I don't think so."

Will come on back and said, "Mr. Waggoner, that is a nice little horse. I like him."

He understood about the horse falling when he stepped in that gopher hole. Mr. Waggoner said, "Will, I'll give you a carload of horses like him."

"That's mighty nice of you, Mr. Waggoner, but oats is high out in my part of the country."

That was all that was said. Will lived in California, and he and Mr. Waggoner just laughed it off. I stayed for the auction, and I bought six or eight carloads of horses. I bought about a hundred and fifty head of them Waggoner horses. They were all registered quarter horses, and in them days they didn't bring too much.

Will came around where I was buying horses. I'd bought over a hundred then, and he said, "Mr. Lum, what do you do with those horses?"

"Oh, I do the best I can with them. I trade them off, sell them, swap them."

He laughed. Tickled him, you know, to think about me swapping them. He said, "That many?"

"Oh yes."

I bought fifty more after I talked to him. Will was just buying one once in a while. When he'd see one he liked, he'd buy it. I was buying them all, 'cause the price was right. And I could sell them all, every one they had there. I remember I bought a little bay filly while Will was talking to me, and Paul Waggoner comes up and says, "Ray, I can give you foreign papers on that little horse if you want them."

"Oh, definitely I want them."

I gave sixty dollars for the little filly, coming a two-year-old, and shipped her to Vicksburg. Mr. Graham was at Rolling Fork, and I called him and said, "Say, run down here. I got in something I want to show you. I got a registered filly that just came in from the Waggoner Ranch, and I got two horses in there that he imported from England."

"Well, I want to see them."

So Mr. Graham came down. "This little mare here is a little bay mare that came from England. Mr. Waggoner said he would send me the papers on her."

"That is perfectly all right. You just send me the papers on her when you get them. What are you going to charge me for her?"

"Three hundred dollars."

"Well, that is all right. That is fine."

He looked over all the horses I had brought in from the sale, and that was the only one he wanted. When Mr. Graham passed away, I bought all of his horses, and that mare wasn't there. He had sold her to someone. I don't know who. He was a curiosity, Mr. Graham was. He had a hundred horses there, and a lot of people thought he was losing money. But he was selling them horses all over the world. The home folks just didn't know where he was going.

So when Mr. Graham passed away, I bought all his horses and sold them at Vicksburg one night. There was people at that sale from as far away as New York. I advertised my sale in every paper I could think of. I advertised in New York and Chicago papers, and people came from them places. And when they came, they came to buy horses. Those horses made a whole barrel of money.

There was one yellow mare in them, I remember, and Bogart

Graf says, "Mr. Lum, I want to tell you about this mare. She killed a man."

"That right?"

"I wouldn't sell her to you without telling you about it."

"Well, that is mighty fine, and I will be sure to tell them about it when I sell her. How did it happen, Bogart?"

"This foreman was riding her and run into a cow. The mare tried to jump over the cow and fell and killed the man. Broke his neck."

"Well, I'll be sure to tell about that."

So when this mare came in that night, I said, "You boys understand that this is the Graham estate's horses. Now this mare is one of them, and I want to tell you about her. The foreman was running a cow. The cow stopped. When the horse tried to jump over her, she fell and killed the man, which was not the fault of the horse. I hope that you boys will appreciate this little mare."

That was the little palomino mare, the one that killed the man. She was the one he wanted me to be sure to tell about, don't you know. I didn't think I could get but fifty dollars a round for that horse, and she brought three hundred and fifty dollars. She went to Lake Providence, Louisiana.

"Now you be sure and tell about that," he told me.

"I'll be sure and do it, Mr. Graf."

It wasn't the horse's fault 'cause the cow run in front of the horse. Most of the time it's not the horse's fault with accidents. It's usually something a person does that causes the accident. All right. We got out of that saddle.

I was in Angelo once, and Mr. Whittaker said, "Come on down and see Mr. Hughes's silo. He just finished one."[100]

We got there, and I said, "How long is that silo, Mr. Whittaker?"

He said, "That's the longest silo that's ever been made. It's three quarters of a mile long."

"How wide is it?"

"Hundred and ninety feet wide."

"How deep is it?"

"Thirty feet deep."

"Is he going to fill it?"

"He's got it damn near filled right now."

"How many of them is he going to put in?"

"He's going to put in three of them."

I don't know how many tons it took to fill that silo, but there was trucks rolling and cattle feed being blown in there all the time. When they got it all in, they covered it up, and that was your silo. Mr. Hughes put mostly corn in there and a lot of sorghum. Sorghum and corn was chopped all up together and blown in there. Don't you think it's not good cow feed. Them damn cows get so fat they can't walk.

A few weeks after that silo business I bought about two hundred bulls from Mr. Hughes and shipped them to Shreveport, Louisiana. I said, "Mr. Hughes, come on and go down with me."

"I'll just do that."

He was a little fellow. Didn't weigh over a hundred and twenty pounds, but he could move mountains. "I'll just do that."

"I guarantee you'll have a good time."

I knew damn well he was going to have a good time. I was going to see to that. Mr. Whittaker, who was my friend, said, "Don't take Mr. Hughes with you. If you do, you'll never buy another cow from him."

"Well, we'll see." Like Jack Benny, I said, "We'll see."[101]

"You're making a mistake taking Mr. Hughes."

"I don't think so."

And I didn't. I'd given him a hundred and fifty dollars a round for them cattle. That's all I'd given him for two hundred Hereford bulls. So Mr. Hughes and I got to Shreveport and went to the best hotel ever. I got him two rooms, and he said, "Why the hell did you rent me two rooms?"

"We ain't going to be in Shreveport but a few days, and, hell, the hotel rooms are cheap down here."

I got hold of a man there, and I said, "I was wondering if there'd be a chance to get the fairgrounds for a cattle sale. I've got two hundred registered cattle that I'm going to sell."

"Well, I don't know about that."

"These cattle came from Mr. Hughes at San Angelo."

"Dwain Hughes?"

"That's him. He'll be with me at the sale to see his cattle sell."

"Well, if Dwain Hughes is coming, you bet, you can have it."

To cut a long story short, I got the fairgrounds, and it didn't cost a goddamn cent. He said, "Tell Dwain I said come by here."

We went over, and, of course, Mr. Hughes was glad to see him. The next day we drove through the country. I was driving a Cadillac then. I got the names of the people who had the most land and drove Mr. Hughes out to meet them. I'd say, "Mr. Hughes and I have two hundred registered cattle up here that we're going to sell next week, and I'd appreciate it if you'd run up and take a look at them."

I'd walk out of the way, and Mr. Hughes would talk to them. I'd come back, and the man'd say, "Why, Mr. Lum. I'll be there. You can look for me." I heard enough of them say, "We'll be there," that I knew we was going to have a good sale.

Them cattle cost me a hundred and fifty dollars, and what do you think they averaged when I sold them? They never had seen no herds of cattle like that in Shreveport. When we got ready to sell those two hundred cattle, you couldn't get within a hundred yards of where the auctioneer was. That was because of all the advertising we had done when Mr. Hughes and I was driving over the country talking to the people. I think they brought close to four hundred dollars a head.

I said, "Mr. Hughes, you got some more cattle there, and them damn cattle brought a lot more than I thought they would." I told him just like it was. I never did lie to nobody about nothing. I said, "The cattle brought more, and I want to buy those other cattle from you."

Mr. Hughes had half a dozen ranches in Texas, and he had some more cattle at another ranch. He was the first man that got a Hereford herd to live in Texas. A few people tried it, and ticks would kill them. But Mr. Hughes didn't quit. He kept bringing them cattle, and after he did away with the ticks, he had the best cattle in Texas.[102]

So I went back and told him, "Now you got a hundred and fifty or two hundred down there."

"I got two hundred down there in that other place."

"Well, I want to give you more for them cattle, and I want you to go with me to Baton Rouge. You'll have fun down there. They are the friendliest people in the world."

"I want to go with you."

"Well, bless your heart."

"Ray, I don't want more money for these. Just give me a hundred and fifty dollars a round."

"Oh no. You got to get more than that for them."

I made him take two hundred dollars for them. I said, "You put on fifty anyhow because we going to sell them cattle like we did that last bunch."

"You think you can sell them as high down there?"

"I don't know, but there's a lot of good people at Baton Rouge."

When we got to Baton Rouge, here comes Frank Barber. I was raised with him in Vicksburg. Frank says, "Ray, I want you to meet Earl Long."

Earl said, "Did you bring your goddamn scrubs down here to rob these people?"

"Let me tell you something, Mr. Long. These cattle that I brought here will make history for Louisiana."

Exactly what I told him is what happened. He kind of quieted down and got all right. Frank says, "Ray, I want to help you a bit. There's a professor here that's been talking about getting a good Hereford bull."

"All right, Frank."

"I'll tell you what I'd like to do. I'd like to bring him here in the morning and let you sell him a bull."

"What ought I to ask for the bull, Frank? Two thousand?"

"Oh hell no. Ask him three thousand."

Three thousand for a hundred-and-fifty-dollar bull. Well, it wasn't a hundred and fifty. I had made Mr. Hughes take two hundred. A two-hundred-dollar bull. It's awful when you have to rob people to make them happy. Down comes the professor. He picked out the bull and just loved him. I said, "I'll let you have him for three thousand, but I'll have to borrow him from you. I'll have to run him through the auction because it won't do to sell stock before the auction."

He said it was all right with him. The next day at the auction I knocked the bull off for four thousand. The professor loved it, you know. He was getting a four-thousand-dollar bull for three. He really did love that bull then. Mr. Hughes said, "Ray, if there's enough professors in the country, you'll get along all right."

It just tickled him to death, you know. Mr. Hughes got along just as well in Baton Rouge as in Shreveport. He said, "Don't throw your money away getting me two rooms. One room's all that I need."

Mr. Hughes never enjoyed anything more than that Baton Rouge sale. It wadn't long after that he passed away. He went where good cattle people go. He told Mr. Whittaker, he says, "I never had as much fun with anybody as I did with Ray Lum." Course I could tell a long story about having fun because I'd always do the best that I could to see that there was entertainment, don't you know. I understood all that. I lost a very dear friend when I lost Mr. Hughes.

Then there was Old Man Goodnight in Texas that lived to be a ripe old age. He was a good cattleman. He had a fine bull there, and every calf the bull sired, he'd sell him for a thousand dollars. Mr. Goodnight was getting ready to sell some cattle at Fort Worth and looked out and saw this same bull in the pen. His cod bag nearly touched the ground, and he had stopped breeding. Mr. Goodnight says, "What are you boys doing?"

His foreman said, "We going to ship that bull to town to sell him." They were going to make hamburger meat out of him.

"Don't ship that bull. Just lay him down. Lay that bull down."

So they laid him down. Mr. Goodnight was seventy-five years old, and he walks over and takes hold of the bull's cod bag. He shoves his balls up about halfway, and he cut that bag off right there with his carving knife and sewed it up again. That was your "goodnight" right there. He goodnighted that bull, and he got about thirty or forty more calves off of him. Isn't that a wonder? That was fifty-some-odd years ago.

They didn't have artificial insemination. If they had had it, no telling how many calves they'd have got out of him, but every calf that old bull got brought a thousand dollars. There wadn't no bulls bringing no thousand-dollar calves but that Goodnight bull. That's how good he was. Not exaggerating, he was the longest[103] Hereford bull I'd ever seen. The idea was to grow these cattle big as you could and get as much meat as you could.

They called that the "goodnight." They'd say, "That old bull, they ought to goodnight him." I saw the bull a number of times after that, after they goodnighted him. He was the longest bull I ever saw, and every one of his calves looked just like him. You have to give Mr. Goodnight credit for being a genius. He knew the score.

My brother W. B. Lum left Vicksburg when he was fifteen years old. He sold papers up at the *Vicksburg Post* till he was nine, and then he worked till he was fifteen as a plumber. So he goes to Clayton, New Mexico, and went to work for a plumber. Wadn't but a few months till he bought the man's plumbing shop. And it wadn't but a few years before he bought a plumbing shop in another town. Ten years later he had plumbing shops in a dozen West Texas towns. When he come to Clayton, he started in homesteading that land out there. Like you would be working for him, he would say, "Bill, you go over to the Court House and sign up there for a section," and to the other boy, "Teddy, you go up there and sign up."

When these boys would leave town, they would come to him, and they would say, "Mr. Lum, I don't need the land, and I've paid a hundred dollars for it."

"Well, here."

He would give them a hundred and fifty and let them leave there happy. To cut a long story short, in ten years Willie had fifty thousand acres. Ten years later—I think it was around 1950—a man come up and said, "Mr. Lum, I want to buy that fifty thousand acres you have there in Clayton, New Mexico."

"I don't want to sell it."

"Well, I'll fix it so you will sell it. We'll give you a million dollars for it."

Of course, a million dollars was more money than my brother ever expected to have, a boy that sold newspapers in Vicksburg for a nickel a piece. He'd buy them papers for two cents and sell them for a nickel. That was the way he started out. He said, "I'll do this. I'll take the million dollars and reserve the mineral rights."

"No, we can't do that. We'll give you half the mineral rights."

Willie thought for a minute. "I've got the million dollars. Half the minerals will be more money than I will ever spend. I'll trade."

They peppered that land with oil wells. Oil wells is as thick as trees, and you can drive fifty miles on the land, and it is still oil wells. His royalty, I imagine, is just deposited in the bank.

My brother Clarence asked Willie what he was worth when he was here, and he laughed. Did you ever see rich people that will talk about what they are worth? Have you ever seen that in your life? You never will. Willie wouldn't say. He would just laugh.

Doc Green and I was together a lot in Texas, and he brought me some squabs[104] one morning at San Angelo. He said, "Ray, I'm going to bring you something for your breakfast this morning you'll like."

He come over with two squabs, and I was with a friend. I couldn't even eat one of them. I said, "Doc, do you care if I let my friend eat some too?"

"Oh hell no. I figured you might have somebody to help you eat them."

I don't remember who I had with me, but he ate the squab too. I never ate such squabs before or since. I don't know just what Doc's recipe was, but they were extra big and awful good. Doc was a genius of a good many things.

The next time I met Doc, he had about fifty little mules about titty-high in Fort Worth. "What are you doing here, Doc?"

"I'm over here with some mules. I've had them here for six weeks, and they are charging me too much to feed them."

I think Doc gave about twenty-five dollars a head for them mules. They'd been there about six weeks when the buyer come, and Doc had run up a big feed bill on them. They was charging him too much, and he couldn't get around it. They was charging him as much for them little mules as they would for big mules. Doc knew they was robbing him, and he was trying to get out the easiest way he could.

"Have you got any prospects for them, Doc?"

"I got a man that's supposed to come from back East."

Well, along comes this man. Doc wined and dined him and got him a new chippy[105] every night. He finally sold them little mules to this man, and he got a hundred and fifty dollars a head for them little sons-of-bitches. Oh, God Almighty, he was a salesman. It wouldn't have surprised me if he had got two hundred. After he paid his feed bill, he was a hundred ahead, or close to it.

I was in Fort Worth one night. At that time you had to get a temperature test on your horses before you could ship them, and it cost a dollar a head. That temperature test was to be sure they didn't have fever. Well, every one of them will have a temperature after he's been handled at a sale. It cost a hundred dollars to do the temperature test, and I was figuring on how to get out of that. The doctor said, "Ray, I got to work pretty fast here."

"You in a hurry, are you, Doc?"

"Yes I am."

"Well, I tell you what you do. There's a hundred head of these horses. You just give me that certificate, and I'm going to give you fifty dollars. We not going to bother those horses. If they don't have temperatures now, they will when we get through monkeying with them."

You'd have to catch them, raise their tail, and put the thermometer in them. We'd have been around there till breakfast. So he says, "I've got to go to Dallas."

"Well, come on, Doc. I'll go with you."

Nice young fellow. He thought a while and said, "All right."

So he pulled out his book and wrote down something. I handed him the fifty dollars and said, "Now come on. I'm going to Dallas with you."

Doc says, "Lady called over there. She's got a cat she thinks so much of, and she's so disturbed and afraid I can't get there in time to save him."

We got to her house and went in, and she told him, said, "The cat's climbing round the ceiling now. Oh, the poor thing's just scared to death. He's suffering so."

"Ray, go out there to my car and get that net."

He went on talking to the lady, and when I got back, I had the net with me. "Oh, Doctor, I'm so glad you came. He just crawls up in the roof. I'm so glad you got here."

Doc takes that net and wadn't two minutes before he had it on the cat. He said, "Now, Mrs. So-and-So, I'm going to have to operate."

The cat had hydrophobia. Doctor knew it, and I knew it too. Everybody knew it but the lady that had the cat. The cat had gone mad and was having fits and climbing around on the ceiling. So Doc got his net over the cat. Then he wrapped him up and put him in the car and said, "I'll have to operate on him."

"Oh, Doctor, I hope you can save him."

"I think I can. I hope so, anyhow."

We lit out back to Fort Worth. I never enjoyed a trip more. My hundred horses were on the way to Vicksburg. That little doctor turned out to be one of the best friends I had there. I done a lot of business with him.

The next morning I called over, and I said, "By the way, Doc, did you talk to the lady about the cat?"

"Oh yes, I did. She wants me to bury him."

So they had to have a cat funeral. I didn't go to the funeral. I said, "Doc, what are you going to have to charge her for that?"

"Oh, it'll be about a hundred and twenty-five dollars for burying him and all."

A cat, don't you know. A hundred and twenty-five dollars to bury a cat.

Next sale I heard of was in El Paso. I got in there one night, and I remember when I went to bed, I heard "Boom! Boom!" God Almighty, I got up and rang the bell. "What the hell is going on around here?"

"We got a war going on."

"Yeah? Reckon they're going to come up here?"

"No. They are down there in Juarez about two miles."

"Well, that's fine."

I went on back to sleep. Next morning I got in my car and went out where they were selling horses. I looked over across the border, and there were three dead horses. I said to this old boy who was with me, "What killed those horses?"

"They got in the line of fire."

"How far apart do they get when they shoot at one another?"

"They get a mile from each other. Them guns they got shoot a half mile, and them horses just got in range of fire."

Bullets wouldn't reach the people, but they would kill the

horses. So there was three dead horses over there. I understood that. At the auction I bought a hundred and fifty mules. That was one of the best deals ever I had. I bought all the mules they sold that day. The only competition I had was one fellow from Arizona, and he wanted some mules to pull a milk wagon. I told him, "I'll let you have all the mules you want, but you're in my way, and you're costing me money."

So he just laid out, and I bought all the mules and let him have the ones he wanted. Time went on, and a fellow told me there was a dairyman in Tucson, Arizona, that wanted to sell his mules."

So I got on a train and went up there. This dairyman had the prettiest mules I believe I ever saw. One of them give milk just like a cow. Had a bag like a cow. That was very unusual to find a mule that would give milk like that. When I got back to Fort Worth, I said to John Yount, the man who ran the auction barn there, "I got a mule I want you to see." She was a pretty black mule that weighed about eleven hundred pounds, and I said, "John, do you reckon she'll breed?"

He said, "I'd sure try to breed her."

She never did get a mule colt. But she gave milk just like a Jersey heifer.

I've had several government contracts in my life. I furnished the government two hundred horses at Mineral Wells, that watering place on the other side of Fort Worth. They was doing army maneuvers there. The next government contract I had, I furnished two hundred horses that went to Alexandria, Louisiana.

Alexandria is where the fence fell down and every damned horse I had got out. Dee Purchell was with me. I had leased these horses to the government. So the night the army gave them back to me, the horses just knocked the fence down and took out. We got busy and gathered them. Dee Purchell and I got most of them two hundred horses. I found a Frenchman down there and said, "I'll give you twenty-five dollars to le' me put them horses in your pen tonight."

He had the gate open and was standing out in front of the gate. "All right. Come on in with them."

In we went. We got them in, and when we counted them, we

had a hundred and ninety-five. We was five short. So I said to the Frenchman, "I'll give you five dollars a head to get the rest of those horses for me."

"I'll get them."

In about two days, here he come with the horses. He had all five of them. I said to Mr. Purchell, "This man's been so nice gathering those horses for us, let's take him over and buy him some beer." So over we went and got a beer.

Next day we billed a sale for the horses. I got a bookkeeper from the bank who knew the score. I went to work on them horses, and they kept bidding even after they was sold. God Almighty.

"Two hundred. Two and a quarter. Two-forty. Fifty. Seventy. Seventy-two. Sold to that man for two hundred seventy-two dollars!"

A fellow was still bidding over there, calling, "Two hundred and eighty," I guess.

I said, "You'll get the next one. There ain't much difference in these horses. Every damn one of them's good. They're like whiskey, just good and better."

Right on with it I went, don't you know. They dropped back down to a hundred and fifty dollars, but I didn't sell many of them under that. It looked like they had all the money you'd ever need there. "Sold for a hundred and fifty dollars."

Them horses didn't cost but fifty dollars a round. And I had already got a check from the government for five hundred dollars for them knocking that fence down and getting loose. I had that money too. All that happened in Alexandria with Dee. He was a Frenchman and a good fellow.

Something went wrong with my car while I was down there, and I pulled out side the road. I sent for a mechanic, and one come from Lake Providence. He worked for two hours and said, "I think I'm going to have to get this car pulled in."

I said, "We'll just try to get another mechanic."

About that time a boy walked up. I didn't know him. He was a little Frenchman, and he said, "Can I help you?"

"Oh, you bet you can."

So he reached down, picked up a wire and put it back on, and said, "You're all right now, Mr. Lum. You're a Lum, aren't you?"

"You bet I am."

I reached over and gave him a pair of boots. I saw his were about worn out. Then I said to the old man that hadn't done nothing, "How much I owe you?"

"Fifteen dollars."

I paid him. I didn't want any more conversation with him. Charged fifteen dollars for coming down there, and the other man was there for three minutes and found my wire loose. If you've had experience with mechanics, you know about these things.

Another time the government had give contracts for thousands of horses, and the acceptance place was in Fort Worth. All right. There was forty or fifty dealers in Fort Worth with horses to show the government.

I was with Charlie and Hugo Strickland, and one was just as good a rider as the other. I don't guess either was ever thrown. There's an old saying, "There never was a cowboy that couldn't be throwed, and there was never a horse that couldn't be rode."

I came in there with my horses. This was the first horses I'd showed the government. I said to Hugo, "I'm going to give you and Charlie five a head for every one of my horses they take."

"Ray, you don't have to do that."

"I want to do that."

I had a little judgment way down the line. I remember this day I just had a hundred horses, and I think they took either ninety-five or ninety-nine of them. I might have had one horse left. Charlie and Hugo done that. When they showed the horse, they'd saddle him. One would take his ear, and the other would saddle that wild son-of-a-bitch. Then they'd sit down on him, and they'd ride him down a certain distance in the pen and then come back. And when they come back, you'd see smoke go up. They were putting the brand on him. It was all over. You had your money then.

I was out in Longview, Texas, and a long-whiskered fellow come down there one day. He loved horses, and he loved to trade. When we'd trade, I'd get twenty-five or thirty dollars boot on the trade, and he had the best horse. He'd be back the next day. "Have you got anything new, Ray?"

"Yes, I have, Dad. I have a little gray mare that you might like."

"How you going to trade here?"

"Give me twenty."

He'd already given me two or three hundred dollars for that horse he was riding. So he'd just tear his pocket out, handing me the twenty like I was going to back out, you know. He'd be back the next day. "You got anything new?"

"Yes, I have. I have a little sorrel here I want you to look at."

If I'd see him coming, I'd get one ready that would handle like pocket dice.[106] "Sit down on her and see if you think you like her."

"I do like her. How you going to trade her?"

"Well, I have to charge you twenty-five dollars boot on that horse."

He'd pull out a roll that'd choke a calf and strip off the damn twenty-five. That went on all the time I was there. He was my meal ticket. He paid for all of my horses.

Three years later I went to Campbell's Clinic in Memphis with a bad back. I stayed there about six weeks, and they had straps on my feet and a brace on my back. Mrs. Lum come on by to see me when she was going on up to see her family in Hopkinsville, Kentucky. She said, "Daddy, you're not getting on very good."

"No, and I'm going to leave here. The damn doctor cussed me out this morning. He come in here, and he said, 'You haven't done a thing that I told you to do!'"

They had my feet all stretched out with that brace on them, and I knew I wasn't no better. So I said, "I'm going to leave here. How much I owe you, Doctor?"

"Fifteen hundred dollars."

I paid him and got away. I had to give an extra hundred and fifty dollars for that damn brace. I got to Mayo's, and they put me with a little old doctor. He took that brace and throwed it bump, bump, bouncing down on the floor. "Be careful of that brace, Doc. Dr. So-and-So charged me a hundred and fifty dollars for that."

"Well, you won't be needing it anymore."

He was just as nice and cool as he could be. Seemed like he liked me, and I liked him. When he found out I was from Texas, that settled it. He said, "Did you ever trade around Longview?"

"Yes, and there was an old long-whiskered fellow there, and every day he'd come to trade. He was my meal ticket there. He never did find a horse that suited him."

He laughed out loud then. "Ray, that was my father."

I couldn't have had a son be any better to me than he was. Every day he'd drive me somewhere. We drove up on the mountain, and I forget what it was we saw, but it was real interesting. The next day we'd take some more scenery. He found out I was the fellow that traded with his daddy, and I told him all about his daddy. When I got ready to go from Mayo's, my bill was just a hundred dollars, and they cured me. They fixed me up.

I remember one West Texas town where a man had some wild horses. He was six-foot-four, a big tall fellow. Walked towards you all the time. We drove up on a peak where you could see those horses down in the valley, them wild horses. These horses had never saw a man, and wadn't any of them branded. When you find a horse there that ain't branded, it's like a maverick calf, you know. It don't belong to nobody.

"What'll you give for them horses?"

"I'll give six dollars a head for all you can put in that pen."

I was watching that fellow, and he never moved a muscle in his body. He kept looking right straight at me, and I don't know what was on his mind. I couldn't read his mind, and I didn't feel very comfortable. He thought it over a while, and then he said, "I'm going to sell them to you."

"Okay."

I bought about six hundred horses from the man, and he says, "I'll have to trap those horses, Ray."

"When you going to start?"

"I'll build a wing[107] tonight."

He got busy and built this wing and caught those horses in pens by the railroad. Then I got them shipped.

I didn't help him any with the wing. I went on somewheres else getting some broke horses. I was getting some you could pet, but I wadn't buying any more for six dollars. His was the cheapest horses I had found. But they didn't cost him anything 'cause he accumulated them. There were lots of wild horses in Texas, of course.

A few weeks after that, that same fellow I bought the horses from was at Coleman, Texas, and killed a man. I knew that day when I offered him six dollars for those horses, and he kept looking at me, he had killing on his mind. I knew what he was thinking about then.

I met a man in Texas once that had an ostrich. You know an ostrich kicks like a mule. I was out in the man's lot, and I had no business getting close to the son-of-a-bitch. I was in front of him, and damned if he didn't kick me. I said, "That's a helluva note. That's the first time I was ever kicked by an ostrich."

He said, "That's the first time ever I saw him do that."

I was hurt pretty bad. I had to limp around there for quite a while to get it straightened out. He said that was the first he ever saw him kick anybody. I said, "I don't know how come the son-of-a-bitch don't like me."

He picked me out. I just walked in front of him and paid no attention to him, you know. Didn't pay no more attention to him than if he was a turkey or a chicken, and the man said that was very unusual.

That's a big country out there in Texas. I was at the King Ranch a number of times, and it was fifty miles from the front gate to the front door of the ranch house and fifty miles from the back door to the back gate of the ranch. That made it a hundred miles across that ranch.

They had some horses that they wanted to dispose of. When a horse got ten years old there, they were usually ready to put a younger horse in his place. Those ten-year-old horses were broke to a queen's taste. They'd turn on a dime and then have a nickel to spend.

When I drove on the ranch, here was four or five fellows at this lake fishing. The foreman says, "Don't you gentlemen come back anymore. If you do, it won't be healthy for you."

I never thought nothing about it. I figured they had sense enough to know that man meant what he said. I come back in two or three days to see about the horses. When I did, I saw five men floating in this lake there.

Kleberg owned that ranch. Kleberg was the man that first started the Santa Gertrudis cattle. Those cattle was raised in Texas, and they all come red. That's the color of them.

I always think about the old man that was up at Oak Ridge. Somebody said, "Uncle Jim, what breed of cattle you like the best?"

"I don't give a damn what breed they are, just so they're red. Just so they're red."

Well, he said a lot there. Them Santa Gertrudis bulls got the longest shelf of any breed I know. I always called a bull's privates his shelf. He carries his dipper in his shelf. S-h-e-l-f.[108] A bull like that wouldn't do good in Mississippi 'cause we got so many briers. He'd pick up too many briers in his shelf, and it would get infected.

I went down about four or five hundred miles south from Angelo to Chihuahua. They was selling mules there, and when I looked in the phone book, everything was "Lum. Lum. Lum. Lum." They was all Chinese. I said, "Good God Almighty. I've found out where I'm from. I'm bound to be a Chinaman." It was nearly all Chinese there. Half of the damn telephone book was Lums.

Somebody asked me once if I was the Lum of "Lum and Abner." That was a radio show we used to listen to. I don't know where that Lum got his name from. That Lum that's in "Lum and Abner," I think Lum was his first name.[109]

Squire Harris was from Vicksburg, and he drove me all over Texas. There wasn't a better car driver than Squire. I would be tired after working all day, and I'd go to sleep. I'd be sound asleep, and Squire would pull the car over and stop. Then he'd go to sleep too.

One day Squire was coming back from Dallas, going about sixty miles in a forty-mile zone. So, "Whr-r-r-r. Pull over there."

He pulled over, and I said, "Officer, I know we was overstepping. We was going too fast."

The officer says, "That driver of yours was watching me in the mirror."

Squire says, "Captain, if I'd had knowed that was you, you'd have had to take out your field glasses to see if I was moving or not."

Well, the fellow got to laughing, and that saved us paying twenty-five dollars or whatever it was. He called them all "Captain," and he could get along fine anywhere he was. They all liked Squire. He had a way of making them like him.

I carried Squire with me to Angelo. He was a genius when it come to riding. So they said, "Ray, do you care if we let Squire sit down on one or two of these horses?"

"Well, it's all right with me if Squire wants to. Squire, do you want to ride one or two of them?"

Squire was awake. His bread was done. "Yes, you got one that don't buck too hard, haven't you?"

"Oh yeah. Why don't you jerk out this one?"

First horse he sat on was a sunfisher. The horse put his belly up to where the sun was, and his back down here, and there wadn't much place to stay on him. First one they put him on was like that, and he rode that dirty son-of-a-bitch. So I told him, "You done rode the worst they got. They give you the top."

Squire rode two or three more, and I couldn't hardly get him away from them. They wanted to keep him there. We left San Angelo and drove down south. Pulled into this town and stopped at the store there. I went in to get me some salmon and crackers, and Squire said, "Get me a can of tomatoes."

He always liked tomatoes. I said, "All right," and went in and got him a box of crackers to go with the tomatoes. When I walked in this fellow says, "Don't let that nigger out of that truck."

I said, "He's a damn sight scareder of you than you are of him, and he ain't thinking about getting out." That was Squire he was talking about. "What's the matter? You don't have no colored here?"

"We did have three years ago. A nigger killed a white woman, and they killed every one in the county. There wasn't one left. They killed every one."

I've often thought about the difference in Mississippi and that part of the world. Mississippi would have tried to get the right one that killed the woman. But there they just killed them all. So that's the difference in countries.

"What makes you call him a nigger? He told me he's a Mexican."

Of course, Squire hadn't told me a damn thing, you know. Anyhow, I got the salmon and the tomatoes and crackers and come back to the truck. We drove on down and started to eat our stuff. We was hungry. And Squire says, "Them that claims to be civilized. Them that claims to be civilized."

I thought about that a lot. We come on up to where they had a horse sale. I called Richard Riley. I wanted to turn some horses over to him, and when he come, he said, "What are you going to do with Squire?"

"Squire, will you be all right in that truck?"

"Oh, I'd rather be in the truck. Just put some blankets in here to keep me warm."

That night Richard and I bought three loads of horses. We all got in the truck and drove on to another West Texas town. They didn't allow a black man in the towns anywhere around there.

I stayed at Stephenville three or four years. Then I was at San Angelo several years. Then I was at Brownsville several years. Brownsville was where it got dry as a bone. Charlie Evans, this friend of mine in Brownsville, had three or four hundred horses. I was wanting to buy the horses, of course. The horses' tanks[110] had dried up, and their bellies had begun to pinch their backbone.[111] So I said, "Charlie, you better sell these horses in a hurry."

So Charlie says, "If it don't rain between now and Sunday, I will." So Sunday came, and Charlie says, "Come on and go to church with me today."

Over we went to church, and the preacher preached a nice sermon. So after the sermon Charlie says, "Oh, Reverend So-and-So, I believe I understood you to say that we don't own anything, that everything in our possession belongs to the Lord."

Preacher said, "That's right, Brother Evans. We don't own anything. It all belongs to the Lord."

"Well, I want you to converse with the Lord and let Him know that if it don't rain awful quick, His horses over there at His ranch can't stand it much longer."

That was Sunday. Monday morning bright and early Charlie and I lit out for the ranch. If I hadn't seen it, I wouldn't have believed it. Just as we went into the gate, here were three horses, and they were about to burst open, they were so full. When I saw them three horses with bellies about to pop, my feathers fell. I knew I wadn't going to get any horses. Charlie saw it too. On down into the pasture we went. First draw we came to, water was running out, and the horses was there drinking. Springs that hadn't run for three years had started running. I was so happy for my friend Charlie. I saw that with my own eyes.

I was with Charlie another time at Brownsville, and he said, "Ray, these boys want you to judge their show there."

When the first colt came up, I flipped his lip and says, "This colt was three years old the first of May."

The boy smiled and led his colt on off. Next boy came up, and I said, "Your colt was three years old in May."

He said, "I know, but what day? What day?"

Charlie said, "You played hell now."

Every one of them wanted to know the day his horse was born. I had a good time with them and give the prize to the horse that I thought was the best. That's been a long time ago, but they judge horses today the same way as they did then.

There's so many things they say things have changed. Well, I don't know. I'm not too good a judge of cats, but I always go back to the story of the cats on the ark. The way I understood it, they had two of every kind of animal on the ark. This is an old, old story. It's bound to be old because it goes back two thousand years. So when they released the cats, this old papa cat came out with his tail straight up, and mamma cat came out with her tail up, and there was ten little cats come behind. And the old big cat says to Noah, "And you thought we were fighting."

That's as old as the cats, but I don't think there's any difference in cats now than two thousand years ago. Just a different set doing it.

I was driving into Brownwood one day, and I looked out and saw two elephants laying in the ditch. I drove on up to the store, and I asked, "What are them damn elephants doing down there?"

"They belong to the circus. They got away when they had the show."

Well, sir, I never had no experience with elephants, but I saw them two there doing business.[112] They was making little elephants. She lays down on her side and lets him crawl right in, and they do it for several days like that.

It was Brownwood where the elephant killed this woman. I was there. The circus was going on, and this lady came by. Just as she did, the damn elephant pulled up his stakes, wrapped his snout around her and throwed her down. Killed her dead as the devil. That was at the Brownwood circus. Not knowing anything about elephants, I asked, "What on earth caused that elephant to do that?"

"Well," they said, "the woman had her monthlies[113] on. She had her sickness on."[114]

He smelled the odor from it, and he went crazy. A lot of other women had been coming by there, and he had never done anything like that before. These gals with their monthlies on should be careful going around elephants.

Frank Norris was a man that could do anything he wanted to. Frank had a call from a man who told him, "Don't you leave there. I'm coming over there to kill you."

Frank said to his stenographer, "You better step out." He was cool and talking a lot lower than I am. "The gentleman that just called said he's coming over to kill me. You better step in the next room."

She hadn't walked out good, when the fellow opens the door and says, "You know what I come for."

"Yes." Frank talked low. He says, "Don't cross over that threshold." There was a little threshold in the floor there. "Don't cross over."

And goddamn, the fellow come right on through, grabbed his gun and throwed it down[115] on Frank. When he did, Frank shot him right through the heart, and down he went. They was trying Frank, and a friend said, "You want to go on to the Frank Norris trial?"

"You bet. I wouldn't miss it."

McLean, the prosecutor, was the best lawyer in Texas, and when he got up, he'd holler and roar, and the place would shake. "Didn't you say so-and-so?" He'd roar, and Frank would just whisper when he'd answer him. "Did you shoot at that man's heart?"

"I can hit an object smaller than a man's heart." He was a good shot, you see. "I can hit an object smaller than a man's heart."

Well, to cut a long story short, that jury just went out and come right on back and let Frank go free. Frank Norris was a mastermind. He built a church in Fort Worth that took up the block. It was about the largest church in Texas. He was a Baptist, and he had it full. I guess the Baptists was the largest denomination in the world.

Did I tell you about the fellow who said, "I'm the law west of the Pecos?" That was Judge Roy Bean. I stopped at his store once. He was a justice of the peace there, and I knew him well. This man came in with his wife once and said, "We going to get a divorce."

Judge Bean said, "You and Mary go back there in that room and talk this over. I'll be with you directly."

He settled them back in the bedroom and give them a little Coca-Cola and locked the door. In about an hour's time he went back to talk to them, and they told him to forget about the divorce. That was kind of the way he worked. Everybody respected him, and he was the law west of the Pecos. No question about that.

Charlie Gorensky was a doodler. He run the commission barn at San Antonio. In Texas when a man gets ready to sell sheep, he's as liable to sell you ten thousand as he would ten. They do things in a big way in Texas. Charlie bought four thousand sheep, and this day Slim Richards and I were there at his mule sale. Charlie said, "Come on over, boys. I got some good barbecued sheep."

So we went over, and it was good. We was eating it and enjoying it, and Charlie said, "God Almighty, that sheep's good. Go back there and tell that boy don't sell another damn one of them. I'll eat every one of them." Going to eat four thousand, don't you know.

The worst desperado I run into was the man that kidnapped Hershel. His name was Pretty Boy Floyd.

They had captured Mr. Hershel and had him as a prisoner. Every day a plane went over, and Mr. Hershel'd say, "What time is it?"

They'd tell him.

Pretty Boy Floyd ransomed Hershel for a million dollars, and Mrs. Hershel give it to him right away. She didn't ring no backup bells. They delivered Hershel to her. Hershel gets hold of the officers, and they went straight as a martin will fly back to that place where they had him. He was a smart man. He found out what plane it was and the time it went over, and he just went right straight to the house where they held him.

I met Pretty Boy after that. I was up buying mules, and a fellow says, "Pretty Boy Floyd's up the street there about a block."

"Yeah? Well, I haven't got any business with him."

He walked right out in the middle of the street that day. I knew who it was, but I didn't pay no attention to him. I went there to ask a man if he had some mules, and he had them. So I went on out and bought them. That was either in Texas or Oklahoma. I don't remember which.

On that same trip I run into the man who wrote a book about the story of his life. I can't call his name, but he's the man that came to Dallas when he was a right young fellow. He came to Dallas, and this con gang got hold of him and talked him into going and getting them five thousand dollars. He went back to Coleman, Texas, and got the five thousand and comes back and give it to those sons-of-bitches. Then he went back to where they told him they was going to be, and when he looked around there, they was gone. He woke up right then. He was awake from then on.

Well, to cut a long story short, he followed them to England. He killed four of them, and the one that was on the boat, he jumped off the boat, and he killed him too. He got all five of them. Then he wrote a book. He wrote the story of his life and called it *Does a Yokel Wake Up?* And don't you think it didn't sell. I met him and his brother at Coleman, Texas. I bought fifty mules from that man. He was ninety-something years old then, and he was a damn sight more active than I am now. I wish I had that book now. I had the book once, and it was a true story, just as true as the Bible.[116]

Eighty
Thousand
Horses

Lum looked on the American West as "another country," where both language and history differed sharply from his own in the Deep South. As a Mississippian who traveled in the West, his tales were inspired by both worlds. The western love for exaggeration in story-telling impressed Lum; and he once recalled a bucking horse who "broke half in two and pitched a man so high, jaybirds built a nest in his hair."

Lum's first visit in the West was in 1918 when the Darnell and Berry auction house in Memphis recruited him to auction a herd of wild horses at a livestock sale in Cheyenne. Lum shipped the animals by rail to New Orleans and resold them there for a considerable profit. Such large sales in isolated areas were a familiar pattern during his trades in Texas and the West.

As he traveled West, Lum felt that he was following in the footsteps of others. He often spoke of Indians and settlers who had traveled western roads before him. Having grown up beside the historic Natchez Trace in Mississippi, he especially loved the Santa Fe Trail, a celebrated route that developed after 1821 between Missouri and Santa Fe. At Santa Fe, New Mexico's capital, it joined the

Chihuahua Trail that ran into Mexico below El Paso.[117] *"Those old trails have seen a lot of men and a lot of stock pass, and I guess they'll see a lot more after I'm gone."*

Lum closely observed the landscape of the West, and the rugged landscape he saw from Pike's Peak impressed him. The mountain rises 14,110 feet above sea level and offers a dramatic view of the Colorado landscape. Lum reached the summit of Pike's Peak by car along a winding road and ate lunch at its Summit House.

Especially vivid was his brief encounter with the outlaws Bonnie and Clyde on a lonely highway in Kansas. Traveling at high speed, the outlaw car seemed to float in the air, and Lum carefully kept his eyes on the road for fear he might be shot. Bonnie Parker and Clyde Barrow swept across the Southwest during the Depression robbing banks and killing twelve people, nine of whom were officers of the law. Frank Hamer, a Texas Ranger who trailed Bonnie and Clyde for four months, killed the pair on May 23, 1934, near Pain Dealing, Louisiana.[118]

The West was the final frontier for Lum's travels. A recognized master trader, he worked in South Dakota, New Mexico, Colorado, and California between the years 1935 and 1950. He traveled to large sales in these states, bought hundreds of mules and horses, and shipped them by rail back to his markets in the South.

When California farmers began to use tractors in the 1940s, Lum bought their mules and shipped them to his southern markets. As farmers in other states sold their mules, Lum followed their sales from the Pacific to the Atlantic. These final sales signaled the end of mules and the men who traded them. He observed that it was "the end of the mule story."

While an important part of his life passed with the end of the mule era, Lum refused to give up trading. True to form, he shifted his trading from mules to cattle and was "back in business again."

One day I ran into Mr. Chappell. He had more horses than anybody in the world. He says, "Ray, what will you give me for eighty thousand horses in La Plant, South Dakota?"

"I'll give you ten a head for them."

"I'm going to sell them to you."

He got an Indian from that part of the country to go with me, and we lit out that night. In two days we was in La Plant and went to gathering horses. I remember the first thing I done, I gathered a hundred mules that was with them horses. I sent them mules to Memphis. Some of them mules brought two hundred dollars.

You could look out on that South Dakota land there, and as far as your eyes let you see was horse manure. You could walk on it here, step on it here. You could walk for twenty miles and never get off of it.

I kept looking at that stuff when I was out there, and one day I was waiting for some horses to come in, and I picked up a piece and went to break it. It was just as hard as a rock. So I got to thinking, "I wonder how long that's been there?"

I finally got a little information from the Indian that was with me. Some of them droppings had been there twenty-five or thirty years. They used them for firewood. You don't see trees much in that part where I was. So they used it for firewood.

One day when I was up getting them horses, I said to this Indian with me, "Let's go over there and see what that woman's doing."

We went over there, and she was roasting this dog. I said, "How much for the horse?"

"How much you give?"

"Ten dollars."

"No sell. I eat him."

So we gathered them horses, and I called my uncle at Corpus Christi, Texas. I said, "Uncle Will, I'm up here in La Plant, South Dakota, and I've got eighty thousand horses that I'm trying to round up."

"Eighty thousand horses! What are you going to do with them horses?"

"Sell them."

"I know you will do that."

That was Uncle Will. He said, "Look, what are they?"

"They are Clydesdales, Percherons, Suffolks, and another two or three breeds of draft horses."

"Ray, cut me out a hundred of those filly colts a year old. What are you going to charge me for them?"

"Twenty-five dollars, Uncle Will."

"Well, send me a hundred."

I was making fifteen dollars a head right there. That was fifteen hundred dollars right there.

Two days later the phone rang, and it was Dr. Harvey. Dr. Harvey was a friend of Uncle Will's. They had both come to Texas from Rocky Springs, where I was born. Dr. Harvey wanted a hundred. All right. I sent his horses on. To cut a long story short, I got out three thousand horses and mules and sent them to Texas. I had boys in Texas, and I shipped them horses by the hundreds.

A little fellow come in one day from Canada. He says, "Ray, I heard you was down here, and I come down to tell you to get those horses out of here. Any morning now snow will be from bank to bank."

I reached over and shook his hand, and I've never seen him since. He just come in the nick of time. I said to him, "Where did you know me?"

"I saw you in Blytheville, Arkansas. You were selling mules and jumped down off a wagon, and you says to the people, 'You think those mules are wild?' You grabbed one by his tail, and you says, 'I can milk every goddamned one of them.' I thought you would have been dead by now."

I'd had a black hostler named Alec Johnson with me there in Blytheville, and he was a good hand. He knew what to do. Alec had super strength. He was awful stout in his hands. But the buyers didn't know that. He was stouter than a horse or mule. Alec would keep the mule's head up, and I would grab him by the tail and milk him. I remember they wasn't bidding on them mules, and I said, "What the hell's the matter with you? You think them mules are wild? I can milk every goddamned one of them."

So I jumped down off the wagon. I had a wagon then. Alec saw me coming, of course, and he knew what to do. He grabbed the mule's ear and twisted it, and I grabbed that mule by the tail, grabbed him by the dick, and he pissed cold water everywhere. He sprayed the place there. I got back up on the wagon and sold that mule for two hundred and went right on selling. They all were as green as him. Anyhow, he said, "I thought you would have been dead."

"I would have if I had kept that up because something would have happened."

He says, "Any morning, any morning now, the snow will be from bank to bank."

I went to the railroad office, billed them horses out, and the next morning I was fifty miles south of there. I called up and says, "How's the snow up there?"

"It's from rooftop to rooftop."

My horses and I would have been submerged, don't you know. So I had my horses and on to Texas I went with them. Ten a head they cost. I shipped out thirty-five hundred head that last week. I sent two hundred to New Orleans. I sent six hundred to Memphis, and all the boys in Fort Worth had horses. Richard Riley bought about six loads. I had all my boys in Texas and Mississippi filled with horses. I'd got out about ten thousand of them in six weeks.

That was Chappell Brothers. They had gone into that deal from a killing standpoint. They raised them for horse meat. That's the reason they had all big breeds. They had Clydesdales, Percherons, and Suffolks. The bigger they was, the more value they had.

Six months later I run into Mr. Chappell, and I asked him, "How many of them horses that I left there survived?"

"Ray, every one of them went to heaven. Every one of them perished."

They all went to sleep,[119] don't you see.

I was in Memphis selling for the Darnell and Berry Commission Company. I was working there for Mr. Darnell, a good old man. He was seventy-five years old. While I was auctioning for him, Mr. Berry said, "Ray, next week I want you to go to Cheyenne with me. I'm putting on a sale in Cheyenne, Wyoming."

He wanted me to come out there and sell three thousand horses for him. He paid me five hundred and fifty dollars. I took Harry Barnett and an Indian with me, and we lit out for Cheyenne.

We got to Cheyenne the first day and started selling those three thousand horses. I started the auction, and there wasn't nobody there to buy but me. I remember the first horse that came in was a pretty sorrel horse. Weighed twelve hundred pounds. A four- or five-year-old. Never saw a man before. He'd just come out of those mountains and never been broke.

"All right, what'll you give for him? Ten dollars? A thousand dollars? Four dollars?"

Nobody got in on him, so I throwed a lot of fives.[120] "I'll give five for him. Five dollars. Five dollars."

I sold four or five of them horses for five dollars. That man that owned these horses, his hand was big as a ham. He put his hand down on me, and it felt like it weighed a ton. He said, "What did you get for that horse?"

I said, "Five dollars." Big twelve-hundred-pound horse. I said, "I'm hoping that it will get better."

He didn't say nothing. He just put his hand on me, and his hand was bigger than a ham. And he wasn't turning loose very fast. I said, "I figure it'll get better. I hope it does."

Nobody but me and Harry Barnett was buying. We was selling, and we was buying. "Come on, Ray! Come on! Come on!"

The next horse come in, "Four dollars. Five dollars. Six dollars. Whack! Six dollars."

Out he went. Well, anyhow, I sold horses there until twelve o'clock noon. I started about nine, and I worked slow. Kept thinking some customers would come in. Well, when twelve o'clock come, I had two hundred and fifty head bought, all charged to Darnell and Berry, and we knocked off an hour for dinner.

After dinner here come a fellow named Joe Grieven from San Antonio. I said, "Harry, tend to business." Harry knew how to tend to business. He saw Mr. Grieven there. Grieven would buy a trainload of horses. Grieven was an angel compared to me. I was giving six dollars a head for them horses, and Joe Grieven would give ten and eleven for them.

So Harry says, "Ray, I'm going to run them horses we bought this morning right back through. We'll make some money to start with on our two hundred and fifty head."

Harry was tending to business, he was. I said, "Well, do you think that will be all right with that man we bought them from? We didn't come up here to stay, Harry, and especially don't want to sleep under the ground."

"Oh, we'll try it."

We got right back with them horses that we bought for five dollars and sold them to Mr. Grieven for ten and eleven dollars.

Then we come on with the other people's horses. I was hoping that the man that I'd bought them horses from who dropped his hand on mine wadn't still around. I don't know whether he was or not, but we went ahead.

Joe Grieven was the man. He was from San Antonio, Texas. He bought a trainload, a trainload with about twenty cars to the train. He bought about five or six hundred horses, and then he lit out back to Texas. When he left, the horses dropped back to five and six dollars a head. I hated to take them any cheaper. I figured there might be another angel the next day. Well, sure enough, the next day here comes this man from Denver, Colorado. He was good for a trainload. After he left, I kept selling horses right on into the night. They dropped back to me, and it wadn't no use me buying them too high. I went ahead and sold the rest of the horses. One or two more buyers come in, but they wasn't much better than I was.

I wound up with most of the horses, and I shipped those horses from Cheyenne to New Orleans and rode the train down with them. When I got to New Orleans, Harry was there, and so was Mr. Darnell, the man who run the sale at Memphis. Mr. Darnell and I was partners on that Cheyenne deal. Before we went up there, he said, "Now, Ray, any of them horses we buy, I want to go fifty-fifty with you."

"That suits me all right, Mr. Darnell."

We got the horses to New Orleans and billed the sale. Here's the people. The sale starts. The first horses come in. "A hundred dollars."

We sold them horses for a hundred dollars a head until we sold might near half of them. When it got down to the other half, they began to get down to sixty and fifty. And it wound up that we sold some of them horses for thirty-five and forty dollars. They'd cost us five and six dollars a head. That's what we'd give for them. Course they had freight on them, but freight was a lot cheaper then than it is now. After we sold the first hundred, we should have sent the other hundred somewhere else. By then we had them New Orleans buyers all filled up.

This is where the fun came. Those New Orleans people bought wild horses from Cheyenne that had never seen a man. They was so wild they would hardly ride on the train, and some of them weighed twelve hundred pounds. So them people come in to get their horses, and night had come. They'd paid for the horses, and they come to get them. Harry said, "Ray, I'm going down to get something to eat."

I said, "I'm going to stay here and see this show."

They didn't know nothing about them wild Cheyenne horses. There'd be ten of them holding one horse, and they'd put a rope on each foot, and two or three of them would hold to the head. Some of them put the horses in tow behind trucks, and some of them hitched them to wagons, and down the street they would go. I never had as much fun in my life, and it was twelve or one o'clock before I went to bed.

When I come back the next morning, they were still there trying to get the horses. There was people lying everywhere, but there was never one killed. They were all small people, and they had sense enough to stay at the horse's head. That was instinct, I guess, for them to stay at the head. They wasn't going to be back there at the firing part,[121] see, where he could kick them. That was the New Orleans auction.

One time I was driving out West, and there was no one but me in the car. I was going through Nebraska, and I smelt an awful stench. I found a cowpoke, and I said, "What is all that stench?"

"See that mountain up there?"

"Yeah."

"The Indians take the cattle up there to cut them and brand them and sort them. A big old bull gored a yearling, and this yearling 'burred'[122] as he fell down that mountain, and three thousand head followed him down into that gulch."[123] It was four or five hundred yards from the top of the mountain to the bottom. "Three thousand head went right into that gulch, and these Indians have been coming here for over a year jerking that meat."

"By golly, I wouldn't think it'd still be any good."

"Do you know this country?"

"No, I don't. In my country that meat would be rotten by now."

You didn't see a buzzard anywhere. Never did see a buzzard. He says, "There is so much salt in the air that it cures the meat."

The Indians were jerking that meat and taking it home. It was good meat. That gives an idea of how pure the air is in that country. Three thousand went off that mountain when that stag gored that yearling. God Almighty, the more cattle that would go over, the more dust they would kick up, and more would follow. It was easy to figure it all out.

Going through Nebraska, I was traveling by myself, and I had a little thirty-two pistol with me. Them doggone pheasants kept running across the road. So I said, "I bet them things are good to eat. I'll get some of them."

I was a pretty good shot. Well, to cut a long story short, I put about twenty of them in the trunk of my car. I shot every one in the head. They was running up the ditch, and I just popped them in the head. After I got the last one in the car, here come a man driving up behind me. I figured he might be a game warden and hoped there wasn't any feathers sticking out of my trunk. He stopped and began to talk. "You is a long ways from home."

"You bet I am. I was wondering about these pheasants. We don't have them in my country. Are they good to eat?"

"Oh yes, and there is a twenty-five-dollar fine for killing them."

"Well, I am so glad you told me."

I didn't tell him he should have told me sooner. I had five hundred dollars' worth in my trunk. He was just as nice as he could be, and I talked to suit him. He didn't look in my trunk, and I was glad to see him leave.

I went on that night to Grand Island, Nebraska. They was having a big horse sale, selling several thousand head. There was all the traders from Fort Worth. I run into Parker Jamison, and I said, "Parker, I got twenty pheasants in the back of my car."

"God Almighty, get them. That's just what we need."

We carried them to the hotel, and Parker told the manager, "We don't care what it costs to pick these pheasants and dress them. We want them fixed up."

I didn't know if they was pheasants or not by the time we got ready to eat them. They cooked them pheasants seven different ways. It costs about ten dollars to buy one. They are high as the devil, but they are good. They were better than any bird I ever ate. We ate those pheasants that night, and the next day we had the sale. I bought lots of horses there. All them traders that I met the next day, I invited them in and had enough pheasants left to go around for all the buyers. I shook hands and got acquainted with a lot of them.

We had a two-day sale, and I bought more horses than any man there. So I started back. I was driving alone, and Parker Jamison was driving alone. I stopped in a town some three hundred miles south of where we had the sale, and here comes a train. A fellow in the hotel there recognized me and said, "Your friend Jamison is on that train. He run his car into a telephone pole, split his head open, and teared himself all to pieces."

I went over to the train, and there was Parker, but he didn't know me. He was all bandaged up with just his nose sticking out. Looked like a mummy. But he got well, and we lived to eat more pheasants after that. He lived several years after that.

My daddy used to say, "Look down, look down that long lonesome road before you travel alone." But I've been a million miles by myself. When I traveled out West, I'd run into mountainous country. I remember I went up on Pike's Peak.[124] I went up there by myself in a little old Ford. A fellow knew me and says, "How're you doing, Ray? How're you feeling?"

"All right. I'm feeling fine."

"Ray, is your nose bleeding?"

"I don't think it is."

I pulled out my handkerchief, put it up, and sure enough my nose was bleeding. By God, I got to feeling kind of dizzy. It's too high, don't you see. I said, "Is that good for you? Is it healthy for you to bleed?"

He laughed it off. He said, "My nose bleeds every time I come up here, and I come up here at least once a year. If I bleed, it must not hurt you any."

I stayed up there as long as I wanted to, and I remember eating lunch about halfway up. They have a restaurant where you can stop and get a drink of whatever you want. I didn't take no drinks. I wanted to make it up there and back, you know. So I was awful particular with that drink. But they got everything in that restaurant.

That Pike's Peak is pretty high. You get up to the top of it and look off down, and there's quite a bit to see. And when I drove along there, there was water in a ditch, and that water was running uphill. Going right up thataway with you. I stopped and looked at it and tried to figure out what the devil was wrong with my eyes.

It wasn't but a few weeks after that, a fellow said, "Ray, they are going to sell a hundred and fifty mules in Chicago." God Almighty, I liked to knocked a hip down getting on that train, and next morning I was in Chicago. When I got there, Mr. McPhillips, an old Irishman, said, "I wish you would have gotten here yesterday. They sold a hundred and fifty mules."

"What did they get for them?"

"Fifty dollars a round."

"Whew." I says, "Who bought them?"

"A fellow from St. Louis."

I said, "Reckon he'll be here today? Can you get him here?"

"I see him coming over here now."

"Call him."

So I got him over there. I said to Mr. McPhillips, "You help me with that fellow now."

I'd done looked at them mules. God, they were good. You know what they were after the government had fed them for six months to a year. So I says, "What you going to take for them mules?"

He said, "I need mules. I've got to have them."

I said, "I need them too, and I'm going to fix it so I can buy them. I'm going to give you seventy-five dollars a round for them."

"Naw, you'll not do that. They cost more than that."

I said, "Well, I'm sure they did."

They cost fifty, don't you see. Well, to make a long story short, I give him a hundred dollars a round for them. I got the hundred and fifty mules and shipped out that evening. I shipped the mules to Vicksburg, and I never had a hundred and fifty mules give more satisfaction. They never sneezed. They never coughed. The government inoculated them mules just like they do boys when they put them in the army. They had mules that were really good.

I used to go up that trail that run through Oklahoma and Kansas. That was an old, old trail, kind of like the Natchez Trace. They called it the Santa Fe Trail. I used to leave every Monday or

Tuesday. I'd leave Fort Worth and go up the Santa Fe Trail to Wichita, Kansas, to buy horses and mules. Wichita was one of the good western markets at that time.

I was headquartered at Fort Worth, and I'd go to Wichita for the sale on Wednesday. Going up was always interesting 'cause the train went through the Miller's Hundred and One Ranch.[125] I'd say we rode twenty or thirty miles going across the ranch. And the buffalo, I don't know how many the Hundred and One Ranch owned, but I do know they had the largest herd of them at that time. There were acres of them there, and you could count them by the thousands. These buffalo would break and run just like cattle when the train come across. It was always interesting to me to see them run.

I traveled in sheep country in the West a lot too. A cowman hates a sheepman, and oh, God Almighty, you can see why. Them sheep eat the grass to the roots, and if you've got enough sheep, they'll starve cows to death.

I was down in Greeley, Colorado, to buy mules. There was lots of sheep in that country and a lot of sheepherders. It was a hot day, and I walked over to the saloon. I walked over to get a glass of beer, and there was a man walking down the street right ahead of me. He had a whip over his shoulder, and he was plaiting a cracker[126] for it. "Baaaaaaaaaa."

So I didn't blink. I followed him a while. Then I saw a native, and I said, "Does that old man know he's bleating?"

"Hell no. That's a sheepherder."

"That's fine."

So I walked right on behind him. "Baaaaaaaaaaaaaaa."

I never heard anybody could imitate a sheep better than he could.

I found out all I wanted to know about sheepherders. They'd be out there herding a bunch of sheep, and if one strays too far, the sheepherder'll bleat at him just like another sheep and call him back a half a mile. If it was a buck, he'd bleat like a ewe and call him back. If it was a ewe, he'd bleat like a buck. He could do it two different ways. He could talk their language. That's the way they worked them, don't you see.

I walked down the street following him, but I didn't talk to him.

I knew as much about him as I wanted to know. Them sheepherders stayed with the sheep too long. When they get out there, they stay a year or two before they ever come in sometimes. When you're in a sheep country, you wouldn't find no mules, so I didn't stay there long.

They had all kinds of animals out West. One time I drove out to a man's place right above Abilene. There was a bunch of antelopes, and when they started running down the road, I sped up. I was driving a good Cadillac car. I can tell you how fast they can run. Sixty miles an hour. I had to stop to keep from running over them, and I was driving up around sixty-five. One of them run on down there and hit the fence, and when he hit the fence, he fell out. I got down there and turned him over. He had the wind knocked out of him, don't you see. I said, "Well, I'll just take that son-of-a-gun back with me."

That was the worst mistake I made. I picked him up and started back to the car. When I went to put him in the trunk, he kicked me alongside the head. He kicked me so hard that I dropped him and let him get loose. I forgot about that antelope.

Another time I was going into Abilene, and I could see a mile down the highway. I'd had the radio on, and it told that Bonnie and Clyde were in that part of the country. It described their car and everything. Well, goddamn, I saw their car coming and knew who it was. The car was driving like hell toward me, and two or three times the son-of-a-bitch had all four wheels off the ground. I said to myself, "By God, I've heard them cars get to flying, but this is the first one ever I saw flying."

On by me they went. I was over to the side just as far as I could get, and I never turned my head to look at them. Course my eyes were looking over there. I had my eyes turned, but I was damned sure not to turn my head. Four or five people had looked at them earlier, and they met their Maker when they sprayed them with the machine gun. I didn't go four hundred yards before I pulled into a filling station, and I said, "I just met Bonnie and Clyde down there."

I breathed easier because I was so glad to be alive. I didn't know whether they were going to take that machine gun and spray me. They killed four or five people on their way down the road before they got killed somewhere in Louisiana. Them fellows in Louisiana killed Bonnie and Clyde one night.

They put that car on exhibition and sent it all over the world. It came to Vicksburg, but I wasn't interested in it. A lot of people I knew ran down to see it. It had around two hundred bullet holes in it.

When my brother Willie lived in Clayton, New Mexico, he called me and said, "Ray, come out here. A man here has got a hundred and fifty bulls, and you can buy them."

I went out to see the bulls. When I got to the man's house, right in his yard was a little baby about six months old, just crawling along in his britches. It was warm weather, and I looked over and saw an eagle sitting up on the post, and his tail was on the ground. He was the largest eagle ever I saw, and I've seen a lot of big eagles. That was just outside Clayton, New Mexico. So I said, "Aren't you afraid that doggoned eagle might take a notion to pick this child up?"

It scared me. He says, "No." Cool and quiet. The people are composed there, you know. He says, "No, I don't have any fear. I've got eight thousand sheep here."

That was enough. He didn't have to tell me any more. He had eight thousand sheep, and that eagle liked sheep. If he got hungry, he'd go for a lamb. He didn't have to explain any more.

But I thought, "I don't give a damn if I had a hundred thousand sheep. I still would be nervous with that son-of-a-bitch out there, and that little baby crawling around in the yard."

I never heard of an eagle packing off a baby, but I guess it has been done. An eagle ain't nothing but a big hawk. He's awful close kin to a hawk. You've got several different-size hawks. You got your little bitty sparrow hawks, chicken hawks, fish hawks, all kinds. Different ones eat different things, don't you see.

I was down in Old Mexico once, and bought quite a few little mules. Mexicans knew what to do with a mule. I've had a lot of experience in Mexico, and during the war I bought lots of little mules there. We would sell these little mules for pack mules. The government was buying pack mules then and was giving about a hundred and sixty dollars a piece for them. I would buy them down in Mexico for about twenty dollars a head.

In Mexico they used them little mules to go in the mines. Now it's all done by electric drags. They've done away with the mules in the mines just like they done away with them up on top of the land. Well, they brought a bunch of them little Mexican mine mules in, and they was all blind.

The man said, "What'll you give me for a hundred of them little mules?"

"I'll give you twenty-five dollars a piece for them."

"I won't take it."

I went down and looked at the little old mules, and every one of them was blind. "I'm still going to give you twenty-five a round for them."

"No, I'm not going to take it."

Well, I wound up having to give him thirty a round for them. I had an old boy with me. He said, "What do you want with them blind mules?"

"They won't stay blind."

You see, they was blind because they had been under the earth. Been down under there for years in the mines, and they had gone blind. A lot of them got their eyesight back after I had them out for a while, don't you know. Yeah, I got along fine with them. They called them "little miners."

I went to Hammond, Louisiana, and carried fifty head of those little Mexican mules down there. None of them was over thirty-six inches high. Wouldn't touch your titties. I got down there, and the man running the filling station said, "What do you have to have for these little mules?"

"I don't have to have anything for them. I could run them in the river and not lose too much. But I brought them here to sell. You know how to sell these little mules, and I'm going to give you five a head to sell them. What are they worth?"

"They'll bring a hundred and fifty dollars here."

"Well," I said to myself, "I'm rich then. I'm already rich if that's the case."

He says, "For that five a head I'll sell them for you."

He was a garage man, but I saw he was smart. The first little mule he sold was for a hundred and fifty, and we didn't sell many of them cheaper than that. He called them "strawberry mules" 'cause they could plow strawberries down the row and not step on the plants. You couldn't use a tractor there, but you could use these little mules. Them little mules was very much in demand in Hammond, Louisiana.

The prettiest mules in the world came from California. They looked just as round as a pencil. Had a lot of shape. It was what they ate that made them so pretty. An animal is what it eats.

When I went to California and started to buy mules, I worked a whole day without buying one. I would flip a mule's lip, and his teeth was three inches long, as long as my finger. I'd flip his lip, see that old long tooth and dodge[127] him. Knock a hip down getting out of the gate.[128]

Night come, and I run into a friend of mine there. I said, "How many you bought, Jim?"

"I bought four hundred. How many you bought?"

"I hadn't bought any. I don't like these damn mules. They are too old."

"Come on down here, and I'll show you two hundred four-year-olds I just bought."

I went down there, and the first thing I done, I flipped a lip. I thought I'd seen them mules before. Here was that long tooth, but I looked over on the corner, and there was that baby tooth. Goddamn, I was thinking how many mules I left that day. "What are you going to take for them, Jim?"

The old boy's name was Jim Harris. "I'm going to take a hundred a round for them, Ray."

Oh, they was good as gold. I shouldn't have give him that much for them. He'd bought them for six bits,[129] but I give him the hundred for them. I said, "It's worth twenty-five dollars a head just to wake up."

You know what made them mules' teeth long? The barley. They was eating barley, and it cut their gums back. Okay. I was awake then. I went right on back and bought the rest I'd passed over. Before I left I bought seven or eight hundred mules and shipped them all to my boys in Texas and Mississippi. I filled up all the boys with mules.

As the tractors would come in, the mules would go out. Wherever they had tractors, you couldn't sell a mule. But they were still using mules in Texas and Mississippi, and that's where I went with mine.

John Yount was a good friend of mine, and him and I was partners on a lot of deals. He loved me and would go to hell and back with me. I'll tell you how strong he was and how good he got to be. One night the government called and said they was going to sell six hundred mules in Oklahoma City. So we went there.

They was a lot of people at that sale. Them Owens brothers who was supposed to be the biggest mule dealers in the world was there to buy too. The auctioneer started in selling, and John and I went to buying mules and bought every son-of-a-bitch we could. We even bought them old long, tall mules, and we run the Owens brothers off. "Goddamn," they says, "that Lum son-of-a-bitch is gone crazy. We're going home."

On the way up to Oklahoma City I had put two cases of whiskey in the car. John said, "What the hell you bringing all that whiskey for?" We could have been put in the penitentiary for this.

"I figured those army officers might like whiskey."

It was during the time you couldn't buy whiskey. The country had gone bone dry, and you wasn't supposed to haul it anywhere. I bought two extra grips to put it in and come on with it. Didn't have no trouble. After the sale was over, John said, "Colonel, Ray brought some tea in his car. We got lots of tea, and we got it over to the hotel."

The colonel said, "What room are you in? It'll be thirty minutes before I can get over there."

John told him what room it was. So here comes the colonel over. He took a shot or two. "Goddamn, that's good."

John said, "Colonel, Ray's got two cases of it out in his car, and he thought you might enjoy it. He brought it to you."

"Goddamn, John. That's fine."

John said, "Wait a minute, Colonel. I am going to put it in your car for you." And he went there to get the cases. There was two cases in our car, twelve quarts to a case, you know.

John come back and said, "Colonel, we got caught in a curve today and bought a lot of mules that's too tall for our area, and you still got a lot of them little bitty mules there. What we want to ask you is, is there any chance we can switch?"

"Oh hell yes. Come on."

Well, to cut a long story short, at midnight we went out to the barn where we'd been all day and swapped back every son-of-a-bitchin' one of them tall cherry-picker mules before we left there. We was there till three in the morning trading them back, and when the smoke cleared away, we shipped out them little short mules, like we wanted. We shipped them on to Atlanta.

Let me tell you what a fellow said about California once. A man came to Fort Worth from California, and he was selling California land by the foot, you know. He had a racket. There have been promoters like him ever since there's been a world. I knew him well, and I liked him. But I didn't have any idea of buying anything from him.

Well, he went to telling us what a wonderful country California was. And Jimmy Adams was a little Irish trader that had been out in California buying mules and had just come back to Fort Worth. He had a different picture of California. Little Jimmy spoke up and said, "It's a land of flowers without odor, fruit without flavor, and more sunflowers and son-of-a-bitches than any country on the face of God Almighty's green earth."

That was his definition of California. It sounded kind of like Jimmy Walker's definition of Texas. It sounded a good deal like Jimmy's.

One day I was driving in California, and I drove into this damn tree and went right on through the son-of-a-gun in the car. I said, "Now, by God, if I'd just heard about that, I wouldn't believe it." They called it a Sequoia. That was in California.

They tell me there's a lot of people got long gray whiskers in California that don't know what beef tastes like. They've ate horse all their life, and they'd rather have horse meat.

I ate horse meat a number of times. I remember I was with Herb Manahan, a friend from Abilene. It was hot, and we were someplace in Nebraska. We pulled in to this cafe, and I said, "Partner, give me a stein of beer."

I was looking to get a little glass. He handed me a stein, and, not exaggerating, there was a quart of beer in it. I cut down on it and said, "Partner, you got a sandwich?"

"Yes. I've got limburger and old brownie."

Herb said, "I'll take limburger."

I said, "I think I know what old brownie is. Give me old brownie."

I bit down on old brownie, and I said, "This is horse meat."

"We sell quite a bit of it here." That was the only comment he made, "We sell quite a bit of it here."

There was your choice, limburger and old brownie. I was like the cat about limburger. You give a cat limburger, and he'll start scratching to cover it up.

California was the first place to put in tractors. I began to buy mules in California 'cause tractors was taking their place. There was the Pacific, and there was the Atlantic. I started at the Pacific, and when I quit selling mules, I was at the Atlantic. I went from one end of the country to the other. It worked just fine for me. Tractors come to California first, Texas next, Louisiana next, Mississippi next, and right on to the Atlantic. The last place they went out was the Carolinas. That was the end of the mule story—from the Pacific to the Atlantic. Finally, I got to where wadn't no place to go but in the water with the last ones.

When Mules
Played Out

In the 1950s Lum shifted his sales from mules to cattle, bought registered Hereford bulls in Texas, and shipped the animals to farmers in the Deep South to upgrade their herds. Elmer Kelton recalled that Texas cattlemen "were always glad to see Ray Lum show up . . . he would bid on just about every bull that came into the ring."[130]

Lum felt he was helping his region by introducing a better grade of cattle and told Kelton that "the low-end bulls in West Texas sales would be considered superior bulls back in Mississippi, and he was helping upgrade the quality of the cattle at home by taking those bulls there for resale."[131] Lum's flare for auctioning horses and mules proved equally effective with cattle. His large sales of Hereford bulls from Texas featured barbecues and drew enthusiastic crowds.

Throughout his life Lum was happiest when he was auctioning. Beginning with his first auction in Clarksdale, he traveled to Memphis, Texas, and the West auctioning stock. His deep voice and rapid-fire speech were familiar to buyers, and even in his eighties he would occasionally auction when asked to "spell" or relieve a tired auctioneer.

At *his livestock barn in Vicksburg, Lum's "singing" style of auctioning was so entertaining that the local radio station broadcast his sales live each week. He embellished his auction with jokes, praise for the animal, and greetings to the buyers. I was with him once when he assisted an auctioneer. The mule entered the auction ring, and he began:*

It's a rare mule, boys, a rare mule.
Now I've got a hundred-forty.
Will you give me five?
A hundred forty-five,
If I never cock another pistol.
If you boys want to bid on him,
Just don't stand there.
These mules are not plentiful.
This one shown,
I don't know when you'll find another one like him.
What do you want to give?
A hundred thirty-six.
Now eight.
Now nine.
Nine.
Nine.
The Lord loves a cheerful giver.
Get in there if you want to.
Hundred thirty-eight.
Thirty-nine.
Will you give nine?
So young to be so tight.
Speak now or hold your peace,
Forever and eternity.
Sold to Willie Jones for a hundred thirty-eight
dollars.
Well, I hope you get two hundred when you sell him.

After *this auction a buyer commented to me, "I just found out how they make an auctioneer. They vaccinate him with a Victrola needle when he is five years old."*

Lum's *success as a trader depended on his ability to quickly "lamp" a horse or mule to judge its defects. He called an animal* with a defect a "snide" or "screw" and taught me how to judge a horse. First examine his teeth to check his age; then feel his eyes. If his eyes are soft, the horse is either weak-eyed or blind. He called a horse with shortness of breath a "heavie,"[132] and one that chews on wood in its stall a "stumpsucker." He warned me that a shrewd trader will polish and file the teeth of a horse to make the animal appear younger and will "inflate" its skin with air to make a withered limb look healthy.

Of all animals, Lum's greatest love was for the mule. With pride he told me that the mule was the backbone of southern agriculture and that George Washington was the first American to breed a mule. He firmly believed mules will again be essential to our lives when we exhaust our oil and gas resources.

Lum explained to me that the mule is a hybrid offspring made by crossing a horse and an ass, and the breed of the horse determines the mule's size and personality. Like all hybrids, the mule cannot reproduce, but on one memorable day he saw a mare mule who had given birth to a colt and compared the wondrous moment to the "Coming of Christ."

The mule's father, the ass or donkey, is shrouded in mystery. Though physically small, the ass can run at great speed, and some believe they never die. Part of the same family (equus) as the horse, the ass has a large head, long ears, small hoofs, and is known for its loud bray. An ass is dun-colored, has a black stripe down its back and across its shoulders, and its height averages four and a half feet. A male ass is called a "jack," and a female a "jenny."

I treasured Lum's advice on horses. He taught me to set the value of a horse, to break a wild one, and, once broken, to safely mount and ride the animal. He believed that as long as people are in this world, they will want to ride horses. He loved horses and people, in that order, and often reflected, "You know, the outside of a horse is good for the inside of a man."

Beneath his tough style as a trader, Lum always identified with children and their love for horses. When children visited his shop, their eyes would light up as he related his tales. Lum always tried to guess the age of children. After checking their age, he offered advice on how they should handle horses. As a child, I sometimes sat in one of the colorful western saddles in his shop and listened to the tales of his trades.

Lum reminisced with me about the meaning of old age and

dreamed of "turning his speedometer back" and reliving his life as a trader. Age was often on his mind, be it his own or his ability to judge that of an animal's, a skill that was essential to his success as a trader. Lum loved to guess the age of children, and as a matter of politeness he always guessed a woman's age as ten years younger than she looked. He stoically reflected on his own age and death as part of a natural cycle that he had seen so often in the lives of men and animals. In spite of his eighty-five years, he continued to attend weekly sales and even bought stock on his final birthday.

He frequently mentioned his favorite phrase, "You live and learn, and then you die and forget it all," as he recalled past trades. His memories of men and animals he had known grew more vivid with age, and he clung to these worlds through his tales. Lum's greatest fear was that at his death his tales would be forgotten.

When mules played out, I started bringing in registered bulls. The first registered bull in Mississippi was Point Compass, and he was owned by a man in Jackson named Davis. He brought that Hereford bull to Vicksburg and showed him off in the hotel lobby. The bull died, and his offspring played out. Ten years went by, and there wadn't no Hereford cattle in Mississippi. They played out. So I began to bring Herefords in. I took up where Mr. Davis left off, and this country's never been without Herefords since.

I had my first sales here at Vicksburg. When we had cattle sales, we'd have a barbecue, and Old Man George Mindrop would barbecue for three days. He'd cook twenty-five or thirty head of cattle, twenty-five or thirty head of hogs, and twenty-five or thirty head of sheep. We had a pit a quarter of a mile long and cooked on hickory coals. You've heard that song, "When the Calliope Plays, They'll All Come." It was the same with my sales. I remember Ben May come down from Yazoo City to one auction. I was selling registered bulls, and he wouldn't give a nickel for a bull. We had butchered a lot of beef and had the barbecue there, and I had a barrel of whiskey with the barbecue. This was in the 'fifties, and Prohibition was over. So Ben goes down and gets full of whiskey. The whiskey was down at the slaughterhouse. I put it down there to give it away, but the people that bought the cattle, hell, they never even tasted the damn whiskey.

The back end of the slaughterhouse was where they throwed the offals out, and the floor was slick. The offals are your guts, and now you save them all. Like the fellow said about the hog, "You know, it used to be, I'd kill my hog, and I'd throw his head away, and I'd throw his feet away. Then I'd skin him and throw his hide away. But nowadays," he says, "they've got it to where all they waste on a hog is his squeal." The squeal is the only thing lost to the packer.

So Ben got drunk on whiskey, and he slipped and fell right over into them offals. And when he come out, you couldn't tell whether he was a man or what he was. Well, Mrs. Lum put one of my suits on the son-of-a-gun. He was about my size, so I lost a suit of clothes.

I advertised them sales, and they come from the forks of the creek to buy cattle. People enjoyed the barbecue, and I'd always have twice too much. People come from all over South Mississippi and Alabama to buy registered cattle. When I got buyers filled up here in Mississippi, I pushed into Alabama and Georgia and Florida. I fixed Mississippi with good cattle and then went into the neighboring states. Florida was some of my last sales.

I went to Florida when a grown cow and calf together didn't weigh over three hundred and fifty pounds. They'd about bred them out. Their bones wadn't much bigger than a pencil. Good God Almighty, I think about what I done for Florida when I brought them white-faced bulls in there. They put my good bulls on their little bitty old cows, and it wadn't long till they had some young cattle weighing five or six hundred pounds. I broke the ice.

If ever there was a place on earth you needed to start improving cattle, it was Florida. I had some year-old registered bulls that weighed nine hundred pounds. Them people was awful nice to me in Florida. There was a man there said, "How about me selling you three hundred of these little cows?"

"How much for them?"

"Twelve and a half a head."

"I'm going to give you ten."

He sold them to me. Three hundred head of cows. Didn't count the calves, don't you see. I should of bought five hundred. I shipped them to Brownwood, Texas. I had a good friend there named Guy Edes. Guy called me and said, "Ray, what have you got to get for them little cows? I been laughing ever since they got here. They're so cute."

"They ain't as cute as a monkey, are they?"

"Naw, but there's people here from everywhere wanting to buy them."

"What can you get for them, Guy?"

"Some of them want to give seventy-five dollars a pair for them."

"Well, I'll tell you what we better do. We're in no financial trouble with them. I don't own them too high. Let's just tell them that we won't sell any till the sale, and all that we don't sell, we'll give them to the buyers. Won't cost them nothing."

On to Brownwood I went. Them Texas people kept coming to see the little cattle. It was like a different kind of jackrabbit had come in there. "Ray, what is that?" They had the best Herefords in the world in Texas at that time. "Ray, what are they?"

"They're the kind of cows you can cross over on these good Texas bulls and make some cattle pretty cheap, and I'm going to auction them on Saturday."

When Saturday came, I didn't have enough little Florida cattle. Texas people want to experiment, and here they come. I remember the old boy that was auctioning. He said, "Ray, you want to sell these cattle, or do you want me to sell them?"

He was a good auctioneer. "I better let you sell them. Reckon you can get a hundred dollars a pair for them? That'd be mighty cheap, wouldn't it?"

Course I was thinking if they bought only fifty how tickled I'd be. Well, to cut a long story short, we had the sale, and the cheapest cattle brought seventy-five. It was the darnedest thing you ever saw and, of course, I had them give to me. I couldn't get back to Florida fast enough, but when I did, those little cattle had advanced in price. I bought a hundred of them, but I had to give twenty-five dollars a round, and I had to dig them up. And they been going up ever since. I never did find any more cattle for ten dollars a head.

I was the first one to bring Brahmas to Mississippi. I remember one sale where a Brahma chased a man out of the ring. A buyer said, "Don't run. That bull won't hurt you."

And the man said, "No, but he'll make you hurt yourself."

Some people are afraid of them. Brahmas are a cattle that, if you lead them, they'll follow you to hell and then jump off with you. But you don't drive them anyplace. See, you have to know more than the Brahma.

A fellow asked me once, "Ray, when do you feel best?"

"I'm at my best when I'm right up there selling."

When I'd be selling at an auction, I'd roll right on. I'd reach up and call every bid. I used to tell them, "Wink your eye or flop your ear, and I'll try to see you there."

Goddamn, I'd be rolling then. You know what rolling is, just traveling on. You don't wait for them to get on. Like the conductor man that a fellow asked, "How do you and your wife do business?"

"I run that just like I run my train. I take off my clothes and get in bed and holler, 'All aboard.' And if she don't get on, I go off without her."

If you come in green to a mule sale, you wouldn't know what the auctioneer had on the carpet.[133] But if you was a mule man buying mules, you had to understand. You can't be a yokel. You got to be awake. Let's have a little auction here:

> *Order in the court!*
> *It's a rare mule we've got here, boys, a rare mule.*
> *I've got a hundred-thirty.*
> *Will you give me five?*
> *A hundred thirty-five.*
> *If you boys want to bid on him,*
> *Just don't stand there.*
> *Those mules are not plentiful.*
> *This one shown,*
> *I don't know where you'll find the next one.*
> *You know how high mules are?*
> *None of you know.*
> *You don't know until they are sold.*
> *What do you want to give?*
> *A hundred thirty-six.*
> *Now eight.*

Now nine.
Nine.
Speak now or hold your peace forever and eternity.
Nine.
Get in there if you want to.
If I never cock another pistol.
I got a hundred thirty-eight.
Thirty-nine.
Come on if you want to.
Hundred thirty-eight.
Thirty-nine.
Will you give nine?
Sold to Willie Jones for a hundred thirty-eight dollars.
You bought it too cheap, you son-of-a-gun. Arrest that man over there. He just give a hundred and thirty-eight dollars for the mule. Oooh, some people are so tight. So young to be so tight. God forgive them, for they know not what they do. Well, I hope you get two hundred for him when you sell him.

I've auctioned, and I've seen auctions all over the world. I seen them in Chicago and St. Louis. St. Louis had the best ring men and the best auction in the world for a while. Then it moved about.

One time Fort Worth was the biggest auction.

Another time Memphis was the biggest auction.

Another time St. Louis was the biggest auction.

And then Chicago had the biggest auction.

That thing moved around in cycles. That's the way it done. And when tractors come, the auctions faded out. They was like mule traders. They didn't die. They just faded away.

It's been a long time since I sold a mule. Been a long time since I sold anything. But I always say it's not a man's age that stops him, it's his health.

The last big sale I made was in Birmingham, and I had a load of registered horses there. This man had a son, a right young man, and the boy wanted to be an auctioneer. I told him, "The only way to be a good auctioneer is to practice."

So the boy went off to school to learn how to auction. When he come back, his daddy says, "Mr. Lum, my boy has just come back from auction school, and I'd like for you to let him sell your stock."

I figured right away what was going to happen. I said, "Well, fine. Let him start with this horse."

I had a horse there, oh hell, must have been worth three or four hundred dollars. The boy said, "All right. What will you give for him?"

A fellow said. "I'll give a hundred."

The boy said, "A hundred, who'll give one?"

"A hundred."

"Who'll give one?"

"A hundred and one."

"Who'll give two?"

I let the boy sell for a while, and then I said to this man that owned the sale, "If you don't mind, I'll rest your boy a spell. Let me rest your boy there."

I got over in the box, and I said, "Gentlemen, you are all strangers to me, and I am a stranger to you, but I've got good horses here. I feel like I can tell you about them better than somebody that is not acquainted with them. This first little horse here is a quarter horse, and I have the papers with him. He's a Texas horse, and out where he come from, horses bring something. He's tops. When you buy this horse, you get the horse and the papers. The transfer is already signed, and all I have to do is fill in your name."

I went to work on it.

"Five hundred."

"Four hundred."

"Three hundred."

"Three hundred and a quarter."

"Three-fifty."

"Three seventy-five."

That was the first one that I sold. The boy had been seeing if he could get a hundred and two for the horse. I was too old a coon to be treed by a pup. While I was selling, the boy that had been to auction school come to me and said, "Mr. Lum, they won't buy a pitching horse."

"Is that so? They won't buy a bucking horse? Well, we'll see about that." I had six pitching horses that had cost fifty dollars a piece. I said, "Folks, out in Texas a good bucking horse is worth lots of money. These are some horses they almost bought to go to England, but they didn't pitch hard enough. They didn't want them unless they was sunfishers. You know a sunfisher puts his back where his belly is and you ain't going to stay on him. Well, these horses wasn't good enough to be sunfishers."

So this first horse come in, and Squire sat down on him. He sat on this horse like he was glued to him. He bent with the horse and never was in danger of being throwed, and that horse would holler. God Almighty, I never heard a horse bellow like that before. This little woman bought the horse for three hundred and fifty dollars. That was one of the horses the boy said wouldn't bring nothing.

Every mule man carried a walking stick or a whip, you know. He didn't hit the mule with the whip. He'd just crack it, and the mule would move. My brother Clarence[134] is a good hand with a whip, and he looks graceful doing it. A whip'll last him three or four years. He never hits the mule with his whip. Another fellow I knew, he'd wear out a whip every week. That's the difference in people.

A lot of people don't want their mules hit. I learned that early in life. I found out people like you better when you respect their stock.

You may forget about the cattle but we'll never forget about the horses and mules. You'll be riding horses as long as you live and as long as our children and their children live, there'll be riding. If one bunch quits another will start. That's so right. If you know about horses, they can't take it from you, and I do know horses. If I lamp[135] a horse, I'll know more about him than the fellow that rides him. When I lamp him, I just glance at him. A man once said, "If that is Ray Lum looking at that mule, he'll know more about him if he lamps him than you would if you had plowed him ten years."

You learn that through loving animals and understanding them. You've got to know the animals that you are handling, and I came up with them. I was a good judge of horses and mules from a twelve-year-old boy on up. I knew them to start with. And then I always prided myself on being a good judge of human nature.

Let me look at this old mule's mouth. Whoa, good man. Hold him there, Squire, like you love him. Whoa, good boy. Get up there! This mule might be a little goosey about his lamps.[136] Whoa back!

Ain't got a pimple[137] on him. This mule's just as clean as a hound's tooth. Hold him, Squire. Take hold of a mule like you mean to hold him.

Some mules are sensitive around the ears. This one is. When that bit hits his mouth, he'll lay his ears right on back. A lot of mules are thataway. If you take his ear and twist it, you can go and do anything you want with him. You just got to have more sense than the mule.

This mule right here is about ten years old. That's close to her age. You go by how broad the teeth are across the back. The older they get, the sharper they get across the back. Now you got it. This mule is awful gentle. You can do anything you want with her. Come here, gal. She's already shod, and she's gentle. That's about as pretty a mule as you'll see. No, you won't have any trouble with her. When the bit hits her mouth, she'll go right on. That's a good mule. Get up, good lady. She'll keep herself fat off what a chicken knocks out of his trough. That will be an easy-kept mule, don't you see, easy-kept.

When you want to mouth a horse, just pull his top lip up. If his teeth are broad like this, he's young. You don't have to look in it for cups.[138] Never mind about the cups. When he gets about seven years old, his teeth will look like my middle finger right here. When he gets about eight years old it will look kind of like this little finger here. The older he gets, the sharper his teeth get. You tell a horse's age by his teeth.

I remember one time I saw a fellow, and he was pulling a horse's mouth open and looking down his throat. So I said, "I've been feeding him oats."

"I'm looking to see how old he is."

"And you're looking down his throat?"

"Yeah."

"Uh huh." Well, you find a man like that, and you can tell him anything you want.

There are a lot of traders can take a rasp and drill to fix an old horse's mouth and make him look young. Back then they would take a horse ten or twelve years old and make a six-year-old out of him. If his old teeth was dirty, they'd take a rag and polish them up white and pretty and pearly. Then they'd go right down in that tooth with the rasp and put the groove right back in the tooth where it used to be.

Fellow would say, "How old is that horse?"

"Mouth him there. Look and see."

If it was one that had been fixed, "Looks like a seven-year-old."

"Does he? Fine. Okay."

You didn't wake him up. Let him sleep. Find him sleeping and let him sleep on, don't you know. And he would be just as happy with him too. A ten- or eleven-year-old would do him more good than a seven-year-old. When you know, you know, and there ain't no use telling nothing.

There was a man here at the barn yesterday with a horse thirty-five years old. He rides him every day. I asked him, "How old do you think your horse is?"

"I think he is about seven or eight years old."

I had already mouthed him. I just went on and left it that way. Let sleeping dogs lie. You can't tell folks about horses.

You know how to tell if a horse is blind? Clap your hands and if he throws up one ear, he's blind on that side. If he's blind in one eye, he'll try to see out of that ear. I remember Old Uncle Dan MacBroom come in once and tied his horse in the stall. I knew he had a screw[139] 'cause when I slapped my hands, both his ears come up. I knew then he was blind in both eyes. I traded with him, and in about an hour or two I swapped him off to somebody else.

I had a blind horse I drove cattle on once. His eyes looked good, but he was just as blind as a bat. He was the best screw ever I owned. Back in them days before the automobiles come along, half the horses were screws. You didn't find too many sound horses. Keeping them in stalls and not letting them have a regular way of life made them turn into screws.

Lots of times traders would say, "That horse is a little dim in the peepers."[140] That meant his eyes was bad. Slip your hand up and push on his eye. If he's got weak eyes, his eyeballs are soft. Put your fingers on his eyes, and if they goes in, you're in trouble.

Some horses got a blue eye or two blue eyes, like a Persian. That's not unusual at all, and a white horse is more likely to have blue eyes than any other color horse. That's from the breed. The majority of your Arabian horses were white, and a lot of them had eyes like people.

When we say, "That horse has a blue eye," that means he's got a bad eye. That's not talking just about the color of his eyes. But some blue-eyed horses have eyes that are plumb good. So you can't always tell just by the color.

I remember when my daddy'd take hold of a horse with blue eyes, the first thing he'd do was put his hand up and feel his eye. If it was firm, he knew he was all right. He found what he was looking for. But if his eyes was bad, he'd say, "He's a little dim in the peepers."

This little fellow traded for a horse I had one day, and he come back awful upset and said, "That horse is blind."

"You think his eyes is bad?"

"Oh, definitely they are. He walked right into that post."

"Well," I said, "it must be a secret. The man I got him from didn't tell me anything about it. Must be a secret."

The man got to laughing, and I swapped him another horse. That's what I wanted to do, of course, and left him happy.

One time I swapped Uncle Dan a heavie. A heavie horse is like asthma with a person. I guess that would be the best way to describe it. Its breath is short, but if you run them and get them emptied out, you can drive them all day.

The worse cheating ever I got, a doctor come up with a pretty horse, and I traded for him. When he left, I found a plug in his windpipe, and there was a big hole in his neck. I forget who I traded him to. I got every kind of snide,[141] but that didn't matter. I didn't pay no attention to that.

Now a lot of stumpsuckers[142] would have a belt around their neck to keep them from sucking on wood. I'd walk down and see a horse with a belt around his neck and, of course, I didn't have to ask any questions. My bread was done.[143] I knew what a stump-sucker was. Usually you could flip his lip and see that his teeth was worn. Sometimes horse and mule people would call a stumpsucker a cribber. Course other people didn't know what that meant.

When you go to buy a horse, don't get one that's too fat. What was it the man said, "A lean hound for a long chase." That's right. You run a potbellied horse, and he'll give out, but take one that looks like a racehorse, and you can ride him all you want to. Just talk to him once in a while, give him a little air and give him a quart of oats, and it'd be the same as giving that potbellied son-of-a-bitch a bushel.

Another thing I never wanted was a big horse. I remember a man wanted a big horse once, and I bought him one in St. Louis. That horse was nearly eighteen hands high, a freak of nature. He just keep growing tall, don't you see, like some people. So I shipped him on to the man I was buying for, and that man phoned me up and called me everything on earth. "I'll never let you buy another horse for me as long as you live. What do you expect me to do with that long, tall son-of-a-bitch you sent me?"

"Drown the son-of-a-bitch! Drown him!"

"Well," the man said, "there ain't enough water. Hell, there ain't a creek or a river that's deep enough to drown him."

Yeah, he ought to have been chloroformed, put to sleep. Get his head out of the feed sack. Good God, good for nothing!

Mules are like Maxwell House coffee. They're good till they drop. Yeah, mules was the backbone of the country, and George Washington bred the first mule. Yes, sir, his bread was done.

You had to have a mule to farm with if you was going to plow. In slavery time a hundred years ago, they didn't have nothing to farm with but mules. They used the mule to build the South, don't you know. Stop and think about it. Mules built the railroads and the levees. They protected us from the river.

They used to say mules is like whiskey. As long as they drink whiskey, they'll make it, and long as they work mules, they'll raise them. I believe that's really true. Long as they drink it, they'll make it, and long as they work them, they'll raise them. So it works both ways.

A man with six or seven acres, all he needs is one mule to work that land. He don't need a tractor. The time is coming when they won't be using big tractors for little farms. If you can't afford to buy a tractor to work five or six acres, you can get you a little mule.

There's a lot of people that'll buy a little mule to plow their crop. The world's not going to stop if they can't get tractors. I've seen it good, and I've seen it bad. But it's not going to stop. It's going to keep right on going. It could be that those bygone days will come back. That's the way I see it. It could be that you'll run out of gas all over the world, and then you'll haul every damn thing with mules again. It's possible.

We don't know how much gas is down under the ground. We don't know whether it's going to last. It could quit. History repeats, they say. I don't like to predict anything bad, but it could happen. If we run out of gasoline, we'll go back to mules. Farmers got to go on. Lots of people now don't know a damn thing about mules, but they can learn.

Time changes, and the time will come when it will be profitable to raise mules. Up in the Delta where they use tractors on big farms, they wouldn't give you a nickel for a mule. But out in these hills where they got just five or ten acres, they still work mules.

What animal is it that you can do away with every one of them, and in a period of time there'll be more? Don't be ashamed if you don't know. I guess I've asked a thousand lawyers, bankers, and doctors, and none of them knew. You don't know the answer even though I been talking about them. If you do away with all of them, in a period of time there'll be more.

Some folks'll holler, "Chickens."

They figure a chicken's got eggs and would go to hatching. Well, I never did consider a chicken an animal. Now what would you say that was?

It's a mule. Mules don't breed. They don't cross. There's two ways to get a mule. If you take a jack and a mare horse and put them together, you get a mule. That's what you call a jack screw. If you breed a saddle mare with a jack, you'll get a mule that'll ride awful good. It'll take after its mother. It'll have more of the mare in it than it has the jack.

Now then, if you want to go the other way, you put a jenny under a stud horse and get a henny.[144] A henny is a mule with little short ears. A cross with a jack and a mare is a different cross from a stud and a jenny, don't you see. You make a different cross.

I'd just as well have a henny. They get to weigh a thousand pounds, and they are awful pretty. They're shaped like a good round horse. I saw one yesterday. A fellow had it in Hazelhurst, and he was riding it. He just fox-trotted him like a horse. Oh, it was nice.

Now, I said that mules don't breed, but there was one down

here at Hazelhurst that had a colt. This man had a mare mule, and one day Mr. Ramsey, an old mule man that had been there some time, called me in Vicksburg and said, "Ray, So-and-So down here's got a mule with a colt."

I lit out down to Hazelhurst and got hold of Mr. Ramsey. He and I went down, and there was the colt nursing the mare. "Hmmmmm," I said, "Mr. Ramsey, you really think that's that mule's colt?"

"Oh hell yes. I saw her a day or two ago, and she was about to burst open and had a bag on her like a Jersey cow. I know that's her colt."

"Uh huh."

I still didn't buy it. But people come from the forks of the creek to see that mule and her colt. It was like the Coming of Christ. I just kept looking at it and wondering. I tried to buy the mare from the man, but he wouldn't sell her. And as time went on, she had two more colts after that.

I know it says in the Bible you don't make the second cross. You breed to make the mule. You make that first cross, but then that mule don't breed. I haven't read the Bible as much as I should have, and I'm getting to the age that if I don't read it now, it'll soon be too late for me. But I think it's in there, and somebody told me definitely that it is. So I'll just leave it at that.

A mule has got twice as much sense as a horse. You won't jump him in the river, and if you get him out of a barn on fire, he won't run back in. Not a mule. But you can pull a horse out of a barn on fire, and the son-of-a-bitch will jerk loose from you, run right back in there, and burn up. You get a mule out, and, goddamn, he'll thank you for it. He won't run back in that fire.

When I walk up to a mule, I always put my hand on him. Looks like he's ready for my hand, and I can do anything I want to with him. Don't go up there nervous with your hand shaking. When you take hold of a mule, grab him like you mean it.

When you touch a mule's face, put your hands up high. Always go up as far as the eyes. When people that don't know put their hands on a mule's nose, the damn mule will paw or bite them. Then they'll say, "He bites."

"Yes, he likes meat."

When you go to buy a mule, look at his feet. When you see a big foot,[145] he's out of a draft-bred mare. But out of a thoroughbred or a saddle mare, you get a little-footer.

A bulldog mule would be a small pack mule. He looks more like a jack than a mare. He's tight-legged, cross-faced, short-backed, and he has a bulldog's features.

The prettiest mules to me are the sorrels. They're bred out of a Suffolk mare, and, God Almighty, they're pretty. They don't weigh over fifteen or sixteen hundred, but they're pretty as dolls. Oh, they're good mules, and every time you hitch one up, they go forward. They're bred to work, don't you know.

A white mule is born black. When you breed a gray mare and a black jack, the colt comes black, and he turns a little more gray every year. He turns whiter and whiter till he gets all white. Yeah, a six-year-old is what I call an iron gray, and that's the prettiest color on earth. Some six-year-olds get dapples on them about the size of dollars.

They called white lightning "white mule" 'cause it was so strong it'd kick you. I used to drink white lightning. It was just as clear as rainwater, but a little spoonful would knock you over. It was about a hundred and forty proof and stout as hell.

The only kind of mule that won't kick you is a big draft mule. They just move off and work. I never saw a big mule kick, and I've had lots of them. But a little mule will kick the back out of your mouth. He'll kick hard enough to kill your whole soul. I've had my pants kicked plumb off by a little mule. Goddamn them, just looks like they do it for meanness. I always thought I was a pretty good judge of a mule, but I was in the stable one night and this mule kicked my britches off. It damn near killed me.

Don't ever sell a mule short. If you've been mean to him, he'll remember and kick you when he gets a chance. I guess a mule is like an elephant in that respect. He keeps it right in his craw and figures he'll get even with you some time. A mule's got more memory than a horse and a lot more sense too.

When you drive a team with more than two mules, you put your best mules next to the wagon by the wheel. Put your heaviest pullers by the wheel and taper it on down to where you have your lightest ones out front. It's like turning your biggest dog loose first.

Put your biggest sons-of-bitches around the wagon tongue, and they start the wagon rolling. Wagon wheels keep on rolling.

The mule skinner drives those mules, and the best ones would almost whisper. They don't have to yell. They know their mules that well.

One of these days I'm going up to Mule Day in Columbia, Tennessee. Every year at Columbia they have a thousand pretty girls riding a thousand pretty mules. Here's the mule, and here's the girl, and they ride bareback, don't you know. It must be a pretty sight to see. If you don't like to look at the girls, look at the mules. You'll have all kinds.

And a damn mule colt, they like to play, you know. If you have two or three mule colts around, and you got a calf in the same pasture, you better get them separated. They don't belong in there together. The mule colts will be playing and will just grab the calf by the neck and throw him over the fence.

A fellow asked another one, "What is a mule?"

"Oh, it's one of those hard tails."

They call them hard tails. You know, you shave a mule's tail. If you don't shave it, he'll have a long, bushy tail just like a horse. They shave the tail so they don't have a lot of hair dragging around in the harness.

I knew more mules named "Maud" than anything else. They'd call a matched team Maud and Annie. "Whoa, Annie, whoa. Gee, Maud." Gee was to your right when you were plowing, and haw was to your left.

If I can get my hand on a mule's jaw, I can tell how old he is. I don't care how dark it is, all I want to do is get my hand on his jaw. The jawbone of an old mule gets sharp. It's wide just like your thumb here when he's young, then when he gets twenty years old, it gets real narrow. And a jack's jaw is the same way.

The jawbone of an ass goes back to the Bible. Methuselah took the jawbone of the ass and whipped off so many thousand of those fellows, don't you know. I remember seeing in the Bible about the jawbone of an ass, and I thought a lot about that old dry bone. You know, if a good stout man got ahold of it, he could whip an awful lot of them. That Methuselah must have been awful strong.

A lot of folks look at a donkey and say, "Them's the laziest sons-of-bitches. I can't get them out of the way."

Well, we had a bunch down here at Willie Ross's place, and Clarence said, "I want to get them in. I sold them to somebody."

So he went down on a good horse to get them. This was twenty-five or thirty years ago. He went down to get the damn donkeys, and when he come back, he says, "I'll have to get another horse and go back tomorrow."

I said, "Did they outrun you?"

Clarence says, "They did, but I'll just go back another time."

Willie Ross told me later, "I was there when Clarence came back with them things, and we started up that bottom in a Cadillac car. I was driving, and them sons-of-bitches was floating right alongside of me just like they was flying. And the car was running sixty-five miles an hour."

I knew they could run, but not that fast. I've had donkeys at the barn there at home, and somebody could come up with a mare and say, "I want to breed this mare, Mr. Ray."

"Yeah. I've got a jack around here somewhere."

Well, that jack would be three quarters of a mile from where the man was unloading his mare. I don't know whether the wind was blowing in his direction or not, but you'd hear that son-of-a-buck holler. He'd open his mouth and bray.

I had a hostler there one day, and a man was unloading his mare. She was already in season, ready to breed, and when the jack hollered, this hostler told me, "You know what that jack said?"

"No. What did he say?"

"Good God! Here I come! Some for me, up! Some for me, up!"

Well, you could hear the son-of-a-bitch braying, and it sounded just like he was saying that. I said, "You don't think they can talk, do you?"

"Well, they talk that kind of language."

You could damn near understand it. That jack'd bray, and by the time they got the mare out of the truck and got her turned around, here was the jack. He'd have the mare bred, and in ten minutes she'd be back on the truck and gone. It worked that fast. You take a jack that will come that far and run that fast coming to a mare in heat, you know when he gets there, he's damn near ready. Yeah, he's damn near ready.

There's a lot of people that believe that a jack don't ever die. But I always figured I knew better than that. I figured they died. Yeah, each gave service.

You know, a jack is one of the heaviest hung animals there is, next to an elephant. One time a train hit this jack and cut his tool off. Along come an old woman, and when she saw the jack's tool laying there on the tracks, she hollered, "Lord God, the train done killed our parson."

So the jack and the parson is kind of alike in some ways, don't you see. Some of them parsons are heavy hung too.[146] "Lord God, they done killed our parson."

I let Victor Bobb have a jack, and the poor thing was awful heavy hung. It was unusual for even a jack to be that heavy. This old jack would step on his tool at night, and he'd just stand there and holler. Vic said he had to get up sometimes in the middle of the night and go out there and knock him off of it. I think he finally sold that jack.

With horses I figure the man is ninety percent of it, and the horse is just ten. If you get a horse, you better know ninety percent more than he does. I was a good hand with a horse till I got too stout. You could lead a horse up and say, "Ray, feel of that horse there. Sit down on him."

When I got ready to sit down on him, I'd cheek him. I'd grab the bridle about an inch above the bit and pull his head back toward me when I put my foot in the stirrup. Sometimes when I forgot to cheek them, I had horses kick my foot out of the stirrup. Out West, every rider does that. Don't cost nothing to cheek him. If you see a man walk out to a horse and just stick his foot in the stirrup, he's asking for trouble.

You should take hold of a horse like you mean business. Don't put your hand on him like it's a dead fish. If you go petting him, he'll think you're tickling him, and any doggone thing can happen to you. But if you put your hand on him like it weighs a ton, then you're safe.

And when you sit down on a horse, take hold of his mane. If you do have to fall off, take that mane with you. Have it in your hand. Most people get scared and turn loose when they fall off. You going to get hurt if you fall off a horse, so try to stay on him.

As time goes on, you will see a lot of changes, but there will always be somebody riding a horse, and there will always be somebody wanting a Shetland pony. I've had people say, "Nobody wants a Shetland pony." As long as they raise children, you will need Shetland ponies. And as long as there are people, they will be riding horses. They have been doing it ever since my daddy come along and my great-granddaddy.

I never did find a horse that I couldn't tame. I had one so wild I had to tie him down overnight. I just tied all his feet together. The next morning he was awful sore, but he was gentle. Way back when I was a boy, nearly all the horses I'd get was unbroke. I was a pretty good handler with a rope, and I'd ride any horse. I'd sit down on lots of them that had never been rode. If they had to be rode before I'd get the money, I'd ride them, you know. But I was always glad when they quit bucking.

A quarter horse has got more sense than most any other horse. If you look at his head, he's broader between the eyes. It's wonderful to have a horse with some sense. If you get one without any brains, they will breed, and their whole damn family will be that way. There was a high-priced stud horse here at Vicksburg, and every colt he got was an idiot. I told you enough.

My favorite animal is a Tennessee walking horse,[147] one of them old horses that speaks to everyone he meets. The best Tennessee walker that I ever had I named Pigeon. People would say, "Why did you ever name that horse Pigeon?"

"Did you see him?"

See, here's a pigeon's head nodding. Every time his foot hits the ground, he'll nod and speak to you. "How do you do. How do you do. Walk, old fox, and shake your tail. Those hounds are searching for your trail."

Yeah, I've had lots of walking horses in my time. Nobody likes a walking horse any better than I do. Your walking horses have a good pastern.[148] That's your pastern joint between the hoof and the ankle here, and that's where you get the comfortable ride from your horse. If you know that, you can look at a horse and tell how he's going to ride before you get on him. If his pastern is short, that son-of-a-bitch will jug your guts out. But if you get that pastern long, your ride will be springy. Now you know why a horse rides the way he does.

War Trace[149] was a beautiful registered walking horse. He got to where they kept him up too much and didn't give him enough stall room. I think he killed a child that got in his stall. This child crawled up in reach of him, and he bit the child and killed it. I think that's what happened with that son-of-a-gun. It happened with War Trace, and it will happen with any stud if you keep him caged up. You take the best horse in the world away from nature, and he'll get cagey, you know. You got to throw him with a mare once in a while. A horse can lose his wits just like a person.

When I give a horse a pill, I just reach in and pull his tongue out. Pull his tongue out with one hand and give him the pill with the other hand, don't you see. A horse pill is as big as an egg. There ain't one man out of a thousand that knows how to do that. Some people say, "Look out, he'll bite you."

Shit, you got his tongue. He'd bite his tongue if he tries to bite you. You pull that tongue out and shove the pill down. It's all done while we're talking, that quick.

This horse meat has jumped in price in the last few weeks. These old killers[150] are now bringing about a dollar a pound. I remember one old horse come in the sale at Natchez that weighed about fourteen hundred. I was sitting out there and was going to buy it for about fifty or sixty dollars, when here comes the man that runs the barn, he says, "Hey! A hundred and forty dollars."

And that was it. He was worth a hundred and forty dollars for commercial purposes, and he was going to Fort Worth. I don't know where he goes from there, but they were not going to ride him. I know that.

There is lots of horse meat consumed. And if beef gets much higher, they'll be eating horses everywhere. Stop and think about it. A horse drinks clean water. He won't drink dirty water. And if you put anything in his feed, he won't eat it. So why wouldn't horse meat be as good as beef? Those people in California would rather have horse meat than beef.

You know, it's hard for me to get out of trading horses and mules. I've been in the horse and mule business all my life, and that's been a long time. I'll go to an auction, and I'll buy two or three horses and then find a truck to haul them home. I've got horses bought now that I haven't got home yet. I'm working a little slow, but I can't help but buy them. I love horses.

And I get a kick out of people talking about horses. They ask me, "How do you tell what a horse is worth?"

Well, a horse is worth what somebody pays for it. That's what it was worth at that time. That's about as far as you can go telling what a horse is worth. People'll ask me lots of time, "What's a horse worth?"

Well, maybe I'd see one, and I'd say, "That one's worth a hundred there. They just sold him for a hundred."

"Hundred dollars?"

"Yeah."

"And that's all he's worth?"

At that time it was. I've always said this, and I'll say it now. If he was thin, you could take Man O' War[151] and stick him in the auction, and he wouldn't bring fifty dollars. Man O' War. Stick him in there fat, and he'd bring a million dollars. Same horse. They used to say, "Man O' War ought to win so-and-so." But if he's thin, they'll buy him for soap. That's the way the horse is.

So it's not what a horse is worth, it's what somebody'll give for him. You may say, "I've got a horse I'm asking two hundred dollars for."

Well, that's fine. If somebody gives you two hundred, he's worth two hundred. There's no way you can set your price on them. As a rule you wind up having to take the other fellow's price, unless you just want to sweat it out and stay with him until somebody comes along and gives you your price, which happens sometimes. People call me at night lots of times and ask, "What's a horse worth?"

"What kind of horse? They're worth different prices."

I try to answer them sensible and help them all I can because I've been in that business always. I sure know how to sympathize with them when they say, "Well, I paid five hundred dollars for him."

"Uh huh. Well, some people paid a lot more than that, and you may have to sell him a lot cheaper if you go to sell him."

"Well, I've got to sell him. I'm going to sell him."

That's the way it goes. If they show me a horse and ask me what he's worth, I'll lamp him once and say, "I'll give you a hundred for him."

I might move him around to see if he's hitting on four.[152] I make sure he's not a bookkeeper. That's a horse that puts down three and carries one. See, if he's carrying one, he'd be limping.

We got names for them all. Every once in a while, somebody'll come up with a weak-eyed horse and say, "Ray, what's that horse worth?"

I'll be looking at him. Maybe I'll put my fingers over his eyes. I can do it in the night. If his eye is soft, then he's weak-eyed. Sometimes they'll bring me out there at night and say, "What's this horse worth?"

"I can't tell you what he's worth, but I'll tell you what I'll give for him."

When I had my barn out there next to the cemetery, a man came up one day. I had a nice walking horse I'd got from somebody down about Summit, and he said, "Mr. Lum, what'll you ask for that horse?"

"Three hundred and fifty dollars."

"Uh huh. Well, I want a better horse than that."

"Oh yes. You do? All right."

Well, along comes Mr. Bocock, and Mrs. Lum sells him the horse for five hundred. I think Mr. Bocock was a diamond dealer. He was some kind of dealer anyhow, but he was dealing in horses that time. So he carried the horse on to Baton Rouge. A week later I was down at Alexandria, and a lady comes by riding a horse, a pretty horse, and I said, "You have a beautiful horse there."

"Well, he should be. I gave Mr. Bocock twenty-five hundred for him."

"Well, he's lovely."

That was the horse I tried to sell the man for three hundred dollars. That same horse I offered to sell him for three-fifty, Bocock sold for twenty-five hundred.

Well, there's a deal stronger than that. I was in Oklahoma City, and a little mare bounced in the auction ring. When the rider pulled on her reins, she stuck her tail in the sawdust[153] about two inches and stopped. I bought her for twenty-seven and a half, and she went out. Here comes a fellow up side of me. He says, "What'll you take for that little horse you just bought?"

"Two hundred dollars."

"But you just give twenty-seven and a half dollars for her."

"To hell with that. You want her—two hundred dollars."

"Well, I'm going to buy her."

So that settled that. He lived in Brownsville. Wadn't long after that I was back in Brownsville, and I ran into him. I said, "How did you get along with the pony I let you have in Oklahoma City?"

"Ray, I had good luck with her. I sold her for twenty-seven hundred and fifty dollars."

She was a polo special. You couldn't train one any better than she was. A cow pony makes a good polo pony. He ain't only good for cows, he can play polo too, don't you see.

So there's a moral to that. A horse is worth what you get for him at that time. And next time you sell him, he's worth what he brings that time. People ask me, "How do you value a horse?"

Well, of course, all my life, ever since I was pretty young, I've been selling at auctions, and I never put a price on a horse. I let the people put one on him during the auction.

I've heard all my life that the outside of a horse is good for the inside of the man. That's just as true as the Bible. Well, I've been in the horse business all my life, and I'm good at answering questions. I may not be right, but I'll have answers, and I'll never tell nobody I don't have an idea. You ask some people a question, smart people, and they say, "I don't have any idea."

They say if you find a fool, don't try to change him. You can change a mule, but you can't change a fool. He'll be a fool as long as he lives. What is it they say? A hint to the wise is sufficient, but a damn fool, you can't knock him down. Son-of-a-bitch, he'll still be a yokel. There's no way to wake him up. You can't hold an umbrella over the world. If it was raining soup every day at twelve o'clock, there'd be some poor fellow out with a fork. He'd starve to death anyhow.

I think that if you treat people good, they will treat you the same way. If you find some fellow that is hard to get along with, take your time and figure out what made him that way. I'm a little like Will Rogers. I like every man I meet. If there is something wrong with him, I figure out what caused it and overlook his trouble because I don't think a man came into this world to be bad and mean.

What was it the old man asked the other one? "What kinds of ticks is the worst ticks?"

The other fellow said, "Them politics is the worst."

Yeah, they're the worst. But you have to have politics. There's no way of getting around them. You will have them as long as you live.

Music is all right for people that love it. The sound of a horse's hooves was my music. I'd like horses, and I would always be busy with them, you know.

I think the more love you can have, the better country we will have. A world without love, I think, would be a sad place to live in. Love thy neighbor. I don't have a wife now. I did love her when I had her, and I loved her family.

Time changes all things. As I get older, I try to look into the future to figure what is going to happen. I try to figure out what is coming tomorrow.

I think that everybody ought to have some religion. The more they have, the better off they are. My religion has always been, "Do unto others as you would like for them to do unto you." I had a common-sense religion. Pay your debts and don't tell any lies. I've had people say, "Oh, that's a horse trader. He will tell you a lie."

I thought to myself I never found where telling a lie was worth a nickel. I always thought the truth would fit in better. A man who tells a lie will get caught, so the lie hasn't helped him very much, you know.

I think that if a man treats his fellow man right, he can lay down at night, go to sleep, and his conscience won't hurt him. A man should treat his fellow man right, pay his debts, don't break the law in any way, and go to church when he can. If he does, I think that he is likely to get to the Pearly Gates. I am hoping that I will go there because I think my mother and my wife have gone there, and I have something to go there for.

A trader is a man that trades in everything. If a man is a trader, and you're looking at one right now, he will trade you for anything you have to trade. If he can't use it, he'll find someone that can.

That's his business. And you are never broke as long as you keep trading. Always keep something to trade on. Lots of people can take a pocket knife and run it into a barrel of money. And there are a lot of people that you can give a barrel of money to, and it won't be long till they won't even have a pocket knife. It's all in who it is trading.

I think traders are born. There ain't nobody that started out trading much younger than I did. I started in trading goats and before it was over I traded horses and mules and cattle all over the country.

The secret of a good trader is he's happy, and he makes a lot of other people happy. He can give you a good trade and still make money for himself. A good trader looks after his customers and keeps people coming back. I trade with people now that I traded with when I was a boy.

When the peddlers first came, they'd put a two-hundred-pound pack on their back and walk all day. They'd spread the pack out when they come up to a house. The lady'd say, "I don't need a thing."

"Well, I just want to show you."

He'd spread his pack out, and maybe she'd find a pair of scissors. Maybe she'd spend a nickel for a package of needles. Maybe she'd find something else she liked. So he'd thank her and beat it on.

Traders had a lot of tricks, and Old Man Maroon would carry a bear with him, and he had an organ. He would play the organ, and that old bear would dance, and he'd pass his hat around and take up nickels. Course he had his pack too. He had you both ways. If you didn't want to buy anything, you would give a nickel to see the bear dance. He was going to get something from you. You wouldn't let him go away without giving him something. I finally sold Old Man Maroon a gray horse, and he got to traveling with a horse and buggy. I never did know whether he ate the bear or not. I bet he didn't waste him.

I always considered that I was a very good trader because I kept a lot of people busy. I had seven or eight brothers younger than me, and I kept them all trading. I started out young with that pair of goats, and that was the best five dollars I ever lost. When I got down to Lorman, I says, "The goats are twenty-five dollars, Mr. Cohn."

"Naw! Twenty."

I come back with the twenty, of course. That was the best five dollars I ever made when he didn't give me the twenty-five. I learned some lessons early in life, and they are still paying off.

When I was trading, I was a lone wolf. I had to travel by myself to do as much business as I did. Being a trader is like the old boy said about the Indian, "When you sleep on the ground, covered with stars, you'll know a lot more than people who haven't done that."

I've got to where I'm fairly good on directions. You could take me a long ways and drop me off, and before long I'd look around and get my directions. I'd know by the sun.

When it comes to cattle, Indians are close observers, and they're a damn sight better with a horse. An Indian handles a horse better than anybody you know. Here's a horse, and here's your Indian. You never saw an Indian put a saddle on a horse, and you never saw an Indian get throwed off a horse.

I remember one time this man had lost his horse, and this Indian was walking down the path. The man says, "Have you seen my horse?"

The Indian says, "Did he have one eye, two teeth out of the middle of his mouth, and a shoe off the right hind foot?"

"Yeah, where is my horse?"

"I haven't seen your horse."

And he hadn't. He explained to the man how he knew all that. By him leaving those two blades of grass in the middle where he grazed, he knew he had two teeth missing. When he'd bite, the grass was left there. And when he saw he'd just graze on the left side, he knew the right eye was out. He didn't graze on the right side, and the grass was just as good there. And he saw from his tracks what shoe was off, you know. He was a close observer, but the man wanted to kill him. He said, "Where's my horse, you son-of-a-bitch? Where's my horse?"

"I haven't seen your horse."

I guess the Indian finally woke him up there after describing why he knew about the horse. A lot of people will fall out with you when you're trying to help them.

I've slept on the ground a lot of times in the summer. I remember the time Richard Riley and I were going to Corpus Christi. We got awful tired this night and pulled off the road to sleep. When I laid down, Richard said, "If you don't get in an ant bed, you'll be all right."

I was so tired I just went on to sleep, and damned if next morning there wasn't fire ants everywhere, all around me. But they wadn't on me. They didn't bite me. Those fire ants can kill a calf.

I remember I had some cows and was coming back from Atlanta. I pulled in someplace in Georgia, and a man was living there that had fire ants all over his place. I said, "You going to stay here?"

"No. I sold this place."

"Well, fine. Sold them ants with it, did you?"

"Yeah, I hope so."

A cow could have a calf, and next morning maybe you wouldn't have a calf. That's how strong those ants were. It was awful.

I road-traded long before they had trucks. I rode in a wagon from Vicksburg to Clarksdale with a bunch of mules. I had a man drive the wagon and carried some feed along for the stock. When I got to Clarksdale, I ran into a bunch of traders camped there. That's where I found the Irish and gypsy traders camped together. Good God, Clarksdale was full of traders. It was nothing to find two hundred traders on trade day, you know. They called it "trade day," and once a month you'd bring in anything you had to sell. Of course, I was mainly interested in horses and mules.

Sometimes I would put livestock right in my car. I used to go to a sale at Summit every week. One day I bought two nice ponies from a man. I really wanted them, and I was driving a Cadillac. So I said, "Well, I'll get these saddles out of the trunk and sell them to make room for a pony."

I got my saddles out and sold them, and then I come back and told the man, "I got two horses I bought here, and I've got to put one in the trunk of my car and one between the seats."

Got this old boy to help me put the ponies in, and we didn't have a bit of trouble with them. We put one between the front and back seats and the other in the trunk, and I come right on to Vicksburg without a bit of trouble. Them horses weighed five or six hundred pounds a piece. They were pretty good-sized ponies.

But the damnedest thing I had happen was at Summit. I bought a bulldog, a full-blooded white bulldog, and I bought a bitch hound. I bought a bunch of turkeys too that day. I don't know why I bought them damn turkeys. So I put those turkeys and the dogs in my car and come on with them. I left the barn and drove about a hundred yards out to the main highway. As a rule, a male dog don't fight a bitch, but by the time I got to the highway, this bulldog started growling, "Grr. Grr. Grr."

I got out and got my walking cane. When I got through working them dogs over, they stayed in there, and I never heard another growl out of them, not another growl. I come on to Vicksburg. Mrs. Lum and I were living down at the corral then. So I took the dogs out of the car and tied them up and fed them. Mrs. Lum said, "Them's pretty dogs."

"Yeah. They didn't like each other at first, but they seem to get along fine with each other now."

The next morning I was going to a sale at Eudora, Arkansas. I fed them dogs good, throwed them back in the car, and drove to Eudora. Eudora's a dog town. Them people know dogs, and I thought I knew dogs pretty well. So I put the dogs in the auction one at a time. I put my bulldog in. He cost ten dollars, and he brought thirty-five. I put my hound bitch in, the one that was fighting the bulldog, and she brought fifty. So my dogs done all right. They both cost just ten a piece. I'd just as soon make money on a dog as a horse or anything else. I couldn't tell the difference in the money after it was made.

I've traded with women a lot of times, but I never knew any women traders. Some widow woman would buy mules and things like that, but I never knew of a woman trader. They've done everything else, and you'd have thought that there was some. I'm sure Tennessee, Kentucky, or some place like that had a few women traders. I'm just surmising. I don't know, but I never knew a woman horse trader. If I had, I'd tell you about some of the trades I had with them.

Now there were some good black traders. Some of them were

geniuses. When I was a small boy, they come through the country trading, and after I grew up, I always traded with them. Ellwood's old uncle, he used to come here and sell mules for me. I'd say, "Give that man whatever mules he wants." He'd be back the next week and would have traded and sold them all. He was a good trader. I've known some black traders that was better than Ellwood's uncle. I knew black traders in Georgia, in Alabama and all around. There's always been some good black traders.

I never tried to sell a man a horse in my life. I'd say, "Let me show you this horse." I never said, "Let me sell you this horse." And I never had any trouble selling horses.

Course if a child came in, I would look and get a horse that would suit him that didn't cost too much money. But when a trader come, I would be on my watch. There was a difference there.

I never found a horse I loved too much to trade. I loved them, but I just thought somebody else would love them better. I never was the kind that keeps a horse.

I knew a lot of gypsies, and I knew them awful early in life. I remember one time I swapped with a gypsy, and when I pushed up the tail, it come off in my hand. I looked, and there was a hook. It was an old bobtailed horse, and they had put a beautiful tail on him. I just hooked it back, brushed it, and kept going. I figured it was a secret. The gypsy didn't tell me about it. Wasn't any use for me to be mentioning it. Never did catch that horse back.[154]

A gypsy will trade for any damned thing on earth, and if he can't use it, he'll find somebody who can. That's the way I am too. Blue Eyes was a gypsy trader who came by Utica, and Grandpa Ray had a little mare with a black mane and tail. Oh, I loved that little mare. When they come to visit us, Grandma would drive the buggy, and she called her Grace. So Blue Eyes come by and traded Grandpa some old plug for his mare and drew ten or fifteen dollars boot. He cheated Grandpa out of that mare. She was worth a whole carload of horses like the one Blue Eyes traded for her.

That was Blue Eyes. He was smart. He worked the Delta and the hills of Mississippi. He'd start trading in the hills and then go on to the Delta. That's the way he done every year. When I got to Clarksdale the year that cotton went to a dollar a pound, the gypsy traders was as thick as them rocks out there. Blue Eyes was living

then, and I traded quite a bit with him. The gypsies would travel by
wagon and trade with everybody, and the best-looking horses they'd
have was the snides.[155] We'd go up to their camp, and I'd say, "You
want to trade one of them pretty ones?"

They'd say, "You Romishel?"[156]

"Yeah. Me Romishel."

They knew I wadn't no gypsy, but I was awake. Good God
Almighty, I run into lots and lots of traders. The gypsies was the
strongest when it come to snide dealings. Of course, they would
have a lot of good strong horses they had just robbed someone out
of. But they would take a snide, and they would straighten him up.
They'd fix him so you wouldn't notice his problem. The gypsies was
good hands with horses.

And the Irish gypsies were the best hands of horses there was.
They could doctor one better than anybody. A lot of Irish gypsies
got to where they'd travel with the black gypsies.

This little old boy come in, and his daddy says, "You didn't
trade with a gypsy did you?"

"No, I traded with a red-faced, blue-eyed fellow."

"Oh, goddamn." Right out of the frying pan and into the fire,
you know. He said, "That was an Irish gypsy. You was robbed. He's
the worst."

One day a fellow said, "What is them white fellows in them
gypsies' camp? Are they gypsies too?"

"Oh, man, don't talk. They are ten times worse than the gypsies, the Irish gypsies, you know."

The Irish gypsies were ten times stronger than the black ones.
The Irish gypsies were the strongest of them all. They'd outtrade
you and they'd rob you. Do both. You was robbed and cheated any
time you traded with them. They called fellows like us yokels 'cause
any time we traded with them, we was robbed. They had the prettiest horses you nearly ever saw, and the prettiest ones was always the
worst ones.

A lot of the Irish used slang when they'd talk among themselves. They understood it, but others didn't. Like they would say
"cat eye" for a hundred-dollar bill. Once a fellow come up with a
little white horse and said, "What are you going to give for him,
Ray?"

"If he's what I think he is, I'm going to give you a cat eye for him."

"If a cat eye is what I think it is, you just bought yourself a horse."

Well, that was all that was said. I got his horse and wished he had a dozen more like it. He was a sweet little horse. I'd have paid more, but I didn't have to.

And a "shade" is another Irish word for a hundred-dollar bill. The Irish would be talking to one another, and some fellow would come up to buy a horse. Richard would say, "If you had about half a shade around here, it'd be nice and cool."

That was his way of saying they'd charge him fifty dollars for that damn horse. A shade and a cat eye is talk that Irish traders use. They'll talk about you all day, and you won't know what the hell they're saying. I learned the talk, but I never let them know that I knew it. I was awake all the time.

I had good trading all over the country. You really get to know a lot of people when you're in the horse business. Yeah, everybody's got something to trade. If they don't want to buy, they may want to sell, and you always try to do something with every man you meet.

Did you ever hear somebody say that a man buying a horse was paying for experience? That is as true as the Bible. There were very few people that knew much about a horse. They'd buy them to drive and ride, and in them days they all used horses. And wadn't but a few people knew about horses.

Them days, nearly every horse was some kind of a snide or screw. You kept your horse in a stall and fed him, and he didn't come out of there except when you got ready to hitch him to your buggy. He stayed in that stall until he went to weaving or chewing on wood. That's where the weavers and the stumpsuckers come from.

If a customer brought back a horse I had traded him, I'd always try to give him another horse. I never did try to give them the old horse back. That other horse would generally be gone, or I'd have him out of the way. All of them would say, "I'll give you anything to get my horse back."

"Uh huh. Well, I traded him off."

Which I had. He'd be already gone. I never saw any place where it was necessary to lie to a man in horse trades, but you handle the truth awful careful sometimes. Like a blind one, you'd say, "This horse don't look good."

"Well, he looks pretty good to me."

"Uh huh. Well, I just wanted to tell you. Okay."

You try to wake them up, but they sleep right on. You can tell them he's a screw, and they'll go right on and trade for him if they like the horse.

A good friend of mine, Tom Mackie, had a blind horse. It was a good horse with a beautiful tail and mane, but he was asleep. He didn't have any eyes, but he rode good. Tom was a good hand with a horse, and he'd ride that blind horse everywhere.

Jokes are like whiskey. They get better with age. I always try to tell a tale in a hurry. If you go too slow, there won't be anybody there but you when you finish. So I don't write a letter. I just send a telegram. Some people take a week to tell you something that turns out to be nothing. When people take that long to tell a joke, I say, "You'll have to send me a telegram, I ain't got time for a letter."

So when you tell a joke, be like the goat, "Ram, bam, thank you, ma'am."

Don't be like the Scotchman. Goddamn Scotchman, you tell him a joke today, and the son-of-a-bitch will laugh about it in church tomorrow. It'll take him that long to get the joke.

You got to tell a joke just right. Talking about just right makes me think of the fellow who had a man that worked for him. He said, "Jim, would you like a little drink?"

"Yes, sir, I sure would."

He give him a drink and said, "How was that, Jim?"

"Just right. Just right."

"What do you mean 'just right'?"

"Well, if it had been any worse I couldn't have drunk it, and if it had been any better, you wouldn't have given it to me."

That's about as true as the Bible.

They tell a lot of good ones on Arkansas. Did you hear the one about the boy that was riding a mule from Texas to Arkansas? Here was the state line, and they was just halfway across. The damn mule had his front feet over in Arkansas and his ass still in Texas, and the man was pulling on him. He was pulling on the son-of-a-gun, and finally the damn mule give in and come on across. The man said, "Good, by God. We've gone to Arkansas."

Well, some people heard him and thought he said, "Good-bye, God. We've gone to Arkansas." You could fix it either way, don't you see.

Yeah, I can tell you a lot of stories on Arkansas. One time I'd sold my mules in Arkansas and started down to listen to the lecture about astronomy. I didn't know anything about astronomy, but I knew a little bit more when I left there.

The lecture was on astronomy, and in the lecture the man told about everything that happens with the stars. He talked about the Jupiter star and the Milky Way and all the stars. He brought up all the stars, and finally he got around to the end of the story. There was a sun dog flying in the east and a moon dog[157] in the west, and they met over here in the northeast. Those sun and moon dogs was pretty close together all down through there.

There was a hog raiser next to me, and all that son-of-a-bitch remembered was those sun dogs. So, the speaker was nice as he could be, and when he got through, he says, "If any of you gentlemen would like to ask questions about astronomy, I'd be so glad to answer to the best of my ability."

The whole crowd liked him, and I don't say that the hog raiser didn't like him too. Well, here comes this long-whiskered son-of-a-bitch walking right down. "I'd like to ask you a question."

"Yes, come right up. Won't you have a seat, please." Just as nice to him as he could be. "Now then. What was your question?"

"I want to know if sun dogs have knots on their peckers."

So I thought, well, that's the damnedest one I've heard. The only dog he knew about was an old hound dog. He didn't know nothing about a sun dog, but he was trying to find out. I was all for him. He was Pete McGraw from Arkansas, chawed more tobacco than his paw could chaw. You see, even an old coon can git treed by a pup, and that astronomy fellow was up a tree and couldn't git down.

I was at Greenville selling mules once, and a fellow said, "Ray, you want to come over to Glory Feed Company?" Glory Company was the biggest feed dealers in Mississippi at that time. They had a big mill at Greenville. "I want to take you over there and show you some ferrets. Did you ever see a ferret?"

"No, I don't believe I did. I've never even read about them."

"I figured you hadn't. Well, this is worth seeing."

So over to the Glory Company we went. They had a warehouse, and the porch came out here where they load the feed. When we got there, the ferrets were stretched out on that porch just like minks. Their heads and tails are about that long. Here they were all stretched out. A man was working in the warehouse, and I said, "How many of these you got here?"

He told me about how many and said, "We got them last year to catch the rats."

"Are they really rat catchers?"

"There's no rats here now."

None. A damn rat comes along, and the ferret runs in a hole after him. And when they come out, they come out with the son-of-a-bitch. They are the greatest. Well, we looked at them, and we couldn't see them work, of course. You would never see a cat catch a rat either, you know. The man said they were losing ten thousand dollars a year to the rats when they got the ferrets. Now there wasn't any feed wasted. There were no rats there.

Come in the shop and meet these folks. This is Dr. Yarborough. That's Mr. Freeman. And these girls here, they won't call their names. They work Uncle Ray to death. This is little Judy here. She's a Lum, and this is Betsy Lum. She's named after her mother. Her mother's got all them kids named pretty near alike.

Now these saddles here, I get most of them from Dallas, and I get my harnesses and bridles from El Paso. I buy most of it in the West cause it's cheaper there. I keep everything here that goes on a horse.

I got leather collars that cost twenty dollars. These are the cheapest collars you'll find in Vicksburg. I stay at the shop out here on Saturdays, and a lot of customers come in. They keep me busy on Sunday too. People are always calling wanting a rope or a whip or a bridle, something pertaining to a horse.

My car stays full of saddles all the time. I'm too lazy, I guess, to take them out. When I go to a sale, I take the saddles out and put them on display on the car, and when I finish the sale, I load back in what I haven't sold.

I sell lots of stuff at cost. People that I've always known come up and expect to buy gear like they bought it twenty years ago. I sell boots for fifteen dollars, and most people sell them for twenty and twenty-five dollars. When I need more gear, I get on the phone, and in a couple of days it's here. So I don't have to make those long trips anymore. When I was young, I'd drive down to Mexico and back. I always liked to go into Mexico. Mexicans make a good many of these saddles.

Come in, young man. How're you doing? Look around my store and see if I've got anything you can use. He wants a wallet just like the one I got right here. That's a good one. Costs three and a half. If you don't like it, I'll try my best to get another. I'm going to talk to that wallet fellow tonight. He's in Dallas. Let me write that down here. "Get wallets." Yours about worn out, huh?

You want a slick saddle?[158] I don't know whether we got a slick saddle or not. No, I don't see one, but I'm looking for some to come today. I've handled saddles always. I don't know why, but I love saddles. I got an order yesterday for one. Somebody called out here, "Ray, can you get an old McClellan saddle?"[159]

"It'll be an old one if I get it." I know they're not making new ones.

Do you need a whip? Let me show you how this one cracks. Oh good God, that is a good whip. Every shot is a pigeon, sometimes two. I've had people pick up a whip and say, "How do you use them?"

Well, I don't ever answer them. You don't want to be rude to them. You know Babe Ruth could stand and knock a home run, and you could stand there and see him do it. But you couldn't do it. So people say, "How do you do that?"

I don't mean to be rude, but I just show them. No trouble for me to crack a whip. Someone said the other day, "No wonder you can do it. You have been doing it for sixty years."

Longer than that, but it didn't take me that long to learn how to use a whip.

You boys help yourself to a Coke when you get ready. You

chewing tobacco, are you? Well, chew my tobacco and spit my juice!

Come in. Shake hands and make yourself acquainted. That's Teddy Conrad. How am I doing? I always say, "Fine."

That's the easiest thing to say. When you get as old as Mr. Ray is, you have to say, "Fine," because if I start telling what is wrong, there won't be anybody left but me when I get through. They'll all be gone. Now then, what was I looking for? I was looking for something.

Hello, young lady. It's good to see you. You get prettier all the time. What makes it, the older a man gets, the prettier the girls get? Meet this young lady. She lives down south of town. Her grandmother's name is Mrs. Owen.

Hey. How you, Snooks? How old are you? I'll guess your age is right at thirteen.

"I'm eleven."

Well, bless your heart. She looked like a thirteen-year-old. After she tells you, it's easier to guess. I'm going to quit guessing these girls' age. I was talking about thirteen, and she's eleven. Maybe I'm getting too old.

Pretty little girl with a cute little figure.

Stay away, boys, till I git a little bigger.

Yeah, she's pretty. She was a cute little girl, wadn't she?

I called a little girl Snooks the other day somewhere, and she said, "How'd you know my name?"

Sure 'nuff, that was her name. They all call her Snooks. I said, "Well, I was just guessing, hon."

Old summer's coming. Won't be long. They call it lazy summer. Oh, I'm getting lazy already. I'm ahead of it. One day I looked at a little boy and said, "You eleven years old?"

He said, "Yeah, but you looked at my teeth."

Now let me guess your age, son. You eleven now? I thought so. Don't shoot, I'm falling. Oh, these kids, I'll put them against the world.

Did you say you need a saddle blanket? Here's a pretty blanket for that little kid you got. You just want one? That one's twenty-five dollars.

How are you, young man? That's my son-in-law. Shake his

hand, by golly. He's got the cutest little wife in the world. I don't get to see her often. Tell her to come by and let me see how that baby boy's growing. He's big enough to get a saddle now.

Hey there. How do you do? That's one of my customers there. You got a horse with you now? Stand up there by the horse. Can you put your chin up on him there?

That horse will grow a little more. What age was he, two or three, when you got him? He's about a five-year-old now. Uh huh. Well, a horse will grow till he's seven years old if you feed him good. Did you know that, son? Oh yeah, you go to feeding them, and they'll grow.

This boy here helps me in the shop all the time. That's his rabbit dog there. He'll run a rabbit all day long, and he'll tree coons too. Oh, he's a smart son-of-a-gun.

How do you think this dog is bred, son? I don't think there is any bulldog in him. Did you get that tick off him, son? Throw it outside, way outside. By golly, I'll be tickie in here.

What was I doing? Oh, I was showing this pretty saddle here. That saddle blanket matches it just right. If you want it, that saddle is a hundred dollars. I'll give you the good blanket with it. Get up on it. Let me see how it fits you.

Now this girl was reared right down here at Yokena. Stayed with her grandmother there. Put your foot in over on the other side of the saddle there, honey. Now raise yourself up in the seat. It's just right for you. You wouldn't have to do anything but put it on your horse. I saw your horse down there, and he's a dandy. Yeah, I let her have a gray mare, and she got a colt off her. The gray mare passed away.

So you're going to buy this saddle. I'm going to give it to you for a hundred and give you the blanket with it. You buy it anywhere else, it will cost you a hundred and fifty. Okay, honey. Good to see you.

Make yourself at home around here. How old would you guess I am? Just guess. You don't have a week. They don't take that long to hang you. I am eighty-five. I'll be eighty-six my next birthday. That's right.

Now these little saddles here are just sixty-five dollars. Here comes your grandmother. She says that is too much? If you want a new saddle, you take this one, and you'll have thirty-five dollars to rattle in your pocket. I'm not trying to sell you any of them. I'm just trying to show them to you.

Howdy. Nice to see you. How you been? Where do you live when you're at home? Oh, you're right at Utica. That's where my mother was born, at Utica. She was a Ray. Utica, Mississippi. You know how to spell Utica? That's one town that spells like it sounds, "U-T-I-C-A," with one "t." Now you got it. Utica.

Hello, honey. You out here with your husband, are you? That's her husband there, folks. He believes he's seen you before. Listen to that. She says eighteen years ago I gave her a belt. Well, bless your heart. I'm proud that I gave it to you. I gave away a lot of belts. Time flies. Yeah, that was eighteen years ago.

I'm fine. I just need to have my speedometer set back. That's all. I'm having too many birthdays. But if I didn't have this many, I wouldn't be here. That's right too. It's an old game, and it will always go on. There will be changes, but it still goes back to the birds and the bees. Yes, sir, it goes back, and you still got to get it out of the soil.

Most of these folks will come in to buy a rope or a bridle or something pertaining to a horse, and I'll visit with them a while. They're all old friends.

Let's see, I needed to phone about them boots. The Acme Boot Company, Operator, please, ma'am. That's still at Clarksville, Tennessee. They've been there a hundred years, so we ought to be able to get them. Yes, you bet you can have my number. Six-three-six, seven-ought-seven-two is my number. Uh huh. Ray Lum. R-A-Y L-U-M. All right, let me talk to him.

Hey, young man. I got a letter from you wanting to know what kinds of boots I wanted from you. What I want is seconds in the best boot you got. I want some pointed toes. That's right. Beg your pardon?

Vicksburg. I been here for a hundred years. I been right here, Ray Lum, for a hundred years, and you been shipping me boots long as you been in business. That's all right. Send me twenty-five or thirty pair. Mix them up there, from sixes to twelves, and send them right away, because I am plumb out. You take care of that, and I'll appreciate it. All right. Okay. Bye now.

I was thinking about Red Nelson and all them old mule men. I guess Red's passed away. Red's gone on to that happy land where good mule traders go.

When you get eighty-five years old, you have outlived so many of your friends. That's the bad part of being old. You can't find anybody to talk to about things that happened back sixty or seventy years ago. They're all gone. I can't find anybody that knows about these landings on the Sunflower River where I used to take my mules. I told you about the fire horses that I took up there. I was trying to find the name of those landings on the Sunflower River, and nobody remembers them. I can't find a soul who remembers that landing where I took the horses and they rung the bell. So I give up on that.

I'm living in past history, don't you see. Yes, sir, there has been a lot of water run under the bridge since I came along. That's why I don't like to plan the future too far ahead. I don't ever like to think about dying, but I know good and well this: Young folks will die. Old folks have to die. Sooner or later we all going to be planted in that marble orchard. They used to say, "They cut down the old pine tree to make a coffin."[160]

Yeah, I was born June twenty-fifth, eighteen ninety-one. On my last birthday, by golly, my family got everything they could think of good to eat, and they cooked and sent it over. I wished you'd have come over, all of you. It was enough for us all to eat. I really had a nice birthday.

I bought five horses on my birthday. Bought five and sold two. I never did consider that it's a man's age that kills him. I think it's his health, and I think most everybody will agree with me on that. Most of the days I feel as good as I did when I was fifty or sixty years old. I still get up every day and make sales. I never miss an auction.

I guess I'm fortunate that I feel good most of the time. I don't have any recipe to give anybody. I got judgment enough to know that time is running out on me, 'cause I've had a lot of birthdays. What was I going to tell you? Oh! I'm planning on having a one-hundredth birthday. I was checking this morning, and I had two or three aunts and uncles that lived to be a hundred. Aunt Mary Reagan down there in Claiborne County lived to be a hundred and five. So my folks is long-living, and I'm hoping that I'll make it to a hundred. I don't know why not. I might be like the old fellow that was talking to the doctor. He said, "Doctor, I'd like to have my speedometer set back."

The doctor said, "I'll see what I can do for you. If you'll quit smoking these doggone cigarettes." The doctor didn't smoke, and he didn't need to quit, I guess. "If you quit smoking and quit drinking this mean whiskey, and quit running after these women, you're liable to live to be a hundred."

The old man says, "What the hell for?"

Done cut out everything he loved, by golly. He just left the doctor alone. He didn't like his prescription at all. You know, the older a man gets, the prettier the girls get. But I believe they were just as pretty then as they are now. By golly, there were pretty girls them days too.

Talking about pretty girls, I had one show up at the sale the other day, and she said she's praying for my health. She hopes I'll live to be a hundred. Bless her heart. If I live that long, I'll be like that fellow Methuselah. Oh, he lived to be two thousand years old. I have a brother that is ninety. People are just living longer now. We are never ready to go.

It's like the doctor that asked the old woman, "Have you ever been bedridden?"

"Oh yes, sir, hundreds of times, and twice in a buggy."

She was truthful, anyhow. She was an old-timer. And I was thinking about how the fellow asked the old woman, "Annie, how old does a woman get before she don't want a man?"

"I don't know, but they have to get older than I am."

All I need is to have my speedometer set back. I'd like to start all over at twenty-one. Let's see, I'm eighty-five now. I'd like to set it back sixty-four years. That would put me back in nineteen-twelve. I was selling mules. Oh good God, I was in business then. Twenty-one years old and doing a lot of business. Started when I was about twelve. Traded my first horse when I was about twelve. Then Little Eatum come along somewhere in there.

I can still auction, but my eyes are bad. That's why I don't auction now. The other day an auctioneer took a coughing spell in

Eudora, Arkansas. So they said, "Come on, Ray, and sell here till that boy gets all right."

Well, the boy never did get all right. He never did come back, and I sold for about two hours.

I still make all the sales each week. Tuesday I go to Fayette. Then on Wednesday I go to Hazelhurst to the auction there. That's my old stomping ground. I've gone to Hazelhurst for years, and I used to sell a lot of horses and mules there. Then on Thursday I go to Natchez, where my brother John[161] had a sale for forty years. Then on Friday I go to Eudora, Arkansas.

They used to tell me I had a photographic memory. If I ever saw anything, I'd remember it. I used to be good at memory, but it slips a little now. I catch myself asking my friends questions, and too many of them, I guess. Memory slips on you. I know mine does. When I was a baby, my father used to quote Scripture all the time. He'd guess at the past and guess at the future, and I catch myself doing it.

Time changes all things, and time waits for no man. Lots of things change in life, and you have to accept them. The old man said when you find your dog dead—it makes no difference how much you loved that dog—kick him. Be sure he's dead. Then look for another dog. There's no use for you to cry about him.

Sometimes I can remember everybody's name, and sometimes I forget them all. They say you live and learn, and then you die and forget it all. If there's nobody to pass it on to, you know you're going to forget it when you die. But sometimes you forget it all before you die. That's the part I was getting at. You don't have to die to forget it. Just stay here long enough, and you'll forget it.

But I'm not thinking about dying yet. Let me tell you the story about the old man that married the young girl. That hasn't been too long ago. Her name was Peaches. The old man had several million dollars, and he said to the girl's father, "I'm eighty years old, and I haven't got too long to stay in this world. I've got plenty of money, and I want to give you folks a million dollars for Peaches. I want to marry Peaches."

Oh, the story was in every paper in the United States and all over the world. That was Browning. He married Peaches.[162] So, anyhow, Browning says, "You don't have to let me know now. You can let me know tomorrow or the next day."

Well, he married Peaches and give her folks a million dollars. He said, "When I pass on, I'll leave Peaches the rest of my fortune."

He did leave her most of it. She was as pretty as a speckled pup under a red wagon. She was just like a flower.

People are like flowers. I don't know anything that compares any better. A rose blossoms, you know, and when it gets old, it fades.

Talking about Peaches reminded me of another young woman who married an old man, and when he started undressing, he took off both his legs and put them right on the floor. Then he took off his wig. He took out his glass eye and took out his false teeth, and whatever else he had that was false. When she come in, she looked and said, "I don't know which pile I'm going to sleep with."

She could jump over there or lay over there. Either one. That could have been a true story. Just 'cause they get maimed or lame, they don't stop. People go on, they do.

I've told you most of the good things that happened to me in life. There are not many states that I haven't seen. I been as far west as California. That's as far as I went, and I been up north too doggone far. Mexico is as far south as I've been. And I went east to Florida on the Atlantic. I run into the water there. I've seen a good bit of this country, and if I die tomorrow, there's not a hell of a lot of it I haven't done business in. That's the nice part of it. Done business in all of them states.

Yeah, Mr. Ray has come down that long, lonesome road. What is it they say? Look down that long, lonesome road before you travel along. Look down that long, lonesome road. I hate to say good-bye. I'll just say so-long.

Wholesale
HORSES AND MULES
CATTLE
GOATS
SHEEP AND
BREEDING BULLS

P. O. BOX 213
Vicksburg, Mississippi

Letters[†]

7/17-50 Mon night

Dear Mother & Sonny,

Came in here this morning and attended the sale. Bought 9 bulls. Already had 4 here. Sent them to Stephenville to sell Wed. Will go to Abilene tomorrow. Looked at a Mr. Trimble's cattle this evening after sale. Didn't trade with him. Called Mr. Hughes. Nice chat. No business. Haven't heard a word from Red. Didn't get him when I called. He was out. I think these bulls will make little money at Stephenville if I don't get orders for them. Bought 2 Reg. Angus Bulls today and Reg. Angus heifer. My car is doing fine. I have never driven it over 50 and don't think I will for 5,000 miles. I believe is best for car—hope you and Sonny feeling fine. And getting some thing done wish some one would buy the heifers there [in Vicksburg] as I can buy heifers here cheaper—than we own them. Will have to try and think of some one for them. I can't think now of any one back there but the Morriseys who might buy them. Hope they're doing good. I have one bunch of cows and calves here they are to let me know about Friday. They are worth coming

† The letters as printed here are direct transcriptions. I've retained Lum's spelling and punctuation.

217

back to see about—I believe there is some place they will make money. And there is 10 cows & calves at winter Texas would make more there. Talk with Allen [Lum's brother]—write me when they are opening. If they want them I will have load them —I think every day I will find something that will make money. I think I will send the Littleton cows to market before I come in. As they're old cows and won't do to go too far. I think in week or so they will make little money. Hope so any way. Well I am tired and will say good night and write again when I have a chance—Love to you and Sonny

Daddy,

Love to Mabel—

Mr Bill Ferris

New Haven Conn.

Dear Bill I miss you like
my Right Arm. Just talked
with your Dad. He was happy
got a good rain although it came
to Late for some Crops. saved lot
of them. Soy Beans are good in most
Places. John Denovan here Yesterday drive
up to my Place on River. Wish you
had been Along. I was down to Hazelhurst
Last Wed. Saw the old Colored Man that
had sign said he would keep it.
So Hury up Come back. I told your Dad
About lawyer Mollison that went
to Chicago. And 40 young blks Visited
me at Hotel there. he asked me if I
gave you that Story I told him
if I didn't I would. Bill
Find Sue For me Tell her to send
me write up I sent her on Abe Lincloln
one more Time Samanthey Playing on Jusie

Harp. I will Put in note to her.
Write me or call Soon Your Friend Ray—

[9/4/76]

Friday Sept 10-76

Dear Friend Bill seems like
ages Since I heard from you. Miss
seeing you so much. I am all alone
now Lady has gone back to N.O.
but said she would come again so
Well she is lots of help and company.
Bill did I send you clipping on Preacher's
Racing donkey. If I didnt you Should
have it. I am giving E. Post article
    Copy from Chicago Paper
on Lester Mollison—I used to Eat
Chicken in his Pick Wick res—
He is a Doodler. I knew him
real well. I am gong to take the
Clipping fron Chicago Press to Cashman
if he doesn't run it I will mail
to you, of course you and I don't
think he will have much choice to
be elected. but he hs going to be
interesting I believe. Bill I believe
these Cattle are going to take of quite
a bit more. you know what they say
about whiskey. Long as the make
it they will drink it
and long as they drink
it they will make it
is way with Cattle. long as they
grow them they will eat them and
long as they eat them they will grow
them. Well we had some rain yesterday I
know your Dad was Proud to get it

if you dont get paper with
Article on matchbox, I will send
you clipping I have from Chicago
Paper—well I will say good
bye for now—have Sue write me
and Send Clipping on Abe where
it says one more Time. Vick was
Out to see me yesterday. I asked him
to be sure and have all your sticks
ready. before you come back. Write
or call me on Receipt of this
    I am Best Wishes Ray—

      9-28-76

Dear Bill Seems like it has been months since
you were here. Talked with your mother Sun.—I told
her try and get you to come for Thanksgiving. Bill
I am guessing your Folks are all for Mr. Ford
I would hate to see Mr. Carter Beat him I
think Ford much better for all the People—
was Surprised at Eastland and Stennis
endorsing Carter. I bet a man at Hazelhurst
last Wed. $100.00 said he was going to bet
me some more. the folks at Utica and
Hazlehurst asked about you Wanted
to know when I was going to bring you
back with me. So Hurry up and make
A Visit to Miss. The N.O. Girl has
gone home. Don't think she will be
back until Xmas. She drove me Places
and was Very good Cook. I am hoping
She doesn't come back until Xmas—
Vic, Elwood and I went last night
to hear Jerry Clower. We had a nice
Visit with him. he knew lots of People
at Yazoo City that I knew—

Elwood told him that he Jerry
Sold the layds[?]—and he first Delivered
them. Went over big with Jerry. And Vick
was in good spirits was bad about Cliff
and Mars Bro—he was Killed in Plane
Crash—near Natchez They are having good
weather to gather the crops. Earl my nephew
got the bean here at home Sat. and is
Picking Cotton over on river Say it will
make over 2 Bales to acre. I had a
fall down in to lake when rope Broke I was
Pulling up hill on. have put me on a new—
Rope now—Yazoo is about to go dry and
Miss. is at it lowest in years was awful
accident on river in N.O. area Pilot
was drunk and ran in to Ferry what
one drunk can do in that case Killed 75
People. well bill will say bye for
now. if you think of any thing I
Can do for you just let me know
And I will be Caught trying
Say Hello to our Friend
Warner has he traded the Alightor yet.
With every good wish for your health
and Happiness Love Ray of Sunshine
Try and get Sue write me a line.

11-30-76

Dear Bill. Was happy to get your letter. Your
mother and Grey ran by on Sat 20—all my folks
were here including W.B. and Family. so we were
having Family reunion. Tell Sue I was happy to
hear from her. Also give my best to Warners—
Every thing out on Lake here about to dry up—
have some of Conn weather this morning down to 17
Earl—has his crop gathered. Soy bean made 40 bu

to acre. Cotton 2½ Bales to acre—river look like it
dry up. hope Mr. Carter makes good President I
think he has lots of us guessing. Well Vick says he
is working on your sticks. I expect to have
another done to sell for some benefit
before or during the Holiday. The Carraways
Asked about you when you come We
will make the Rounds. Write Soon

                    Ray of Sunshine
                    Every good wish.

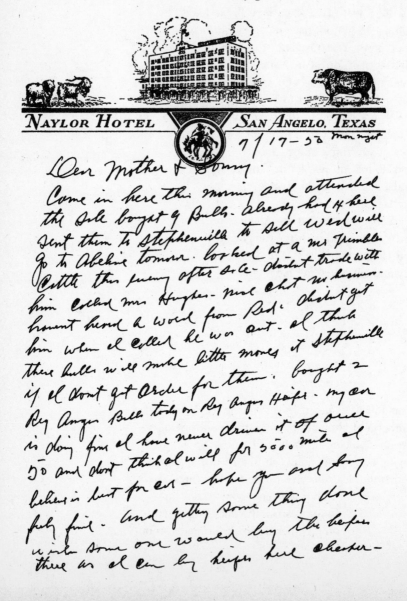

than we own them will have to try
and think of some one for them. I cant
think now of any one back there but the
morriseys who might buy them. hoke they are
doing good. I have one hunder of cow & calves
here they are to let me know obot Friday
they are worth coming back to see obot —
I believe there is some place they will
make money. And there is a cow & calves
at winter flefor would make more than sold
to Allen — write me when they ore sfering if
they want them I will have lost they —
I think every day I will find some thy
that will make money I think I will
send the littleton cows to market before I
come in. As they ore old cows and was
ols to fo to fos — I think in week

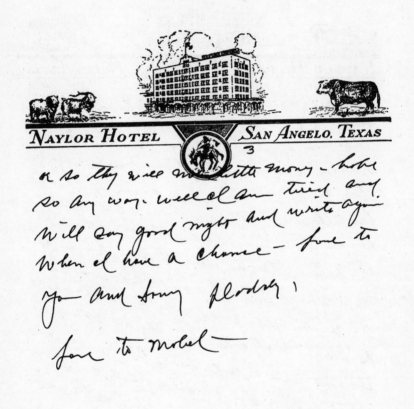

NAYLOR HOTEL · SAN ANGELO, TEXAS

3

or so they will me a little money - hope
so any way. well I am tired and
will say good night and write again
when I have a chance - love to
you and Tommy gladly -

love to Mabel —

Bibliographic Essay

MULES IN AMERICAN HISTORY

During the colonial period an active trade in mules and horses existed in New England. An excellent overview of the role of mules in the United States is James Westfall Thompson, *A History of Livestock Raising in the United States,* Agricultural Historical Series No. 5, U.S. Department of Agriculture (November 1942). William B. Weeden treats the role of mules in New England in *Economic and Social History of New England,* vol. 2 (Boston, 1891). Two interesting general studies of mules are Theodore H. Savory, "The Mule," *Scientific American* (December 1970), pp. 102–9, and Charles W. Burkett, "Mule," *Cyclopedia of American Agriculture,* vol. 3 (New York, 1908), pp. 507–10.

The most comprehensive survey of the mule in southern history is Robert Byron Lamb, *The Mule in Southern Agriculture* (Berkeley, 1963). Lamb and W. B. Tegetmeier, *Horses, Asses, Zebras, Mules and Mule Breeding* (London, 1895), describe George Washington's role as the "father" of American mule breeding. Ulrich B. Phillips explores the preference of Southerners for mules in *Life and Labor in the Old South* (Boston, 1957), pp. 134–35. Frederick Law Olmsted penned vivid firsthand accounts of mules in the antebellum South in *A Journey in the Seaboard Slave States in the Years 1853–1854, with Remarks on Their Economy* (New York, 1904), pp. 55–56. Similar accounts are included in James Silk Buckingham, *The Slave States of America,* vol. II (London, 1842), p. 203. J. V. Harper describes Irish traders who drove herds of mules into the South during the antebellum period in "Irish Traveller Cant," M.A. thesis, University of Georgia, 1969, p. 24.

MULES IN THE SOUTH

Ulrich B. Phillips explores the common fate of mules and black slaves in two books, *American Negro Slavery* (Baton Rouge, 1966), p. 242, and *Plantation and Frontier Documents, 1649–1863,* vol. I (New York, 1969), p. 175. Eugene D. Genovese describes how black lives were linked with mules in *The Political Economy of Slavery* (New York, 1965), pp. 244–46, 276–77. Jack Temple Kirby eloquently traces the role of mules' southern history in "Men, Mules, Moonshine, Music—Destiny," *Rural Worlds Lost: The American South 1920–1960* (Baton Rouge, 1987), pp. 195–204.

Blacks developed a large body of songs, tales, superstition, and jokes about the mule. Examples are included in Paul Oliver, *The Meaning of the Blues* (New York, 1966), pp. 47, 112; Richard Dorson, *American Negro Folktales* (New York, 1967), pp. 114, 139, 306; Zora Neale Hurston, *Mules and Men* (New York, 1970), pp. 154, 217; William Ferris, "Black Folklore from the Mississippi Delta," Ph.D. Dissertation (University of Pennsylvania, 1969), pp. 140–41, 199, Newbell Niles Puckett, *The Magic and Folk Beliefs of the Southern Negro* (New York, 1969), pp. 45–46, 114, 139, 319, 354, 461, 475, 506, 533, 545.

William Faulkner writes about the skill blacks showed in handling mules and the belief that they could read the animal's thoughts in his novel *Light in August* (New York, 1950), p. 9. Frank T. Welch reflects similarly in *The Plantation Land Tenure System in Mississippi,* Mississippi Agriculture Experiment Station Agricultural College, Bulletin No. 385 (June 1943), p. 40.

Alfred G. Smith presents southern arguments favoring mules over other animals in "Our Migratory Mules," *Country Gentleman,* vol. 88 (February 17, 1923), p. 9, and *House Executive Documents, U.S. Patent Office Report of the Commissioner of Patents for the year 1849,* 31st Congress, 1st Session (Washington, D.C., 1850), p. 160. Susan Dabney Smedes recalls in detail how mules were worked on her family plantation in *Memorials of a Southern Planter* (New York, 1890), pp. 69–70, 92, 100.

George M. Rommel details advice on how to raise mules in the South in "Suggestions for Horse and Mule Raising in the South," *Twenty-third Annual Report of the Bureau of Animal Industry for the Year 1906* (Washington, D.C., 1908); Will Rogers and others describe impressive large sales of southern mules in: Will Rogers, "Maury County Mules," McNaught Syndicated Article (March 3, 1935), reprinted in *The Daily Herald* (Columbia, Tennessee, April 13, 1975), p. 20; Lorraine A. Allen, "The Largest Mule Farm in the World," *Overland Monthly* (April 1914), pp. 379–82; "Columbia Is Mule Market," *Nashville Tennessean and the Nashville American* (November 11, 1916), p. 2; "Big Mule Day at Columbia," *Nashville Tennessean and the Nashville American* (December 7, 1916), p. 7.

Researchers at agricultural experiment stations in both the nineteenth and twentieth centuries published numerous bulletins on mules. These include B. D. Raskopf and M. T. Danner, *Public Horse and Mule Market at Nashville,* Tennessee Agricultural Experiment Station, Rural Research Series, Monograph No 219 (Knoxville, 1947), p. iv; Lewis E. Long, *Farm Power in the Yazoo Mississippi Delta,* Mississippi Agricultural Experiment Station Agricultural Bulletin No. 295, pp. 1–30; J. J. Csorba, *The Use of Horses and Mules on Farms,* Agricultural Research Service ARS 43-94, U.S. Department of Agriculture (Washington, D.C., March 1959); H. R. Duncan and R. L. Murphree, *Breeding of Jackstock,* Agricultural Experiment Station Bulletin No. 262, the University of Tennessee at Knoxville (June 1957); J. L. Jones, "The Mule; Its Uses, How to Breed, Grow, Prepare for the Market and Sell," *Eighth and Ninth Reports of the Bureau of Animal Industry for the Years 1891 and 1892* (Washington, D.C., 1893), pp. 335–42; R. Kuykendall, "Feeding Experiments with Farm Work Mules, Delta Experiment Station, Stoneville, Mississippi," *Bulletin* (Mississippi

Agricultural Experiment Station Agricultural College, 1935), pp. 1–24; G. S. Templeton, "Mule Feeding Experiments" (in two parts), *Bulletin,* Mississippi Agricultural Experiment Station, No. 244, 1927, pp. 1–31, and No. 270, 1929, pp. 1–38; J. T. Warder, "Mule Raising," *Report of the Commissioner of Agriculture for the Year 1863* (Washington, D.C., 1862), pp. 180–90.

MULES IN THE WEST

The mule was essential in the settlement of the American West. Albert C. Leighton details the animal's contributions in "The Mule as Cultural Invention," *Technology and Culture,* vol. 8 (January 1967), p. 51; Floyd F. Ewing, Jr., "The Mule as a Factor in the Development of the Southwest," *Arizona and the West,* vol. 5 (Winter 1963).

John Ashton describes the use of mules in nineteenth-century western pack trains in "History of Jack Stock and Mules in Missouri," *Monthly Bulletin,* Missouri State Board of Agriculture (August 1924), pp. 1–63; Joseph T. Hill, *Ewing Young in the Fur Trade of the Far Southwest, 1822–1834* (Eugene, Oregon, 1923), pp. 25–30; Vincent Geiger and Wakeman Bryerly, *Trail to California* (New Haven, 1962); Max L. Moorehead, *The Apache Frontier* (Norman, Oklahoma, 1968), pp. 39–40, 91–112, 191, 195, 206, 230, 264; Moorehead, "Spanish Transportation in the Southwest, 1540–1846," *New Mexico Historical Review,* vol. 32 (April 1957), p. 109; Moorehead, *New Mexico's Royal Road: Trade and Travel on the Chihuahua Trail* (Norman, Oklahoma, 1958) p. 86; W. D. Smithers, "Mule Packs and Wagon Trains" (in three parts), *The Western Horseman* (February 1965), pp. 52–53, 102–3 (part 1); (March 1965), pp. 28–29, 96–98 (part 2); (April 1965), pp. 60–61, 96–99 (part 3).

Western writers repeatedly stressed their preference for mules over oxen and horses. R. L. Duffis eloquently presents their arguments in *The Santa Fe Trail* (New York, 1931), pp. 133–34; see also Josiah Gregg, *Commerce on the Prairies,* Max L. Moorehead, ed. (Norman, Oklahoma, 1954), p. 24; Vincent Geiger and Wakeman Bryerly, *Trail to California* (New Haven, 1962), p. 40; Merrill T.

Mattes, *The Great Platte River Road,* vol. 25, Nebraska State Historical Publications, 1971, p. 38; James Josiah Webb, *Adventures in the Santa Fe Trade, 1844–1847,* Ralph P. Bieber, ed. (Glendale, California, 1931), p. 70.

Colorful teamsters with mule teams pulled loads of 45,000 pounds of cargo in the nineteenth century. Arnold R. Rojas chronicled the exploits of these men and their animals in *Last of the Vaqueros* (Fresno, California, 1960), p. 142; John Randolph Spears, *Illustrated Sketches of Death Valley* (New York, 1892), p. 83; Robert Rineland, "Death Valley Borax Beds," *Overland Monthly,* vol. 54 (July 1909), p. 359; A. W. Whitehead, "Handling a Wagon Train," *Journal of the United States Cavalry Association,* vol. 17 (April 1907), p. 649; and James W. Steele, *Frontier Army Sketches* (Albuquerque, 1969), p. 306.

H. W. Daly details the key role of mules in western military campaigns by leaders such as General Custer in "The Geronimo Campaign," *Arizona Historical Review,* vol. 3 (July 1930), pp. 31–32; John A. Rand, "Nine Hundred Mules," *The New Yorker* (November 27, 1954), p. 174; Fairfax Downey, *Army Mules* (New York, 1946), p. 34; *House Executive Documents, Report for the Year Ending 30th June 1877,* vol. 2, 45th Congress, 2nd Session, 1877, 1794, pp. 180–81; Edward S. Farrow, *Camping on the Trail* (Philadelphia, 1903), p. 128; Randolph B. Marcy, *The Prairie Traveler* (New York, 1859), p. 27; H. W. Daly, "Pack Transportation," *Journal of the United States Cavalry Association,* vol. 17 (July 1906), p. 78.

Military manuals detailing the skills required to pack mules using saddles and ropes include: Captain H. W. Lawton, *Instructions for Using Moore's Improved Pack Saddle,* Quartermaster General's Office (Washington, D.C., 1881), pp. 8–9; Daniel F. McCarthy (Captain), *Manual of Instructions for Quartermasters Serving in the Field* (Washington, D.C., 1900), pp. 71–83, 95–99, 105–14; and J. L. Hines (Major General), *Training Pack Animals,* Training Regulations no. 360-20, prepared by Quartermaster General, War Department, Washington, January 11, 1926.

Emmett M. Essin describes skilled packers in "Mules, Packs, and Packtrains," *Southwestern Historical Quarterly,* vol. 74 (July 1970), p. 63, and H. L. Scott, "The Skilled Packer," *Journal of the United States Cavalry Association,* vol. 17 (January 1907), p. 52.

THE TRADER

Anthropological studies of markets and marketplaces suggest why the trader is a familiar figure in every culture. Sidney W. Mintz, Luis Mott, and Robert H. Silin list important studies in "A Supplementary Bibliography on Marketing and Marketplaces," Exchange Bibliography 792 (Monticello, Illinois, n.d.). Folklore scholars explore the lives of traders and their tales in books and articles. Antti Aarne and Stith Thompson list folktales celebrating the trader found in cultures throughout the world in *The Types of the Folktale* (Helsinki, 1964), p. 463. Roger J. Welsch published an outstanding anthology of horse-trading tales collected by the Nebraska Federal Writers Project in *Mister, You Got Yourself a Horse* (Lincoln, Nebraska, 1981). Amanda Dargan and Steven Zeitlin profile American street markets and the lore of their traders and auctioneers in "American Talkers: Expressive Styles and Occupational Choice," *Journal of American Folklore* (January–March, 1983), vol. 96, no. 379, pp. 3–33. Simon Bronner presents similar traditions of street markets and traders in "Street Cries and Peddler Traditions in Contemporary Perspective," *New York Folklore Quarterly* (1976), vol. 32, pp. 2–15. Richard Bauman describes dog traders in Canton, Texas, and includes an excellent bibliography of folktale scholarship in " 'Any Man Who Keeps More'n One Hound'll Lie to You': A Contextual Study of Expressive Lying," *Story, Performance, and Event* (Cambridge, 1986), pp. 1–10, 117–27. Leroy Judson Daniels recalls his horse trades as told to Helen S. Herrick in *Tales of an Old Horsetrader: The First Hundred Years* (Iowa City, 1987).

Numerous British and American publications warned horsemen about the trader. Two of the more colorful are: *How to Buy a Horse . . . An Exposition of the Tricks Frequently Practiced in the Sale of Unsound Horses* (London, 1840); Henry Bracken, *Ten Minutes Advice to Every Gentleman Going to Purchase a Horse Out of a Dealer, Jockey, or Groom's Stables. In Which Are Laid Down Established Rules for Discovering the Perfections and Blemishes of the Noble Animal* (Philadelphia, 1787); and Stephen Van Rensselaer, *Points on Buying a Horse* (Newark, N.J., 1904).

Will Rogers acknowledges that though he is "the world's worst horse trader . . . I love to trade" in *The Autobiography of Will*

Rogers (Boston, 1949), p. 326. Ben Green presents the horse trader's philosophy in *Horse Conformation and Hoss Trades of Yesteryear* (Cumby, Texas, 1963) and S. G. Thigpen offers similar reflections in "The Horse Trader," *A Boy in Rural Mississippi* (1966). John Ashton discusses one of the great nineteenth-century mule traders, Luke McClure Emerson, and compares him to P. T. Barnum in "History of Jack Stock and Mules in Missouri," *Monthly Bulletin* (August 1924), pp. 41–42. Two excellent guides to the terms that traders use are J. Warren Evans, Anthony Borton, Harold F. Hintz, and L. Dale Van Vleck, *The Horse* (San Francisco, 1977), and Margaret Cabell Self, *The Horseman's Encyclopedia* (New York, 1963).

GYPSY TRADERS

Jean-Paul Clebert offers an excellent description of gypsy horse traders in Europe in *The Gypsies* (Baltimore, 1969), pp. 135–37; Jan Yoors, *The Gypsies* (New York, 1967), p. 101; and Kamill Erdos, "Gypsy Horse Dealers in Hungary," *Journal of the Gypsy Lore Society,* vol. 38 (pps. 1 and 2). Irving Brown describes storytelling and humor among gypsy traders in the United States in *Gypsy Fires in America* (Port Washington, N.Y., 1972), p. 159.

IRISH TRADERS

Patrick Green [Padraig Mac Greine] surveys the history of Irish tinkers and travelers in nineteenth-century Ireland in "Irish Tinkers or 'Travelers,' " *Bealoideas,* vol. 4 (1931), pp. 170–86. Green discusses the language of the Irish traders in "Some Notes on Tinkers and Their 'Cant,' " *Bealoideas,* vol. 4 (1934), pp. 259–63, and "Further Notes on Tinkers' 'Cant,' " *Bealoideas,* vol. 3 (1932), pp. 290–303. Other discussions of Irish cant include Kune Meyer, "On the Origin and the Age of Shelta," *Journal of the Gypsy Lore Society,* (1891), pp. 257–66, and "The Secret Languages of Ireland," *Journal of the Gypsy Lore Society,* vol. 2 (January 1909), pp. 241–46; H. L. Mencken, *The American Language: An Inquiry into the Devel-*

opment of English in the United States (New York, 1965), p. 578; Albert Thomas Sinclair, *American Gypsies* (New York, 1917), p. 9; Alistair Reid, "A Reporter at Large: The Travellers," *The New Yorker* (August 18, 1962), pp. 37–66; Ian F. Hancock, "Shelta: A Problem of Classification," *Pidgin-Creole Studies: Current Trends and Prospects* (Washington, D.C., 1974), pp. 130–37.

Marguerite Riordan captures the colorful lives of Irish traders in the twentieth-century South in "The Irish Mule Traders," *American Cattle Producer* (October 1950), pp. 9–10, 25–28; Edwin Muller, "Roving the South with the Irish Horse Traders," *Reader's Digest* (July 1941), pp. 59–63; George E. Ryan, "The Irish Travelers," *Ave Maria* (March 18, 1967), p. 16; J. V. Harper, "Irish Traveler Cant: An Historical, Structural, and Sociolinguistic Study of an Argot," M.A. thesis (University of Georgia, 1969); and J. V. Harper and C. Hudson, "Irish Traveler Cant in Its Social Setting," *Southern Folklore Quarterly,* vol. 37 (June 1973), pp. 101–4.

YANKEE TRADERS

Yankee traders were a favorite topic for writers in the nineteenth century. Thomas Chandler Haliburton has one of the earliest accounts of a Yankee trader in *The Clockmaker; or The Sayings and Doings of Sam Slick, of Slicksville* (Philadelphia, 1840). P. T. Barnum argues that Yankee traders had a prominent place in nineteenth-century American culture in *Funny Stories* (New York, 1890), pp. 83–90, 103–5, 161–62. Barnum's arguments are seconded by Josh Billings [Henry Wheeler Shaw], "The Kuntry Hoss Jockey," in *Old Probability* in *The Complete Works of Josh Billings* (Sidney, 1919), and by Alice Morse Earle, *Stage Coach and Tavern Days* (New York, 1900), pp. 388–93. Richard Wright describes Yankee traders who dealt in both clocks and mules in *Hawkers and Walkers in Early America* (Philadelphia, 1927), pp. 66, 80. B. A. Botkin describes New England horse traders and their tricks in "Horse Jockeys (Dealers or Tricks)," *A Treasury of New England Folklore* (New York, 1965), pp. 22–29.

SOUTHERN TRADERS

Joseph Baldwin describes the culture of nineteenth-century traders in the American South in *The Flush Times of Alabama and Mississippi* (New York, 1853), p. 236, as does Robert Byron Lamb in *The Mule in Southern Agriculture* (Berkeley, 1963), pp. 18–19. An excellent study of the tales of southern horse traders is Page Holmes, "An analysis of Horsetrading Narratives," M.A. thesis, University of North Carolina (Chapel Hill, 1972). An interesting description of twentieth-century Georgia traders is "Horse Trading," *Foxfire*, vol. 10, no. 1 (Spring 1976), pp. 40–71.

Thad Snow presents descriptions of twentieth-century southern traders in "Proud Kate, the Aristocratic Mule," *Harper's Magazine* (July 1954), pp. 64–65; Alfred G. Smith, "Our Migratory Mules," *Country Gentleman* (February 17, 1923), p. 9; and John Ashton, "History of Jack Stock and Mules in Missouri," *Monthly Bulletin*, Missouri State Board of Agriculture (August 1924), p. 55.

S. G. Thigpen recalls Manuel Allen, a black trader in Mississippi, in "The Horse Trader," *A Boy in Rural Mississippi* (Picayune, Mississippi, 1966), pp. 168–70. Nate Shaw, a twentieth-century black farmer in Alabama, describes his mule trades in Theodore Rosengarten, *All God's Dangers* (New York, 1974), pp. 198–99.

WESTERN TRADERS

Many southern traders moved West to find their fortunes. One of the best known of these nineteenth-century traders, D. H. Snyder, is described in John M. Sharpe, "Experiences of a Texas Pioneer," *The Trail Drivers of Texas,* John Marvin Hunter, ed. (Nashville, 1925), pp. 722–23, and in James K. Greer, *Bois d'Arc to Barbed Wire* (Dallas, 1936). Twentieth-century western traders from the Deep South, such as Ray Lum and Jim Merritt, are recalled in Ben Green, *Horse Conformation and Hoss Trades of Yesteryear* (Cumby, Texas, 1963), pp. 85, 90. Green was a veterinarian whose books about his career as a trader include *Ben K. Green Goes Back to Back* (Austin, 1970); *Horse Tradin'* (New York, 1971); *The Last Trail Drive Through Downtown Dallas* (Flagstaff, 1971); *Some More Horse*

Tradin' (New York, 1972); *The Village Horse Doctor* (New York, 1971); and *Wild Cow Tales* (New York, 1972).

J. Frank Dobie stressed the love of Westerners for the trade in his *Guide to the Life and Literature of the Southwest* (Dallas, 1969), p. 100; Howard Lamar offers an excellent portrait of the western trader in *The Trader on the American Frontier: Myth's Victim* (College Station, Texas, 1977); Rupert Richardson, *Comanche Barrier to South Plains Settlement* (Glendale, California, 1933), pp. 72–73, 89; Francis Harris, *Horses in America* (New York, 1971), pp. 74–75; Andy Adams, *Log of a Cowboy* (Lincoln, 1971), p. 104; David H. Coyner, *The Lost Trappers* (Albuquerque, 1970), pp. 19–20. J. Evett Haley chronicles the career of Texas rancher, Charles Goodnight, in *Charles Goodnight, Cowman and Plainsman* (Boston, 1936).

In both the sale and purchase of horses and mules, western military leaders usually were outmaneuvered by seasoned traders. Descriptions of their problems that are both fascinating and humorous are in *Manual for the (U.S.) Quartermaster's Department, United States Army, 1904* (Washington, D.C., 1904), p. 113; *House Executive Documents for the Year Ending June 30, 1884,* vol. 1, 2nd session, 48th Congress, 1884–85, p. 466; "Rules and Regulations (Regarding Procurement and Disposition of Horses and Mules)," General Orders, No. 43, Quartermaster General's Office (Washington, D.C., September 23, 1864).

Philip Ashton Rollins notes cowboys who at times engaged in horse trades in *The Cowboy: His Characteristics, His Equipment, and His Part in the Development of the West* (New York, 1936), p. 156. John A. Rand recalled one such cowpuncher, who was stationed in China in World War II and continued to trade for Chinese horses in Kunming, China, in "Nine Hundred Mules," *The New Yorker* (November 31, 1954), pp. 173–74.

THE TRADER IN AMERICAN FICTION

Traders and their stock of folk humor have provided an important resource for American writers. Walter Blair discusses this relationship in *Horse Sense in American Humor* (Chicago, 1942), pp. v–viii.

Mark Twain and Josh Billings joked with each other about mules, and Cyril Clemens describes their humorous exchanges in *Josh Billings* (Webster Groves, Missouri, 1932), pp. 124–26. Billings was an auctioneer and affirmed his love for the trade and its humor in *Essays* (Sidney, n.d.), p. xxiii, and in *Old Probability* (New York, 1879), pp. 18, 20, 28. P. T. Barnum, a contemporary and friend of both Twain and Billings, loved to trade and used the trader's style in his many promotional schemes. Neil Harris traces this fascinating story in *Humbug: The Art of P. T. Barnum* (Chicago, 1973).

Mark Twain celebrates both horses and storytelling in *A Horse's Tale* (London, 1907) and in *How to Tell a Story* (New York, 1897). Studies of Twain's use of storytelling in his fiction include Ray W. Frantz, Jr., "The Role of Folklore in Huckleberry Finn," *American Literature,* vol. 28 (1956), pp. 314–27, and Victor Royce West, *Folklore in the Works of Mark Twain* (Lincoln, 1930).

Southern traders and their humor shaped the fiction of nineteenth-century writers like Augustus Baldwin Longstreet whose "The Horse Swap" describes a trade in his *Georgia Scenes* (Gloucester, Massachusetts, 1970). An excellent overview of this literature is Henning Cohen and William Dillingham, *Humor of the Old Southwest* (Atlanta, 1975).

John Steinbeck includes a twentieth-century trade of mules for a truck in *The Grapes of Wrath* (New York, 1967), pp. 86–87. This is particularly interesting because many horse and mule traders became used-car dealers when their customers sold their animals.

William Faulkner celebrates the southern horse trader through the character of Pat Stamper in "Spotted Horses," *The Portable Faulkner,* Malcolm Cowley, ed. (New York, 1967). Cleanth Brooks feels Faulkner viewed the trader as "something of a conjurer and a magician" and offers a detailed study of Faulkner's work in *William Faulkner: The Yoknapatawpha County* (New Haven, 1964), p. 182. James Webb recalls Faulkner's love for the mule in James Wilson Webb and A. Wigfall Green, eds., *William Faulkner of Oxford* (Baton Rouge, 1965). Daniel Hoffman thoughtfully explores Faulkner's use of the trader and his lore in *Faulkner's Country Matters* (Baton Rouge, 1989), pp. 82–89.

THE AUCTION

Joan Samson explores the auction and the auctioneer in *The Auctioneer* (New York, 1975) and Ralph Cassady offers a contemporary view of the tradition in *Auctions and Auctioneering* (Berkeley, 1967). Robert Bethke compiled a "Bibliography of Auctioneering" in *Keystone Folklore Quarterly,* vol. 16 (Fall 1971), pp. 149–50. Daniel W. Steed, Jr., studies the southern auction in "Auctioneering as Folk Art" (1976), M.A. thesis, The Center for Intercultural and Folk Studies, Western Kentucky University.

Government bulletins on livestock auction markets include Clayton F. Brasington, Jr., *Livestock Auction Markets in the Appalachian Area: Methods and Facilities,* U.S. Department of Agriculture Marketing Service Research Report No. 309 (Washington, D.C., 1959); Clayton F. Brasington, Jr., and George E. Turner, *Livestock Auction Markets in the Southeast: Methods and Facilities,* U.S. Department of Agriculture Marketing Service Research Report No. 141 (Washington, D.C., 1956); Lewis D. Malphrus, *Livestock Auction Operations in South Carolina,* South Carolina Agricultural Experiment Station, Clemson Agricultural College, Bulletin No. 467 (December 1958); B. D. Raskopf and M. J. Danner, "Public Horse and Mule Market at Nashville, etc.," *Rural Research Series Monograph,* Tennessee Agricultural Experiment Station, No. 219 (Knoxville, 1947).

Daniel J. Steed, Jr., describes a traditional auctioneer in "To Be an Auctioneer, You've Got to Get It in Your Blood," *Kentucky Folklore Record,* vol. 20 (April–June 1974), pp. 42–43, and in "Traditional Auctioneering as a Folk Art," Folklore Research Paper, Western Kentucky University, 1974.

RAY LUM

Edward H. Lum traces Ray Lum's ancestry in his *Genealogy of the Lum Family* (Somerville, N.J., 1927). An interesting feature on Rocky Springs, Mississippi, Lum's birthplace, is "The Saga of Rocky Springs," *Southern Living* (March 1975), p. 22. Katy McCaleb

Headley describes the history of Rocky Springs in *Claiborne County: The Promised Land* (Port Gibson, Mississippi, 1776), pp. 77, 96, 176. In 1974 Lum participated in the Smithsonian Folklife Festival and was featured in "Profile of an Auctioneer (Ray Lum)," *Festival of American Folklife* (July 7, 1974), p. 2. The following year Lum visited Yale University, where he spoke at the National Humanities Institute and related his tales to a large audience of faculty and students on the Cross Campus Green. The visit was featured in the *New York Times* (October 1, 1975). Lum hosted a benefit auction for the American Field Service in Vicksburg, and Jamie Wilson Smith profiled his life in "Lum Is Auctioneer for AFS Attraction," *Vicksburg Sunday Post,* February 22, 1976, p. 16.

William Ferris and Judy Peiser presented Lum's folktales on a long-playing record and transcription, *Ray Lum: Mule Trader* (Memphis, 1976) [SF102-11-76] accompanied by an essay by Ferris, and in a twenty-minute film, *Ray Lum: Mule Trader* (Memphis, 1973). Both the record and the film are distributed by the Center for Southern Folklore, P.O. Box 226, Memphis, Tennessee 38103.

For published selections of Lum's tales and discussions of his life as a trader see William Ferris, "Ray Lum: Muletrader," *North Carolina Folklore Journal,* vol. XXI, no. 3 (September 1973), pp. 105–19; "Ray Lum's Horse and Mule Lore," *Mid South Folklore,* vol. vi, no. 2 (Spring 1978), pp. 15–50; "More of Ray Lum's Horse Sense," *Mid South Folklore,* vol. vi, no. 3 (Summer 1978), pp. 43–50; "The Horse Trader in Anglo-American History," *Mississippi Folklore Register,* vol. xii, no. 1 (Spring 1978), pp. 4–24, and "Mules in the South," *Mules and Mississippi* (Jackson: Mississippi Department of Archives, 1980), pp. 5–14, 46; "Ray Lum: Mule Trader, An Essay" (Memphis, 1976) accompanies the above-mentioned record, "Ray Lum: Muletrader." Ferris published a biographical portrait, "Ray Lum," in Charles Reagan Wilson and William Ferris, co-editors, *Encyclopedia of Southern Culture* (Chapel Hill, 1989), p. 509.

William Ferris's collection of personal correspondence, taped recordings and transcriptions, 16mm film, 35mm black and white negatives, and color slides of Ray Lum are part of the

University of Mississippi Archives and Special Collections. The University's Archives and Special Collections also holds the Ray Lum papers, which include personal letters, business ledgers, canceled checks, and other memorabilia of both Lum and his wife.

Endnotes

1. J. J. Csorba, *The Use of Horses and Mules on Farms,* Agricultural Research Service ARS 43-94, U.S. Department of Agriculture (Washington, D.C., March 1959), p. 4.
2. Rufus F. Briggs, "Friendly Neighbors," printed in a newspaper column by Briggs entitled "World" and pasted in Lum's photo album. No date or newspaper title was included. Western writer and newspaperman Elmer Kelton in San Angelo, Texas, recalls Lum's presence at local cattle auctions was always welcomed. "Everyone was always glad to see Ray Lum show up. He had a smile and a handshake for everyone and always brought me a can of black strap molasses. Ray always started the bidding on bulls and was an important asset to the sales" (telephone conversation March 12, 1990).
3. Note pasted in Lum's photo album. The full text read: "Ray, if we had you up here we would elect you to Congress. Your friend, Henry Clark." Beside the note Lum wrote "Stephensville, Texas. Passed away."
4. Ben Green, *Some More Horse Tradin'* (New York, 1972), pp. 214–15.
5. Letter from Elmer Kelton, March 22, 1990.
6. Tomas O'Crohan, *The Islandman* (Oxford, 1965); Theodore Rosengarten, *All God's Dangers: The Life of Nate Shaw* (New York, 1975). Other important books in the tradition of O'Crohan are Eric Cross, *The Tailor and Ansty* (London, 1964); Maurice O'Sullivan, *Twenty Years A-Growing* (New York, 1933); and Peig Sayers, *An Old Woman's Reflections* (London, 1972).
7. Katy McCaleb Headley discusses the Mason and Harpe gang in *Claiborne*

239

County, Mississippi: The Promised Land (Port Gibson, Mississippi, 1976), pp. 90–95. Patti Carr Black describes the history of the Natchez Trace in *The Natchez Trace* (Jackson, Mississippi, 1985). A special issue of *Southern Quarterly* (Summer, 1991) is devoted to the Natchez Trace and includes features on its relation to Indians, Andrew Jackson, Afro-Americans, John James Audubon, William Faulkner, Eudora Welty, and Richard Wright.

8. The Vicksburg campaign was critical to the Union's effort to close the Mississippi River and supply routes from Texas. Samuel Carter III describes Grant's effort in *The Final Fortress: The Campaign for Vicksburg 1862–1863* (New York, 1980); James M. McPherson shows how the Vicksburg Campaign influenced the outcome of the Civil War in *Battle Cry of Freedom: The Civil War Era* (New York, 1988), pp. 627–36.

9. *Gave him the wheel:* Ran over him.

10. *Browse:* To graze randomly.

11. *Dressed:* Butchered.

12. *Lights:* Intestines.

13. Joseph Jett was a prominent citizen in Rocky Springs who in 1891 built a new shop that he declared "will add materially to the Main Street of that village." Katy McCaleb Headley, *Claiborne County, Mississippi: The Promised Land* (Port Gibson, Mississippi, 1976), p. 77.

14. *Drummer:* Traveling merchant.

15. *Bush:* To negotiate a lower price than the figure originally bid; often traders pointed out defects in a horse or a mule bought at an auction that were not "called" by the auctioneer and "bushed" a lower price out of the auctioneer for the animal.

16. *Sorghum mill:* A mill where sorghum cane was ground to produce a sugary liquid that was then boiled to make sorghum molasses. A lone mule walked in a circle and pulled one end of a pole that was connected to a machine that crushed juice from the cane.

17. *Sorghum chews:* Crushed sorghum cane; the by-product of a sorghum mill that was discarded. If allowed to eat the sweet-tasting chews, an animal would bloat and die.

18. *One percent:* One hundred percent.

19. Bob Corritore, Bill Ferris, and Jim O'Neal, "Willie Dixon," Part I, *Living Blues* (no. 81, July/August 1988), p. 16.

20. William Ferris, *Images of the South* (Memphis, 1977), p. 33. In a conversation with Evans he explained that he photographed the Lum barn in Natchez first. He suggested to Ben Shahn, whom he knew well in New York, that he photograph the barn during a photographic trip Shahn was about to make through the South.

21. Ray Lum letter, December 28, 1932, University of Mississippi Archives.

22. Pete Daniel captures the human suffering wrought by the flood in *Deep'n as It Come: The 1927 Mississippi River Flood* (New York, 1977). Delta planter William Alexander Percy, the uncle of Walker Percy, describes

his efforts to aid its victims in *Lanterns on the Levee* (Baton Rouge, 1973), pp. 249–69.

23. Nelson Blake surveys the Corps's role in building levees in "Flood Control and Drainage," *Encyclopedia of Southern Culture,* Charles Reagan Wilson and William Ferris, co-eds. (Chapel Hill, 1989), pp. 335–37.

24. *Bounce:* To ride; to demonstrate an animal for a customer.

25. *All Saints School:* A private Episcopal school in Vicksburg. *The Park* is the Vicksburg National Military Park which commemorates the battle and siege of Vicksburg during the Civil War.

26. *Pitch:* To buck.

27. *Broke in two and lost his coupling pin:* Bucked so violently it seemed the animal was coming apart.

28. *Giraffe:* A tall lanky horse.

29. *Boot:* Cash paid to cover the difference in value between two animals traded.

30. Jean-Paul Clebert describes such tricks in *The Gypsies* (Baltimore, 1969), p. 138, and Kamill Erdos notes similar trading techniques among gypsies in "Gypsy Horse Dealers in Hungary," *Journal of the Gypsy Lore Society,* vol. 38, pts. 1 and 2, p. 5. As Lum observed, horses like Little Eatum were the gypsy trader's "taw," his "meal ticket."

    Arkansas folklorist Vance Randolph published a folksong, "The Horse Trader's Song," that warns against Gypsy traders in *Ozark Folksongs,* vol. 2 (Columbia, Missouri, 1946–50), pp. 261–62:
    It's do you know those horse traders?
    It's do you know their plan?
    It's do you know those horse traders?
    It's do you know their plan?
    Their plan it is for to snide you,
    And git whatever they can,
    I've been around the world.

    The song describes how gypsy traders "send their women from house to horse/ to git whatever they can," and one verse refers to the gypsy trick of trading a "snide" like Little Eatum, that the customer will have to return:
    Go saddle up your snides, boys,
    And tie 'em to the rock,
    The first man that gets 'em
    Will pay us to take 'em back,
    I've been around the world.

    Jan Yoors notes that gypsy fathers taught their sons to bring out a horse's good points and to disguise his weaknesses in *The Gypsies* (New York, 1967), p. 101. Not content to simply buy and resell animals, their greatest art lay in "putting right" a horse's defects (Clebert, p. 137). Tired, old horses became spirited animals through "gingering," the insertion of a piece of ginger into their anus. Another gypsy trick used with old horses was to bore their teeth and fill them with lunar caustic or rosemary. Teeth were also filed with an auger to disguise the animal's age (Clebert, p. 137; Erdos, pp. 3–4). Lorraine A. Allen discovered that gypsies occasionally allowed outsiders to travel with them, and describes how the largest mule dealer in the world learned his skills in a gypsy wagon in "The Largest Mule Farm in the World," *Overland Monthly,* April 1914, p. 382.

31. *Snide skin:* A horse with a defect; usually the buyer did not discover the defect until after the trade was completed.

32. *Dray:* A wagon used to haul materials that often did not have sides.

33. *Hostler:* One who takes care of horses. A hostler often worked at a livery stable and assisted the livestock dealer in showing animals to his customers. He might also travel on the road with a trader and help show stock.

34. *Boll weevil:* An insect that devastated southern cotton crops. The insect migrated from Mexico and reached Mississippi in 1907. The boll weevil lays its eggs in the cotton square and thereby prevents its development of cotton fiber. Douglas Helms traces the boll weevil's history in "Just Lookin' for a Home: The Cotton Boll Weevil and the South" (Ph.D. dissertation, Florida State University, 1977).

35. *Out of a jack:* Bred from an ass.

36. *Roach:* To cut and trim. Most mule owners cut their animals' manes completely off and severely trimmed their tails to facilitate their work in harness.

37. Thomas Jonathan "Stonewall" Jackson (1824–1863) was a general in the Confederate Army. He received his nickname from Confederate General Barnard E. Bee, who praised him and his troops for standing "like a stone wall" during the first battle of Bull Run (July 21, 1861). Charles Wilson offers an excellent summary of his life and impact on the South in "Jackson, Stonewall," *Encyclopedia of Southern Culture,* Charles Wilson and William Ferris, eds. (Chapel Hill, 1989), pp. 690–91.

38. *Hand:* A hand's breadth, or 4 inches (10.16 cm).

39. *Pommel:* The knoblike section at the front and top of a saddle.

40. *Carved:* Closely trimmed.

41. Hiroshima, the capital of Hiroshima prefecture in Japan, was the target of the first atomic bomb that was dropped on a populated area. American forces dropped the bomb on August 6, 1945, and almost 130,000 people were killed.

42. *Ears laid back:* A mule or horse flattens his ears back before kicking.

43. *Out of the woods:* Recovered; well.

44. *His bread wasn't done:* He was lacking in intelligence.

45. Maurice Cockerham describes the visit of Theodore Roosevelt to Vicksburg in October 1907 and his famed bear hunt in "Teddy's Tensas," *Louisiana Conservationist* (September/October 1983), pp. 12–17. Cockerman says that Roosevelt hunted the bear in a tract of virgin timber with a companion named Ben Lilly who had killed bear by the "hundreds, tracking them on foot through the canebrakes, sometimes with a dog and sometimes alone, and bringing them to bay. According to many accounts, he often closed with his quarry armed only with a long knife of his own making." Gordon Cotton

recalls Holt Collier who is also said to have led Roosevelt on his bear hunt in "If It Hadn't Been for Holt Collier, the Teddy Bear Wouldn't Be," *Vicksburg Evening Post* (October 14, 1990), p. E-2.

46. Theodore Gilmore Bilbo was born October 13, 1877, in Pearl River County, Mississippi. Bilbo's forty-year political career in Mississippi led him to the governor's office and to the United States Senate. Bilbo was best known for his strong segregationist views and for his political corruption. Chester M. Morgan examines Bilbo's role in southern populism in *Redneck Liberal: Theodore G. Bilbo and the New Deal* (Baton Rouge, 1985).

47. *Grip:* Suitcase.

48. *Gar:* A fish with a long, pikelike body and long, narrow jaws. Freshwater gars in North America are known for attacking other fish.

49. *Green mules:* Unbroken mules.

50. *Loess:* An unstratified, yellowish-brown loam found in North America, Europe, and Asia. Extensive deposits are found along the Mississippi River and its tributaries. It is thought to have been deposited by wind.

51. W. C. Handy, *Father of the Blues* (New York, 1970), p. 74.

52. Norman L. Crockett discusses the history of Mound Bayou and other all-black towns in *Black Towns* (Lawrence, Kansas, 1979).

53. David L. Cohn, *Where I Was Born and Raised* (Boston, 1948), p. 12.

54. *Colonel Meals:* Colonel M.[arvin] R.[oswell] Meals (1908–1964) held his largest mule auction on the Twist Plantation in Arkansas in January 1939. The sale lasted three days, and he organized it like a circus. He erected two large tents and hired several assistant auctioneers. To feed the crowds Meals bought 25 hogs, 1,000 loaves of bread, and 150 pounds of coffee.

Meals wore tailor-made suits and hand-made, knee-high laced boots that cost $27 a pair. During his free time he watched wrestling matches and was a friend of Jack Dempsey.

Journalist Ernie Pyle recalled a memorable visit with Meals in his hotel room. According to Pyle, Meals claimed "a mule-trader is the shrewdest man in the world, bar none."

Pyle recalled that "Colonel Meals's speaking voice is not at all unusual . . . But the second he starts spieling he switches to a high, penetrating tone . . . He has talked for three days straight, and it [his voice] has never given out yet, even when he has a cold." Ernie Pyle, "He Auctions Off Mules and He Loves His Work," *Press Scimitar* (May 5, 1940) and "Mules Are His Business, Movies His Relaxation," *Press Scimitar* (May 9, 1940).

After World War II, Meals argued that mules would regain their place in the hearts of farmers because "there aren't many farmers who raise spark plugs, tires, gas, and oil on their farms. But most of them do raise hay." After the mule market disappeared, Meals turned to cattle and then to second-hand autos and farm machinery. "The Colonel Shifts Gears," *Press Scimitar* (March 18, 1954). Two lengthy obituaries on Colonel Meals that appeared in

Memphis newspapers are Hila Van Hook McGee's "Col. Meals, Famed Mule Auctioneer, Is Dead," *Press Scimitar* (March 21, 1956), and "Saturday Rites Set For Col. M. R. Meals," *Commercial Appeal* (March 22, 1956).

55. *Blood-based:* Red.

56. *Two percent:* Two hundred percent.

57. *Pick up a nail:* Stick a nail in their hooves; the horses were so healthy that a nail could not penetrate their hooves.

58. The economy of the South and the Mississippi Delta, in particular, was wedded to the cotton economy. Pete Daniel traces the rise and fall of cotton in *Breaking the Land: The Transformation of Cotton, Tobacco, and Rice Cultures since 1880* (Urbana, Illinois, 1985). Annual prices for cotton are recorded in *Historical Statistics of the United States: Colonial Times to 1970* (U.S. Government Printing Office, 1975), pp. 517, 518.

59. *Wiggly:* Worm.

60. *Bored with a pretty big auger:* Did business on a large scale.

61. *Yearling:* Year-old.

62. *Sorrel:* A brown, red-yellow hue.

63. *Bays:* Brown, red-yellow hue.

64. *Single tree:* The pivoted or swinging bar to which the traces of a harnessed horse or mule are fixed.

65. *Gyp water:* Water containing gypsum (hydrous calcium sulfate).

66. *Trace:* One of two straps or chains of a harness that attach a mule or horse to a wagon or plow.

67. *Five-thirties:* Five and a half years old.

68. *Didn't ring no backup bell:* Didn't waste time.

69. *Ring man:* A man who stands inside the ring with the stock and makes the animal move before customers. The ring man opens the gate to bring the animal into the ring, sets the opening price for bidders, and drives the animal out the exit gate when bidding is completed.

70. *Angel:* An inexperienced buyer.

71. *Wheel horse:* A person with exceptional strength and dependability. Teamsters placed their strongest, best animal at the back of the team next to the left wagon wheel and referred to it as their "wheel horse." The wheel horse moved out first and bore the wagon's heaviest load.

72. Knox Kinard traces the history of the Waggoner family and their ranch in "History of the Waggoner Ranch" (M.A. thesis, University of Texas, 1941). See also "Waggoner, William Thomas" and "Waggoner Ranch" in Walter Prescott Webb, ed., *The Handbook of Texas* (Austin, 1952), vol. II, p. 851.

73. Will[iam Penn Adair] Rogers was part Cherokee and was born in 1879. He worked as a cowhand in Texas and later joined Texas Jack's Wild West Show in South Africa. William Brown traces his life and influence as a humorist in *Imagemaker: Will Rogers and the American Dream* (Columbia, Missouri, 1970).

74. John Ashton has an excellent description of the history of the King Ranch in "King Ranch," *The Handbook of Texas,* Walter Prescott Webb, ed. (Austin,

1952), p. 961. Frank Goodwyn traces the development of the ranch in *Life on the King Ranch* (New York, 1951).

75. Earl Long served as lieutenant governor (1936–39), as governor (1939–40, 1948–52, 1956–60), and died several days after his election to the U.S. House of Representatives in August 1960. A. J. Liebling describes Long's political career in *Earl of Louisiana* (1961). Michael L. Kurtz and Morgan D. Peoples explore Earl Long's political career and how at times he opposed his brother Huey's political positions in *Earl K. Long: The Saga of Uncle Earl and Louisiana Politics* (Baton Rouge, 1990). Long was also the subject of a recent film, *Blaze*.

76. Goodnight was born in Macoupin County, Illinois, and moved to Milam County, Texas, with his mother and stepfather in 1846. In Texas he became a ranger and an Indian scout, and by 1865 owned a herd of cattle. In 1876 he moved his herd of 1,800 head of Durham cattle to Palo Duro Canyon in the Texas Panhandle and the following year went into a partnership with John G. Adair. In 1887 their ranch was divided between Goodnight and Adair's widow, Cornelia Adair, and two years later Goodnight sold his portion. J. Evetts Haley describes Goodnight's life in *Charles Goodnight: Cowman and Plainsman* (Boston, 1936).

77. German settlers in Texas moved to Comal, Gillespie, Llano, Guadalupe, Kerr, Kendall, Calhoun, Victoria, DeWill, Lavaca, Colorado, Austin, Washington, Fayette, and Bastrop counties. Terry G. Jordan explores the history of these settlers in *German Seed in Texas Soil: Immigrant Farmers in Nineteenth-Century Texas* (Austin, 1966).

78. [Alexander] Frank[lin] James (1843–1915). William A. Settle traces the history of the James brothers in *Jesse James Was His Name* (Columbia, Missouri, 1966).

79. Charles Arthur "Pretty Boy" Floyd (1901–1934). After several robberies and a short prison sentence Floyd joined Bill "the Killer" Miller and robbed banks from Kansas City to Ohio. When Miller was killed during a robbery in Bowling Green, Ohio, Floyd's partner in crime was George Birdwell, a former church deacon from Oklahoma. The two traveled together until Birdwell was killed during a bank robbery in 1932. In 1933 Floyd was labeled Public Enemy No. 1 and continued to elude police until 1934 when F.B.I. agents trapped and killed him in a cornfield near East Liverpool. Carl Sifakis, "Floyd, Charles Arthur 'Pretty Boy' (1901–1934): Public Enemy," *The Encyclopedia of American Crime* (New York, 1982), pp. 256–58.

80. Bean was born about 1825 in Mason County, Kentucky. In 1882 Bean was appointed justice of the peace in Eagle's Nest Springs near the present location of Langtry, Texas. Two biographies of Bean are C. L. Sonnichsen's *Roy Bean* (New York, 1943) and Everett Lloyd's *Law West of the Pecos* (San Antonio, 1931).

81. Carry Nation (1846–1911) was born in Kentucky in a slave-owning family. Important biographies of Nation are Carleton Beals, *Cyclone Carry: The Story*

of Carry Nation (Philadelphia, 1962) and Robert Lewis Taylor, *Vessel of Wrath: The Life and Times of Carry Nation* (New York, 1966).

82. Ian Hancock describes the group's history in "Gypsies," *Encyclopedia of Southern Culture,* Charles Reagan Wilson and William Ferris, co-eds. (Chapel Hill, 1989), p. 432, and in *American Speech* (Fall 1986) and *The Pariah Syndrome* (1987).

83. Lum's friend and fellow Texas trader Ben Green once visited a gypsy camp and recalled a "little short, fat, squatty trader [who] had every appearance of being an Irishman or some other breed of white man" in *Horse Conformation and Hoss Trades of Yesteryear* (Cumby, Texas, 1963), p. 72.

84. The first Irish traders emigrated to the United States in the early 1800s and established a livery stable in Washington, D.C. After the Civil War their leader, Pat O'Hara, led the group south to Atlanta. From this center, groups settled in Nashville and Fort Worth and began trading with farmers. Typically they would sleep on a four-poster mahogany bed with a crucifix hung from the tent's center pole. Stew, large loaves of bread, and quart-size bowls of tea were served on Haviland china, and after the evening meals Irish tales and ballads were the entertainment.

    Once Irish traders arrived in a community, local farmers brought their worn-out mules to the camp to trade for young five-year-olds. The farmer usually paid cash or "boot" to cover the difference between the two animals. Their field mules could still be used for light hauling in cities, and one of the trucks shuttled between stockyards and the camp to supply fresh stock and to haul the old mules back. While the men traded mules, their wives sold hand-sewn lace to the women of the community. Edwin Muller, "Roving the South with the Irish Horse Traders," *Reader's Digest* (July 1941), pp. 60–61.

    George E. Ryan describes how each year, on April 28, Irish clans gathered in Atlanta to bury their dead, celebrate marriages, and review the year's work in "The Irish Travelers," *Ave Maria* (March 18, 1967), p. 16. When traders met on the road, their parting words were "See you at the funeral." They set up as many as two hundred colorful tents outside Atlanta and observed funerals at the Church of the Immaculate Conception. Mourners wept and lamented at each grave among dogwood and azaleas in the church cemetery. Designs of a mule, a walking stick, a broken wheel, and a ladder were often placed on the graves. One Irish trader lost two wives in a single year and gave each a two-thousand-dollar funeral (Muller, p. 52). According to Patrick Green, funerals were also very important among the tinkers in Ireland. He describes their funeral ceremonies in "Irish Tinkers or 'Travellers,'" *Bea-loideas,* vol. 3 (1931), p. 173.

    At weddings barbecue was served on a two-hundred-foot table to cele-brate. Newlyweds received money from their families plus a tent, a car and trailer, a truck and a string of mules. Once married, the young man was expected to launch his own career as a trader. J. V. Harper notes how one Irish trader recalled, "My father, he gave me one mule when I got married and a hundred dollars in money. Some gets more, I know. But I know what I got was a hundred dollars and a little young mule," in his impressive study, "Irish Traveler Cant: An Historical Structural and Sociolinguistic Study of an Argot," M.A. thesis (University of Georgia, 1969), p. 13. When the week's cycle of mourning and celebration ended, the traders returned to the road and would not see each other for another year (Muller, pp. 62–63).

85. Speakers today refer to their speech as "Shelta," "Bog Latin," "Tinkers' Cant," and "The Ould Thing," while for outsiders it is "the gibberish of tinkers." Kune Meyer, "The Sacred Languages of Ireland," *Journal of the Gypsy Lore Society,* vol. 2 (January 1909), p. 245; see also H. L. Mencken, *The American Language: An Inquiry into the Development of English in the United States* (New York, 1965), p. 578.

86. J. V. Harper, "Irish Traveler Cant: An Historical Structural and Sociolinguistic Study of an Argot," M.A. thesis (University of Georgia, 1969), p. 21.

87. Alfred E. Smith (1873–1944) was born in New York City, the son of a truckman who drove a horse-drawn wagon. Both of his parents were Roman Catholic. After his presidential defeat Al Smith served as chairman of the board of the New York Trust Company and assisted in the erection of the Empire State Building. His biographies include Richard O'Connor, *The First Hurrah* (New York, 1970), Matthew and Hannah Josephson, *Al Smith: Hero of the Cities* (Boston, 1970), and Norman Hapgood and Henry Moscowitz, *Up From the City Streets* (New York, 1928).

88. James John "Jimmy" Walker (1881–1946) was born in New York City of Irish-American parents. The second-born of nine children, he studied law at New York Law School after which he launched a career as a songwriter in Tin Pan Alley. He served in the state senate from 1921 to 1925 as a Tammany protégé of Al Smith. Walker was recruited from Albany by Tammany leaders to run for mayor of New York City and won in 1925. After being accused of corrupt payoffs by Judge Samuel Seabury, Governor Franklin D. Roosevelt ordered a hearing, and on September 1, 1932, Jimmy Walker resigned his office as mayor of New York City. His life is detailed in Gene Fowler, *Beau James: The Life and Times of Jimmy Walker* (New York, 1949) and Milton Mackaye, *The Tin Box Parade* (New York, 1934).

89. *Anchored:* Stayed.

90. *Sale barns:* Livestock barns used to temporarily house livestock before and after auctions. *Livery barns:* Barns that housed horses and mules. Horse owners often kept their animal in a livery barn where it was fed and groomed.

91. *Pitch:* To buck.

92. *Cheek:* To turn the horse's head back toward the rider by pulling on the bridle or one of the reins. This keeps the horse off balance so that he cannot buck until the rider is in the saddle.

93. *Sunfisher:* A horse who bucks so violently he turns over in the air, placing

"his belly where his back ought to be." Even the best riders were thrown by such a horse.

94. *Draw:* A gully or deep ditch through which cattle and horses could circulate.

95. *Chunk:* To throw.

96. *Bag:* Udder or mammary gland on a cow.

97. *Dipper:* Penis.

98. *S.B.:* Son-of-a-bitch.

99. The quarter horse is built low to the ground and is heavily muscled in his front. Quarter horses are known for their speed over short distances and their ability to turn quickly, qualities that have made them a favorite horse among cowboys. Margaret Cabell Self notes that the breed is descended from Janus, an English thoroughbred that lived in Virginia between 1756 and 1780. *The Horseman's Encyclopedia* (New York, 1963), pp. 285–86.

100. Dwain Hughes was a banker and rancher who operated a ranch east of Spring Creek near Mertzon, Texas. Hughes specialized in Hereford cattle and sold Lum registered bulls on several occasions. Western author Elmer Kelton recalled that Lum was always a welcome presence at the Hughes sales (telephone conversation, March 13, 1990).

101. Jack Benny (1894–1974) was born *Benjamin Kubelsky* in Chicago, Illinois. He first appeared as a comedian on the vaudeville stage in Waukegan at the age of seventeen. In 1929 Benny appeared in his first of more than a dozen motion pictures. In 1932 he launched a radio program that continued for over twenty years and established him as one of America's favorite comedians. He first appeared on television in 1950 and had a weekly program from 1960 to 1965 that presented Benny as a comic miser.

102. While several species of ticks infest cattle, only one *(Margaropus annulatus)* transmits splenetic (or Texas) fever. The "Texas" fever infected large numbers of cattle in Pennsylvania and the Midwest in the 1800s. Colonel R. J. Kleberg is said to have built the first vat for dipping cattle in chemical "dips" that killed the ticks. By 1945 the fever tick was eradicated in twelve of the thirteen states formerly infested. T. C. Richardson traces the history of ticks and Texas fever in "Cattle Tick," *The Handbook of Texas,* Walter Prescott Webb, Editor-in-Chief (Austin, 1952), vol. I, pp. 315–16.

103. *Longest:* The largest in length from the animal's head to his hindquarters.

104. *Squabs:* Young pigeons.

105. *Chippy:* Prostitute.

106. *Pocket Dice:* Small dice that can be easily carried in the pants pocket.

107. *Wing:* A fence that leads the animals to pens where they are caught.

108. *Shelf:* The skin covering the penis.

109. The "Lum and Abner" show ran from 1931 to 1955 on the radio. Lum was played by Chester Lauck, and Abner by Norris "Tuffy" Goff. The two actors also made several films.

110. *Tank:* Waterhole.

111. *Their bellies had begun to pinch their backbone:* They were dying from lack of water and feed.
112. *Doing business:* Making love.
113. *Monthlies:* Menstrual napkins.
114. *Had her sickness on:* Had her menstrual period.
115. *Throwed it down:* Aimed.
116. Lum is referring to Frank Norfleet, a Texas rancher who was swindled and turned detective, tracking down those who had swindled him. He wrote a highly successful book entitled *Norfleet* and lived to be almost a hundred. Norfleet was said to have celebrated his ninetieth birthday twice, once by mistake, and then again when he actually reached it.
117. The most comprehensive study of the Santa Fe Trail is Max L. Moorehead's *New Mexico's Royal Road* (Norman, Oklahoma, 1958).
118. Bonnie [Parker] (1910–1934) and Clyde [Barrow] (1909–1934) are two of the most notorious outlaws in American history. Their career ranged from Dallas, Texas, and Joplin, Missouri, to Louisiana. In 1967 the career of Bonnie and Clyde was chronicled in a popular motion picture, *Bonnie and Clyde.* H. Gordon Frost and John H. Jenkins describe Frank Hamer's pursuit of the outlaws in *I'm Frank Hamer: The Life of a Texas Peace Officer* (Austin, 1968).
119. *Went to sleep:* Died.
120. *Throwed a lot of fives:* Bid five dollars a head frequently.
121. *Firing part:* Back feet. A horse or mule is most likely to kick with its back feet, and it is especially dangerous to stand behind an animal.
122. *Burred:* Bellowed.
123. *Gulch:* A deep ditch.
124. Pike's Peak is named for Zebulon Montgomery Pike who discovered the mountain in 1806. The mountain rises 14,110 feet above sea level in central Colorado and is in the southern part of the Front Range of the Rocky Mountains. A cog railroad and a highway carry visitors to its summit, which is usually covered with snow.
125. Although Lum is technically correct, the Miller's ranch is usually called the One Oh One Ranch.
126. *Cracker:* A plaited string at the end of a whip which makes a loud sound when the whip is popped.
127. *Dodge:* To avoid; to escape.
128. *Knock a hip down:* To hurry; to move quickly.
129. *Six bits:* Seventy-five dollars.
130. Personal letter from Elmer Kelton, March 22, 1990.
131. Personal letter from Elmer Kelton, March 22, 1990.
132. *Heavie:* A horse that suffers from pulmonary emphysema. The disease develops in horses five years and older. The animal usually coughs after exercise. Such horses can be used for pleasure riding but are not able to do hard work.
133. *On the carpet:* In the auction ring; being sold.
134. *Clarence:* Clarence Lum, Lum's younger brother.

135. *Lamp:* (verb) To glance quickly. Seasoned traders could judge a horse's merits with a quick look or "lamp."

136. *Lamp:* (noun) Eyes. If a horse was said to have "one lamp burning," he was blind in one eye.

137. *Pimple:* Defect or shortcoming. If a horse or mule "ain't got a pimple on him" he is in perfect condition.

138. *Cup:* The concave opening on the top of a horse or mule's tooth.

139. *Screw:* A horse or mule with a defect. A blind animal raises his ears when he hears a strange sound. By clapping his hands Lum discovered that this horse was blind in both eyes because both of his ears were raised.

140. *Peepers:* Eyes.

141. *Snide:* A defective animal.

142. *Stumpsucker:* A horse that chews on wood, a nervous habit developed by horses that are confined in stalls for too long. Anthony Bornton notes that a cribber has a habit of force-swallowing gulps of air. The horse usually grasps an object with its incisor teeth and pulls its neck back in a rigid arch as it swallows air. The practice can create gastric upsets or colic. *The Horse* (W. H. Freeman and Company, 1977), pp. 234–35.

143. *My bread was done:* I was awake.

144. *Henny:* The offspring of a female ass or jenny and a stallion. Mules are bred from a male ass or "jack" and a female horse or mare.

145. *Big foot:* A mule with large feet. The animal is the offspring of a large "draft-bred mare" or workhorse and an ass.

146. *Heavy hung:* Had a large penis; "well endowed."

147. The Tennessee walking horse is a recent breed that traces its ancestry back to Black Allan who was descended from Hambletonian and Morgan ancestors. The walking horse was developed for use by plantation owners who wanted a horse with a comfortable gait that could be ridden between rows of crops. The Tennessee walking horse has a gait between the walk and the trot that is especially comfortable during long rides.

148. *Pastern:* The section of a horse's leg between his fetlock and his coffin joint.

149. *War Trace:* One of the most famous Tennessee walking horse sires.

150. *Killers:* Horses that will be slaughtered for their meat.

151. Man O' War (1917–1947), known as "Big Red" because of his unusual size and chestnut coloring, was one of the most celebrated American racehorses. He was born at Nursery Stud, Kentucky, and was owned by Samuel D. Riddle. Man O' War's unusual strength, his long stride, and his speed were unique, and he won twenty of his twenty-one races. His only loss—to Upset —was caused by a mixup at the starting gate. He was put out to stud at four, and his offspring included War Admiral and Blockade.

152. *Hitting on four:* Walks well on all four feet; not limping.

153. *Stuck her tail in the sawdust:* Used her back feet to stop abruptly.

154. *Catch that horse back:* To get the horse back in a later trade.

155. *Snides:* Defective animals.

156. *Romishel:* Gypsy (from Romany gypsy).

157. *Sun dog* and *moon dog:* Constellations of stars.

158. *Slick saddle:* A saddle without tooling and other decoration.

159. *McClellan saddle:* A cavalry saddle that is smaller and lighter than western saddles used for work on the range. The McClellan saddle was used primarily on army posts. Glenn Vernam offers an excellent history of saddles and saddle-making in *Man on Horseback* (New York, 1964).

160. Lum's line ''They cut down the old pine tree'' is from Billy Hill's 1929 song, ''They Cut Down the Old Pine Tree.''

161. *John:* John Lum, Lum's younger brother.

162. ''Peaches'' Browning (1910–1956) and ''Daddy'' Browning (1875–1934) were a major cause célèbre in 1925.

WILLIAM FERRIS, a native of Vicksburg, is Director of the Center for the Study of Southern Culture at the University of Mississippi. A leading scholar on Mississippi folklife, he is the author of six books and numerous articles on folklore and the co-editor of the highly acclaimed Encyclopedia of Southern Culture. He is co-founder of the Center for Southern Folklore, Memphis, a nonprofit multimedia corporation dedicated to preserving indigenous and ethnic cultures of the South through films, books, records, exhibits, and community presentations. With the Center staff, Ferris has produced over a dozen highly praised and award-winning films on southern life. Ferris is a former professor at Yale University where he was a protégé of Robert Penn Warren and is now a Professor of Anthropology at the University of Mississippi.